Why? Why? Why?

Why? Why? Why?

BARDFIELD
PRESS

First published as hardback in 2005 by
Miles Kelly Publishing Ltd
Bardfield Centre, Great Bardfield, Essex, CM7 4SL

This edition published in 2006 by Bardfield Press

Bardfield Press is an imprint of Miles Kelly Publishing Ltd

2 4 6 8 10 9 7 5 3 1

Editorial Director
Belinda Gallagher

Art Director
Jo Brewer

Editorial Assistant
Bethanie Bourne

Authors
Camilla de la Bedoyere, Catherine Chambers,
Chris Oxlade

Designers
Jo Brewer, Venita Kidwai,
Sophie Pelham, Elaine Wilkinson

Jacket Designer
Tom Slemmings

Indexer
Helen Snaith

Production
Elizabeth Brunwin

Reprographics
Anthony Cambray, Mike Coupe, Ian Paulyn

Cartoons
Mark Davis, The Maltings Partnership

ISBN 978-1-84236-777-3

Printed in China

British Library Cataloguing-in-Publication Data
A catalogue record for this book is available
from the British Library

www.mileskelly.net
info@mileskelly.net

Contents

Space 6

Weather 36

Science 66

Your Body 94

Dinosaurs 120

Birds 150

Mammals 168

Ancient Egypt 190

Knights and Castles 212

Pirates 230

Index 252

Far-out questions about...

Which star keeps us warm? 8
When is it night time during the day? 9
Why is the Sun spotty? 9

Is Earth the only planet near the Sun? 10
Do other planets have moons? 11
What are other planets like? 11

What is inside the Earth? 12
Why does the Moon change shape? 13
Why do we have day and night? 13

What is the hottest planet? 14
Why is Mars called the red planet? 15
Which planet has the biggest volcano? 15

What is the smallest planet? 16
Why does Mercury look like the Moon? 17
Which planet is baking hot and freezing cold? 17

What is the biggest planet? 18
Which planet has rings? 19
Is there a giant made of gas? 19

Which planet rolls around? 20
Why does Neptune look so blue? 21
Why do Neptune and Pluto swap places? 21

Space

Are there snowballs in space? 22
What is a shooting star? 22
Does the Sun have a belt? 23

How are stars made? 24
What is a group of stars
    called? 25
Are all stars white? 25

What is the Milky Way? 26
Can galaxies crash? 26
Do galaxies have arms? 27

How does a shuttle get
    into space? 28
How fast do rockets go? 29
When is a shuttle like a glider? 29

Why do astronauts float
    in space? 30
Where do astronauts go to sleep? 31
Why do astronauts wear
    spacesuits? 31

Are there robots in space? 32
Which probe has travelled the
    furthest? 33
Have probes been to Mars? 33

Quiz time 34

Which star keeps us warm?

The Sun does. It is a star like all the others in the night sky, but it is much closer to Earth. The Sun is a giant ball of hot, glowing gas and it gives off heat that keeps the Earth warm. It also gives us light.

Hot hot hot!

The Sun's surface is so hot that it would melt a metal spacecraft flying near it! It is 15 times hotter than boiling water.

When is it night time during the day?

Sometimes the Sun, the Earth and the Moon all line up in space. When this happens, the Moon's shadow falls on the Earth, making it dark even if it's daytime. This is called an eclipse.

Eclipse

Sunspot

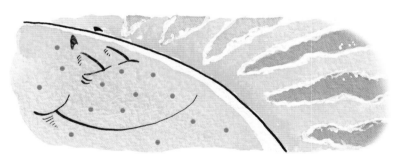

Why is the Sun spotty?

Some parts of the Sun's surface are cooler than the rest of it. These cooler parts appear darker than the rest of the Sun, like spots on its surface. They are called sunspots.

Remember

Never look straight at the Sun. Your eyes could be badly damaged.

Is Earth the only planet near the Sun?

There are eight other planets near the Sun. Mercury and Venus are nearer to the Sun than the Earth is. The other planets are further away. All the planets move around the Sun in huge circles. The Sun and its family of planets is called the Solar System.

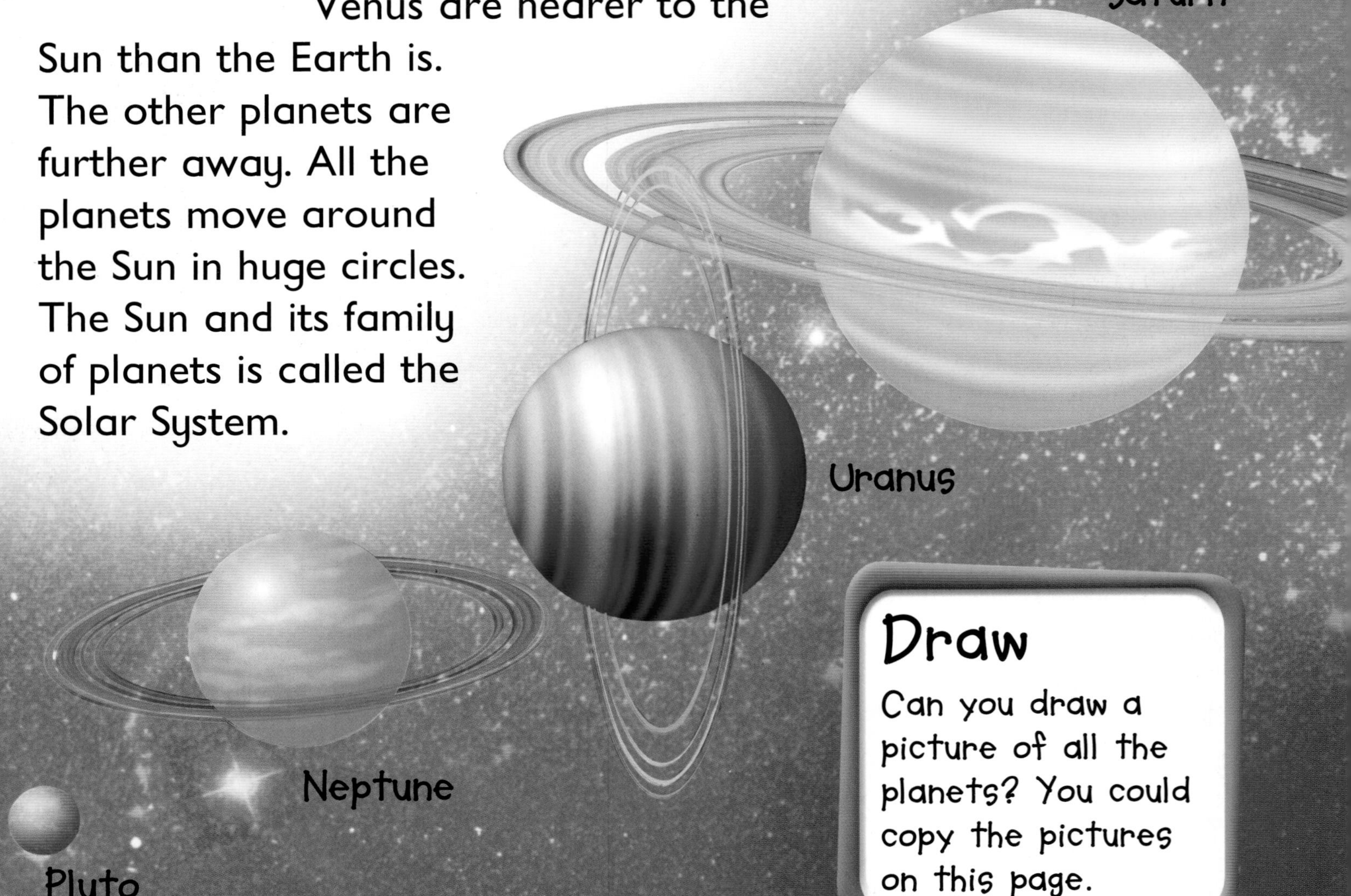

Saturn

Uranus

Neptune

Pluto

Draw

Can you draw a picture of all the planets? You could copy the pictures on this page.

Do other planets have moons?

Earth is not the only planet with a moon. Mars has two moons. Jupiter and Saturn have more than 30 moons each. Venus and Mercury are the only planets with no moons.

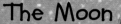

The Sun

Mercury

The Moon

Venus

Earth

Mars

Jupiter

What are the other planets like?

Mercury, Venus and Mars are rocky planets, like the Earth. They have solid surfaces. Jupiter, Saturn, Uranus and Neptune are balls of gas and liquid. They are much bigger than the rocky planets. The last planet, Pluto, is solid and icy.

One big, happy family!

There are millions of smaller members in the Sun's family. Tiny specks of dust speed between the planets along with chunks of rock called asteroids.

What is inside the Earth?

There are layers of hot rock inside the Earth. We live on the Earth's surface where the rock is solid. Beneath the surface, the rock is hot. In some places, it has melted. This melted rock may leak from a volcano.

Crust

Mantle

Inner core

Outer core

Living it up!

Earth is the only planet with water on its surface. This means that people, plants and animals can live here. No life has yet been found on other planets.

 **New Moon**

 **Crescent Moon**

 **First quarter Moon**

 **Gibbous Moon**

 **Full Moon**

Why does the Moon change shape?

The Sun lights up one side of the Moon. The other side is dark. As the Moon circles the Earth, we see different parts of the lit side. This is why the Moon seems to change shape.

The Moon

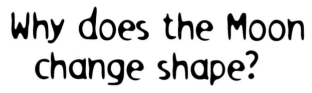

Why do we have day and night?

The Earth spins round once every day. When the part you live on faces the Sun, it is daytime. When this part faces away from the Sun, the sunlight can't reach you. Then it is night time.

Look

Look at the picture of the Moon. The circles are called craters. They were made by lumps of rock smashing into the Moon's surface.

What is the hottest planet?

Venus is the hottest planet in the Solar System. Its surface is hotter than the inside of an oven. Venus is covered in a blanket of thick, yellow gas. The gases trap heat from the Sun but don't let it escape. This means that Venus can't cool down.

Back in a year!

Nobody has ever been to Mars. It is so far away that it would take a spacecraft six months to get there. It would take another six months to get home again!

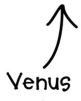

Venus

Why is Mars called the red planet?

Mars looks red because it is covered with red rocks and red dust, the colour of rust. Sometimes, winds pick up the dust and make swirling dust storms. In 1971 dust storms covered the whole planet. The surface completely disappeared from view!

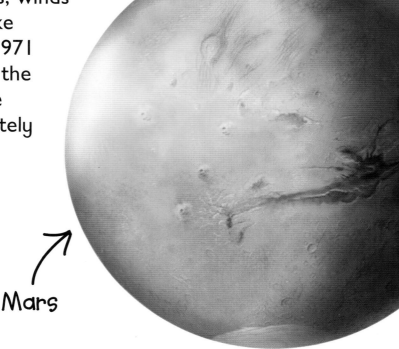

Mars

Which planet has the biggest volcano?

Mars has the biggest volcano. It is called Olympus Mons and it is three times higher than Mount Everest, the highest mountain on Earth. Olympus Mons has gently sloping sides, like an upside-down plate. Mars has many other volcanoes, too. There are also giant canyons and craters.

Discover

Try looking for Venus in the night sky. It looks like a bright star in the early morning or evening.

What is the smallest planet?

Pluto is the smallest planet in the Solar System. It is smaller than our Moon. Pluto has one moon, called Charon, which is half the size of Pluto. Because Pluto is a long way away, the Sun is just a tiny speck of light.

Charon, Pluto's moon

Pluto

Pluto's surface

Why does Mercury look like the Moon?

Mercury looks a bit like our Moon. It is covered in dents called craters. These were made when rocks crashed into the surface. There is no wind or rain on Mercury, or the Moon, to wear away the craters.

Mercury

Sun trap!

Mercury is very close to the Sun. It gets much hotter there than on Earth. If you travelled to Mercury, you would need a special spacesuit and shoes to protect you from the heat.

Think

Pluto is the coldest planet. Can you think why?

Which planet is baking hot and freezing cold?

Mercury is hot and cold. It spins very slowly. The side that faces the Sun is baked until it is hotter than the inside of an oven. When this side faces away from the Sun, it cools down until it is colder than a freezer.

What is the biggest planet?

Jupiter is the biggest planet. It is 11 times as wide as the Earth. All the other planets in the Solar System would fit inside it! Jupiter is covered in swirls of red and orange gas. These are giant storms.

Giant storm

Jupiter

Moon pizza!

Io is one of Jupiter's moons. It is covered in yellow and orange blotches. Io looks like a pizza in space! The blotches are made by hot liquid that comes out of volcanoes.

Saturn's rings

Saturn

Which planet has rings?

Saturn is surrounded by rings that shine brightly in the sunlight. The rings are made from millions and millions of lumps of ice. Some lumps are the size of ice cubes. Others are as big as cars!

Count

Can you count how many planet Earths there are on these pages?

Is there a giant made of gas?

Not really! However, Jupiter and Saturn are called gas giants. This is because they don't have solid surfaces like the Earth. They have a thick layer of gas and then liquid. You couldn't land on them in a spacecraft.

Which planet rolls around?

 **Uranus is different to the other planets.** Most planets are almost upright. They spin as they move around the Sun. Uranus is tipped right over on its side. This planet spins, too, but it looks as though it is rolling around!

↑
Uranus

New new moons!

Astronomers (scientists that study space) keep finding new moons around Uranus. They have found 27 so far. There are four big moons and lots of small ones. But there may be more!

20

Why does Neptune look so blue?

Neptune is covered in bright blue clouds. Sometimes there are streaky, icy white clouds, too. One white cloud is called The Scooter because it scoots around Neptune at high speed. There is also a giant storm called the Great Dark Spot.

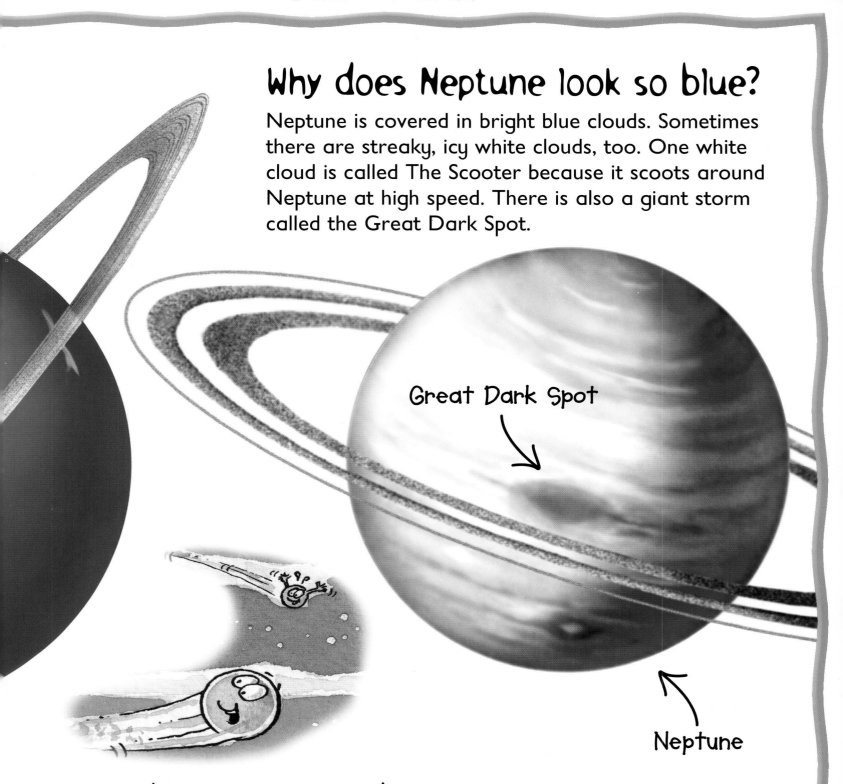

Great Dark Spot

Neptune

Why do Neptune and Pluto swap places?

Most of the planets move around the Sun in huge circles. Pluto's circle is a bit squashed. This means that it is sometimes closer to the Sun than Neptune. Then it is Neptune's turn to be the planet that is furthest from the Sun!

Remember

Uranus and Neptune have rings. Which other two planets have rings, too?

Are there snowballs in space?

Not really! However, comets are a bit like giant snowballs. They are made up of dust and ice mixed together. When a comet gets close to the Sun, the ice begins to melt. Then dust and gas stream away from the comet. They form a long, bright tail.

What is a shooting star?

A shooting star is a bright streak across the night sky. It is not really a star. It is made when a small lump of rock shoots into the air above the Earth. Because the rock is going so fast, it burns brightly.

Comet

Asteroid belt →

Does the Sun have a belt?

The Sun has a belt made up of lumps of rock called asteroids. We call this the asteroid belt. The asteroids move around the Sun between Mars and Jupiter. The biggest asteroids are round, but most are shaped like giant potatoes.

Discover

Can you find out the name of a famous comet?

How are stars made?

Stars are made from huge clouds of dust and gas. Gradually the cloud shrinks and all the gas and dust clump together. The centre of the cloud gets hotter and hotter and a new star begins to shine. The star gives off heat and light.

1. Cloud of gas and dust

3. Star begins to shine

Shine on!

Stars can shine for thousands of millions of years! The Sun started shining five thousand million years ago. It will stop shining in another five thousand million years.

4. New star

What is a group of stars called?

A group of stars is called a star cluster. A star cluster is made from a giant cloud of gas and dust. Some clusters contain just a few stars. Others contain hundreds of stars and they look like a big ball of light.

2. The cloud begins to spin

Star cluster

Are all stars white?

Only the most giant stars shine with a bright white light. This is because they are extremely hot. Smaller stars, such as our Sun, are not so hot. They look yellow instead. Very small stars are cooler still. They look red or brown.

Draw

Can you paint white, yellow and red stars on a sheet of black paper?

What is the Milky Way?

The stars in space are in huge groups called galaxies. Our galaxy is called the Milky Way. All the stars in the night sky are in the Milky Way. There are so many that you couldn't count them all in your whole lifetime!

Can galaxies crash?

Sometimes two galaxies crash into each other. But there is no giant bump. This is because galaxies are mostly made of empty space! The stars just go past each other. Galaxies can pull each other out of shape.

Count

Look at the pictures on these pages. How many different shapes of galaxies can you find?

The Milky Way

Elliptical galaxy

Irregular galaxy

Spiral galaxy

Do galaxies have arms?

Some galaxies have arms that curl in a spiral, like the Milky Way. Other galaxies, called elliptical galaxies, have a round, squashed shape. Many galaxies have no shape and are called irregular galaxies.

Great galaxies!

There are thousands of millions of galaxies in space. Some are much smaller than the Milky Way. Others are much larger. They all contain too many stars to count!

How does a shuttle get into space?

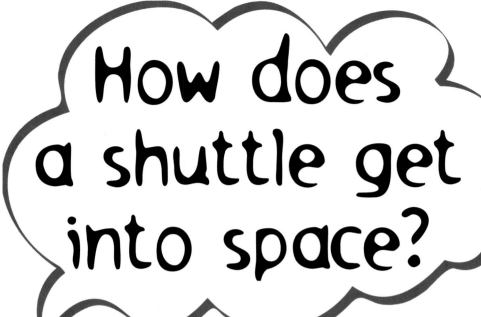

Booster rocket

Tower

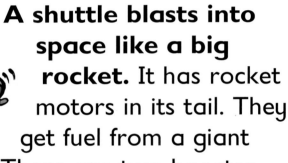

A shuttle blasts into space like a big rocket. It has rocket motors in its tail. They get fuel from a giant fuel tank. There are two booster rockets, too. The fuel tank and the booster rockets fall off before the shuttle reaches space.

Rocket power!

Rockets are filled with fuel. The fuel burns in the rocket motor to make hot gases. The gases rush out of the motor and push the rocket upwards.

Fuel tank

Space shuttle

Rocket motors

How fast do rockets go?

Very, very fast indeed! After blasting off, a rocket goes faster and faster and higher and higher. When it reaches space, it is going 30 times faster than a jumbo jet. If a rocket went slower than this it would fall back to Earth.

Rocket

Make

Blow up a balloon and then let it go. The air rushes out and pushes the balloon along, like a simple rocket.

When is a shuttle like a glider?

When a shuttle travels back to Earth it slows down. Then it begins to fall. It does not use its motors to fly down. Instead, it flies like a giant glider. The shuttle lands on a long runway and uses a parachute to slow to a stop.

Why do astronauts float in space?

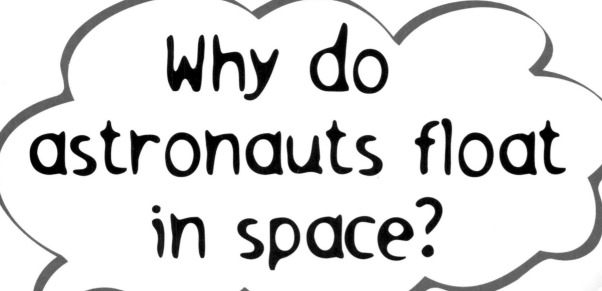

When things are in space they don't have any weight. This means everything floats. So do astronauts! This makes them feel sick, too. In a spacecraft everything is fixed down to stop it floating away. Astronauts have footholds and handholds to grab onto.

All packed?

Astronauts must take everything they need into space. In space there is no air, water or food. All of these things have to be packed into the spacecraft and taken into space.

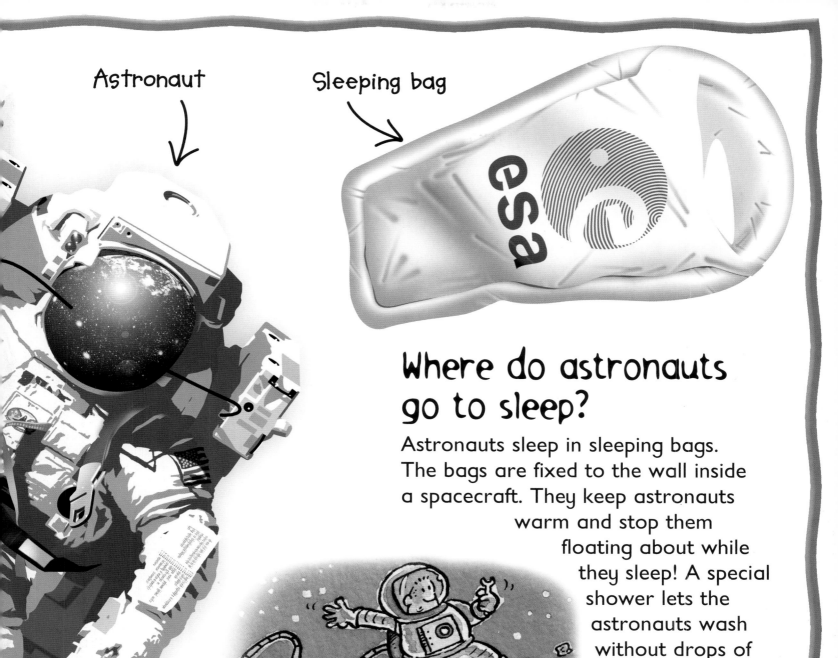

Astronaut

Sleeping bag

Where do astronauts go to sleep?

Astronauts sleep in sleeping bags. The bags are fixed to the wall inside a spacecraft. They keep astronauts warm and stop them floating about while they sleep! A special shower lets the astronauts wash without drops of water floating everywhere.

Why do astronauts wear spacesuits?

Space is a dangerous place. Spacesuits protect astronauts when they go outside their spacecraft. There is no air in space. So a spacesuit has a supply of air for the astronaut to breathe. The suit also stops an astronaut from getting too hot or too cold.

Remember

Can you remember why astronauts have to carry air with them in space?

Are there robots in space?

There are robot spacecraft, called probes, in space. They have visited all the planets, except Pluto. Some probes travel around the planets. They send photographs and other information back to Earth. Other probes land on a planet to take a closer look.

Snap happy!

A probe called *Voyager 2* was the first to visit Uranus and Neptune. It took photographs of the planets and sent them back to Earth.

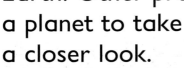
Viking probe on Mars

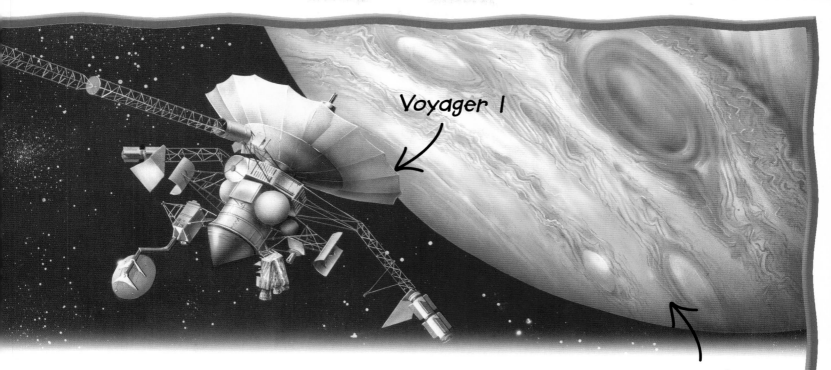

Voyager 1

Jupiter

Which probe has travelled the furthest?

A probe called *Voyager 1* was launched from Earth in 1977. It visited Jupiter in 1979 and then Saturn in 1980. Then it kept going, out of the Solar System. *Voyager 1* is now 14 thousand million kilometres from Earth!

Draw

Try designing your own robot explorer. You can take some ideas from these pages.

Sojourner

Have probes been to Mars?

More probes have been to Mars than any other planet. In 1997 a probe called Pathfinder landed on Mars. Inside Pathfinder was a tiny robot vehicle, called *Sojourner*. Scientists steered it using remote control. It investigated the soil and rocks on Mars.

Quiz time

Do you remember what you have read about space? Here are some questions to test your memory. The pictures will help you. If you get stuck, read the pages again.

1. Which star keeps us warm?

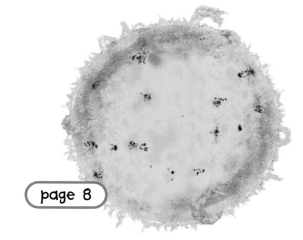

page 8

2. Why is the Sun spotty?

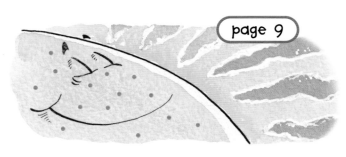

page 9

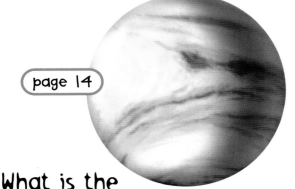

page 14

3. What is the hottest planet?

4. Why is Mars called the red planet?

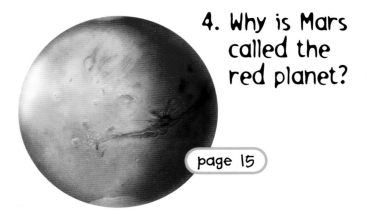

page 15

page 16

5. What is the smallest planet?

page 22

6. What is a shooting star?

7. Does the Sun have a belt?

page 23

11. How does a shuttle get into space?

page 28

8. What is a group of stars called?

page 25

12. When is a shuttle like a glider?

page 29

13. Why do astronauts float in space?

page 30

9. What is the Milky Way?

page 26

10. Can galaxies crash?

page 26

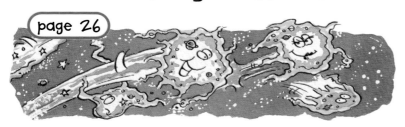

Answers

1. The Sun
2. Cooler parts look darker, like spots
3. Venus
4. It is covered with red rocks and dust
5. Pluto
6. A lump of rock burning in the sky
7. Yes, the asteroid belt
8. Star cluster
9. A huge group of stars
10. Yes
11. Like a giant rocket does
12. When it travels back to Earth
13. Because they have no weight in space

Breezy questions about...

Why is summer warm and sunny? 38
Why are days longer in summer? 38
Why do leaves fall in autumn? 39

What is the sunniest place? 40
When is a lake not a lake? 41
What happens when it
   doesn't rain? 41

Where does rain come from? 44
Are all clouds small and fluffy? 45
What rain never lands? 45

What happens in a flood? 46
Did Noah build an ark? 47
Can there be a flood in a desert? 47

What is snow made of? 48
When is snow dangerous? 49
Are all snowflakes the same? 49

Does Earth have a blanket? 42
Where does it rain every day? 42
How deep is the atmosphere? 43

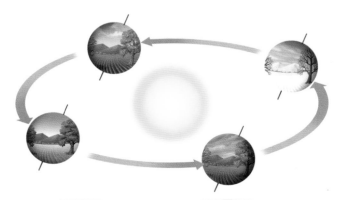

Weather

Where are the fastest winds? 50
Which storm has an eye? 51
How do we measure wind? 51

What makes the sky clap? 52
When is lightning like a fork? 53
Does lightning hit buildings? 53

What is a rainbow made of? 54
When does the sky have curtains? 55
When can you see three suns? 55

What is a rain dance? 56
Who first recorded the weather? 56
Are weather sayings true? 57

Which bird spins in the wind? 58
What is a weather house? 59
How do we know how hot it is? 59

Can planes tell the weather? 60
Why do scientists fly balloons? 61
How do we watch
    weather from space? 61

Did weather kill the dinosaurs? 62
Is Greenland green? 63
Is our weather changing? 63

Quiz time 64

Why is summer warm and sunny?

The Earth is tipped to one side as it moves round the Sun. Some of the year, the north half of the Earth faces the Sun. Then the Sun is higher in the sky, making the weather warm. This is summer. When the southern half of the Earth faces the Sun, it is winter in the north.

Spring in the north

Summer in the north

The Sun

Why are days longer in summer?

Summer days are longer because the Earth is tilted and spins round. In summer, the Sun rises earlier and sets later. This makes daytime last longer than night. In the middle of summer in Sweden it is light for 21 hours!

Winter in the north

Why do leaves fall in autumn?

Autumn comes between summer and winter. Many trees lose their leaves in autumn because it is hard for them to grow in the dark winter months. The leaves turn from green to red, orange or brown. Then they fall to the ground.

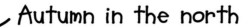

Autumn in the north

Find

Can you find photographs of red, orange and brown leaves in autumn?

Sunshine at midnight!

At the North and South Poles, the Sun never sets in summer. It is light all day. In winter, the Sun never rises. Then it is dark all day long!

What is the sunniest place?

The Sahara Desert in North Africa is the sunniest place on Earth. It is sunny for nearly 12 hours every day! It hardly rains, which makes it hard for plants and animals to live here. People dress in loose clothes to stop being sunburnt.

Sea makes fire!

Water flowing around the sea can change the weather. El Niño is a warm water current in the Pacific Ocean. Scientists think that this could cause droughts.

When is a lake not a lake?

When it's a mirage! A mirage often happens on a hot day. Hot air near the ground makes light from the bright sky bend upwards. This makes it seem as if there is a lake on the ground in the distance. Really the ground is dry!

← People living in the desert

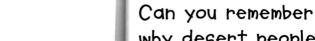

Drought

Remember
Can you remember why desert people wear loose clothes, even when it is very hot?

What happens when it doesn't rain?

Sometimes it is dry for a long time in places where it normally rains a lot. This is called a drought. There was a drought in the United States in the 1930s. Crops didn't grow and fields turned to dust. Many people had to leave their farms.

Does Earth have a blanket?

Planet Earth

Yes, it does. The Earth is wrapped in a thick blanket of air. It is called the atmosphere. This is where all the weather happens. The atmosphere also helps to keep the Earth's surface warm at night. In the day it protects us from harmful rays coming from the Sun.

Where does it rain every day?

In a tropical rainforest the weather is always very hot and very wet. The Sun shines every day, and there are downpours of heavy rain, too. Rainforest plants grow very quickly in this steamy weather.

Monsoon downpour!

In some countries it pours with rain for a few weeks every year. This is called a monsoon. In India, enough rain falls in one year to cover the ground with water 26 metres deep!

How deep is the atmosphere?

The atmosphere stretches hundreds of kilometres above our heads. If you go up through the atmosphere, the air gets thinner and thinner. High up in mountains, mountaineers find it difficult to breathe so they take breathing equipment with them.

Mountaineer

Look

Look at the picture of the Earth above. What do you think the white swirly patterns are?

Where does rain come from?

Most rain comes from the sea! Some seawater turns to gas in the air. If the air rises, the gas becomes water drops. These make clouds. If the drops get big enough, they fall as rain. The water flows back to the sea.

3. Rain falls

2. Water from plants rises into air

4. Water runs into rivers

1. Seawater rises into air

The water cycle

Head in the clouds!

The tops of tall mountains are often in the clouds. At the top it looks misty. Mountaineers sometimes get lost in these clouds!

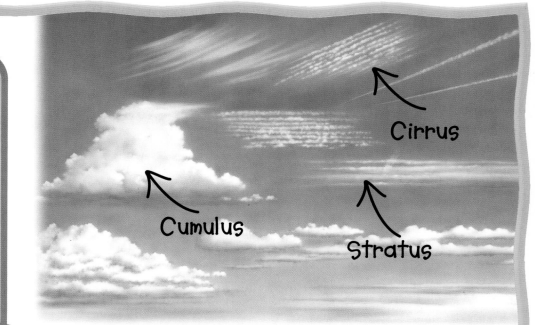

Cirrus

Cumulus

Stratus

Are all clouds small and fluffy?

Clouds come in lots of different shapes and sizes. Weather experts give the different clouds names. Fluffy clouds are called cumulus clouds. Some are small and some are giant. Flat clouds are called stratus clouds. Wispy clouds high in the sky are called cirrus clouds.

What rain never lands?

Sometimes rain that falls from a cloud never reaches the ground. If the drops of rain fall into very dry air, the water in them turns into gas. This means that the drops disappear and never reach the ground.

Look

Look at the clouds outside today. Are they fluffy or flat? The picture above will help you.

What happens in a flood?

Sometimes a lot of rain falls in a few hours. So much water flows into rivers that they fill up and burst their banks. The rivers flood the land on each side. Sometimes houses disappear under the flood water.

Floods of tears!

The river Nile in Egypt floods every year. Thousands of years ago, the Egyptians made up a story about the flood. It said that a goddess called Isis cried so much that the river filled up with her tears.

Did Noah build an ark?

The Bible tells the story of a man called Noah. He built a great boat called an ark to escape a flood. We don't know if Noah's ark existed. Scientists have found out that there probably was a huge flood thousands of years ago.

Noah's ark

Flooded house

Find

Can you find the country of Egypt and the river Nile in an atlas?

Can there be a flood in a desert?

Yes there can. Most of the time there is no rain in a desert. The hot Sun bakes the ground hard. Once in a while, it rains heavily. The water flows off the ground instead of soaking in. This can cause a flood.

What is snow made of?

Snow is made of ice, which is water that has frozen. When it is very cold in a cloud, tiny bits of ice (crystals) begin to form, instead of water drops. The pieces clump together to make snowflakes that fall to the ground. The weather must be very cold for snow to fall. If it is too warm, the snowflakes melt and turn to rain.

Shiver!

Antarctica is the coldest place on Earth. The lowest temperature ever recorded there is −89°C. That's much, much colder than inside a freezer!

Snow drifts

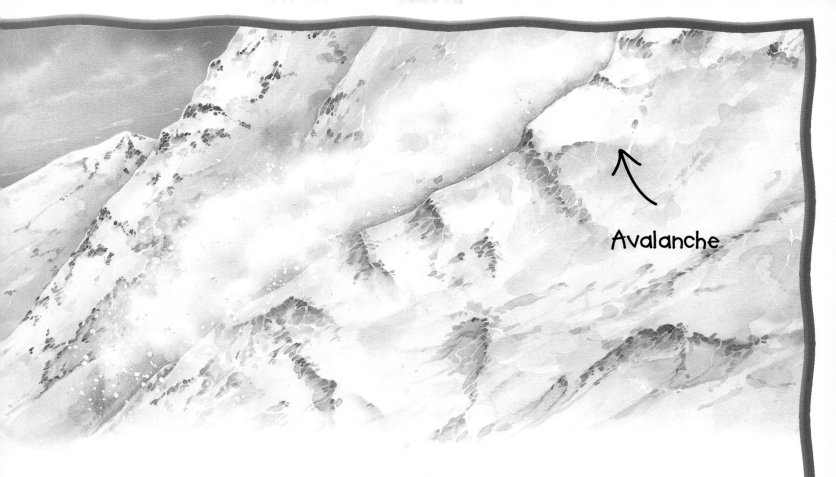

Avalanche

When is snow dangerous?

When lots of snow falls on mountains, deep layers build up on the slopes. The snow may suddenly slide down the mountain. This is an avalanche. A big avalanche can bury a town. A loud noise or even a person walking on the snow can start an avalanche.

Are all snowflakes the same?

It's hard to believe, but all snowflakes are different — even though there are millions and millions of them. This is because every ice crystal in a snowflake has its own shape. No two crystals are the same. Most ice crystals in snowflakes looks like stars with six points.

Think

Can you think why it could be dangerous to ski across a steep hillside covered with snow?

Where are the fastest winds?

Inside a tornado. A tornado is like a spinning funnel made of air. They reach down from giant thunderstorms. The winds can blow at 480 kilometres an hour. That's twice as fast as an express train! Tornadoes can rip trees from the ground and destroy houses.

Tornado ⟶

Which storm has an eye?

A hurricane is
a giant spinning
storm made up of
super-strong winds.
The centre is a hole called
the eye. Here it is calm and sunny.
If a hurricane reaches land, the winds can
damage buildings and heavy rain causes
floods. Hurricane hunters are planes that fly
into hurricanes to measure the wind speed.

Eye

Hurricane hunter

Stormy names!

A tropical storm that starts in
the Atlantic Ocean is called a
hurricane. In the Pacific Ocean,
a tropical storm is called
a typhoon. In the
Indian Ocean it is
called a cyclone.

Draw

Look at the
pictures on this
page. Can you
draw a picture of
a tornado and a
hurricane?

How do we measure wind?

We measure the wind on a scale
called the Beaufort Scale. The
slowest wind is Force 1 on the
scale. This is called a light
breeze. The strongest wind is
Force 12. This is called a
hurricane. Force zero means
there is no wind at all.

What makes the sky clap?

A thunderstorm! Inside a big thundercloud, water drops and bits of ice move up and down, bumping into each other. This makes electricity build up. When the electricity jumps around, we see a spark of lightning and hear a loud clap of thunder.

Huge hail!

Hail is made up of lumps of ice called hailstones. Hail can fall from thunderclouds. The biggest hailstone ever fell in Bangladesh in 1986. It was the size of a grapefruit!

When is lightning like a fork?

When lightning jumps from a thundercloud to the ground, it looks like huge forks in the sky. If lightning jumps from one cloud to another, the clouds light up. This is called sheet lightning. Lightning can be red, blue, yellow or white.

Lightning ⟶

Does lightning hit buildings?

Lightning often hits tall buildings. The buildings have a metal spike on top called a lightning conductor. When lightning hits a building, the lightning conductor carries the electricity to the ground. If there was no lightning conductor, the building could be damaged by the lightning.

Thundercloud

Count

Count the seconds between a flash of lightning and a clap of thunder. The bigger the number, the further away the thunderstorm.

What is a rainbow made of?

Rainbow

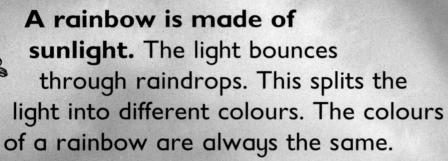 **A rainbow is made of sunlight.** The light bounces through raindrops. This splits the light into different colours. The colours of a rainbow are always the same. They are red, orange, yellow, green, blue, indigo and violet.

Remember
Can you remember all seven colours of a rainbow?

Northern lights

When does the sky have curtains?

In the far north and the far south of the world, amazing patterns of light sometimes appear in the sky. They look like colourful curtains. The patterns are called auroras (or-roar-rers). They happen when tiny light particles from the Sun smash into the air.

Rainbow with no colour!

A fogbow is a rainbow that is white. You might see a fogbow when the Sun shines through fog. It is white because the water drops in fog are too small to split up the light into rainbow colours.

When can you see three suns?

If there are thin clouds high in the sky, you might see three suns. The clouds are made of bits of ice. These bend light from the Sun. This makes it look as if there are two extra suns in the sky. We call these mock suns, or sun dogs.

What is a rain dance?

 **In many hot places, such as Africa, it only rains once or twice a year.** People may dance traditional rain dances if the rain does not fall. In the past, people believed that rain dances really could bring clouds and rain.

Who first recorded the weather?

 Over 3000 years ago in China, people made notes about the weather. They studied how windy it was, or if it rained or snowed. They carved the information onto pieces of tortoiseshell.

Rain dance

Are weather sayings true?

There are many sayings about the weather. Most of them are true. One saying is 'Clear Moon, frost soon'. If there are no clouds in the sky you can see the Moon clearly. It also means it will get cold quickly at night. So the saying is true.

Full Moon

Weather cows!

Some people think that cows lie down when it is going to rain. But this weather saying is not true. Cows lie down on sunny days, too!

Discover

Can you find some more sayings about the weather? You could ask your teacher, or try looking in a book.

57

Which bird spins in the wind?

A metal cockerel on a weather vane. The cockerel spins so it can point in any direction. When the wind blows, the cockerel spins and points to where the wind is coming from. If the wind is blowing from the north, it is called a north wind. The wind blows from the north, south, east and west.

Weather vane

Groundhog Day!

In the USA, February 2 is called Groundhog Day. If people see an animal called a groundhog, they think that it will stay cold for another six weeks!

What is a weather house?

A weather house is a model that can tell how much moisture is in the air. If it is going to be dry, a lady in summer clothes comes out. If it is going to be rainy, a man with an umbrella comes out.

Weather house

How do we know how hot it is?

By reading a thermometer. A thermometer shows the temperature, which is how hot the air around us is. The first thermometer was made in 1714 by Gabriel Daniel Fahrenheit.

Think

From which direction does a southerly wind blow? North or south?

Can planes tell the weather?

Weather planes don't carry any passengers. Instead they fly through the air recording the weather. They measure the temperature of the air, the speed of the wind and how much water is in the air. This information helps weather forecasters tell us what the weather is going to be like.

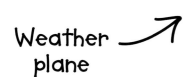

Weather plane

Astronaut snaps!

Astronauts who travel on the space shuttle and live on space stations take cameras with them. They often take amazing photographs of clouds and thunderstorms from space.

Why do scientists fly balloons?

Scientists fly balloons to find out about the weather. The balloons are filled with a gas called helium. They float up through the air and carry instruments that measure the weather. The information is sent back to the ground by radio.

Weather balloon

Remember

Can you remember how information gets from a weather balloon down to the ground?

How do we watch weather from space?

With weather satellites. A satellite moves around the Earth in space. It takes photographs of the clouds below and sends them back to Earth. Satellite photographs show which way hurricanes are moving. They help forecasters to warn people if a hurricane is heading their way.

Did weather kill the dinosaurs?

Dinosaurs lived millions of years ago. Scientists think that they may have died because the weather all over the world got colder. They think this happened when a giant rock (meteorite) from space hit the Earth. This threw lots of dust into the air, which blocked out the Sun.

Meteorite hitting the Earth

Is Greenland green?

Greenland is a big island in the Atlantic Ocean. It is covered with a thick sheet of ice. Hundreds of years ago, Greenland was green because it was not so cold and icy. People from northern Europe called Vikings farmed there. They moved away when the weather got colder.

Vikings in Greenland

Windy tower!

The Tower of Winds is a tower in Athens, Greece. It was built 2000 years ago. It had a giant wind vane on top to measure the direction of the wind.

Find

Can you find Greenland on a map of the world?

Is our weather changing?

Weather experts think the weather is getting warmer. This might be happening because we are cutting down forests. When trees are burned, they release a gas called carbon dioxide. This traps heat from the Sun in the atmosphere.

Quiz time

Do you remember what you have read about weather? These questions will test your memory. The pictures will help you. If you get stuck, read the pages again.

1. Why do leaves fall in autumn?

page 39

2. When is a lake not a lake?

page 41

3. Where does it rain every day?

page 42

4. How deep is the atmosphere?

page 43

5. Are all clouds small and fluffy?

page 45

6. What rain never lands?

page 45

7. What happens in a flood?

page 46

8. Did Noah build an ark?

page 47

9. When is snow dangerous?

page 49

10. Which storm has an eye?

page 51

11. What makes the sky clap?

page 52

12. Who first recorded the weather?

page 56

13. What is a rain dance?

page 56

Answers

1. Because it is hard for them to grow in the dark winter months
2. When it's a mirage
3. In a tropical rainforest
4. Hundreds of kilometres
5. No, they come in different shapes and sizes
6. Drops that fall into very dry air
7. A lot of rain falls and floods the land
8. We don't know if Noah's ark existed
9. In an avalanche
10. A hurricane
11. A thunderstorm
12. The Chinese
13. A traditional dance to bring on clouds and rain

Electrifying questions about...

Is science in the playground?	68
What is a wheel?	69
What makes things stop and start?	69
Why do fireworks flash and bang?	70
Do I need energy?	71
What is a thermometer?	71
What is in an electric motor?	72
Where do rainbow colours come from?	73
What is the loudest sound?	73
Where is science in a city?	74
Who works railway signals?	75
How do skyscrapers stay up?	75
How do you make magnets?	76
Does a magnet have a field?	77
What are poles?	77
Where does electricity come from?	78
What is a circuit?	79
When is electricity in the sky?	79
What waves are invisible?	80
What is an X-ray?	81
What waves can cook food?	81
Are computers clever?	82
Does a computer have a brain?	83
How does a computer remember?	83

Science

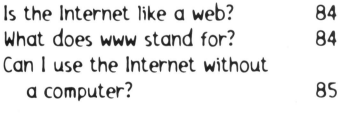

What do scientists do at work?	88
Who is the most famous scientist?	89
Do scientists help doctors?	89

Is the Internet like a web?	84
What does www stand for?	84
Can I use the Internet without a computer?	85
Can a car be made from card?	86
What materials grow?	87
Does glass grow?	87

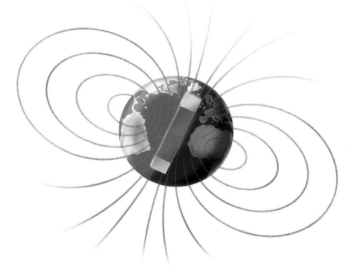

Are we harming the Earth?	90
What is recycling?	91
Does electricity harm the Earth?	91

| Quiz time | 92 |

Is science in the playground?

Yes, it is! Lots of science happens in a playground. The playground rides could not work without science. A see-saw is a simple machine called a lever. It has a long arm and a point in the middle called a pivot. As you ride on the see-saw, the lever tips up and down on the pivot.

See-saw

Lever

Pivot

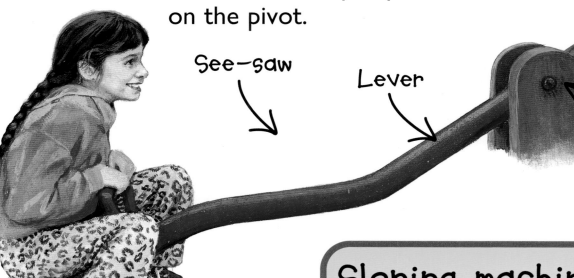

Sloping machine!

A ramp is the simplest machine of all. It is easier to walk up a ramp to the top of a hill than it is to climb a steep hillside.

What is a wheel?

A wheel is a very simple machine that can spin around. Wheels let other machines, such as skateboards, bicycles, cars and trains, roll along smoothly. They also make it easy to move heavy weights in carts and wheelbarrows.

Feel

Press the palm of your hand onto a table. A force called friction stops you sliding your hand along.

What makes things stop and start?

Pushes and pulls make things stop and start. Scientists use the word 'force' for pushes and pulls. Forces are all around us. The force of gravity pulls things downwards. It makes a rollercoaster car hurtle downhill. It also slows the car on the uphill parts of the track.

Rollercoaster

Why do fireworks flash and bang?

Bread

Cheese

Butter

Fireworks flash and bang because they are full of chemicals that burn. The chemicals have lots of energy stored in them. When they burn, the energy changes to light, heat and sound. We use chemicals that burn in other places too, such as cookers, heaters and car engines.

Fireworks

Milk

Do I need energy?

Yes, you do. Your body needs energy to keep working. It even uses energy when you are fast asleep! You get energy from food. Some food, such as bread, is full of energy. You have to eat other kinds of food as well. They have chemicals in them that keep your body healthy.

Fruit and vegetables

Hot! Hot! Hot!

The hottest-ever temperature recorded was in a science laboratory. It was four hundred thousand million degrees Celsius (400,000,000°C). Now that's hot!

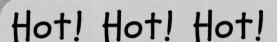

What is a thermometer?

A thermometer tells us how hot something is. This is called temperature. The numbers written on a thermometer are normally degrees Celsius (°C). If you put a thermometer in cold water, it shows 0°C. If you put it in boiling water it shows 100°C. A thermometer can also measure your body temperature.

Remember

Look at the picture of food above. Can you remember a food that gives energy?

What is in an electric motor?

Magnets and wires. Electricity from a battery passes through the wires. This turns the wires into a magnet. Two more magnets on each side of the motor push and pull against the wires. This makes a thin metal rod (spindle) spin around.

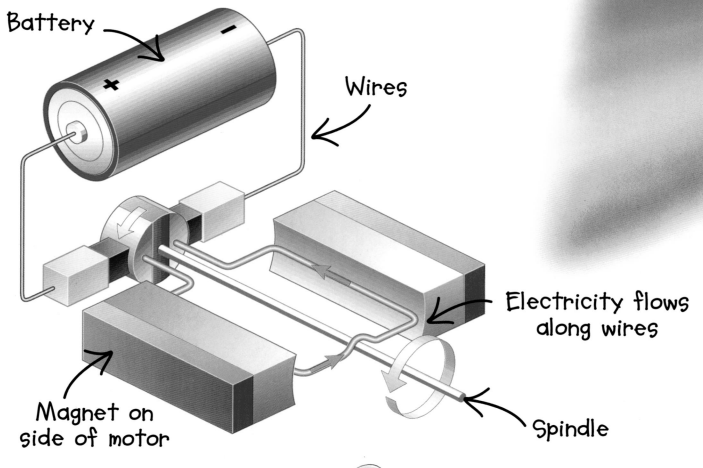

Battery

Wires

Electricity flows along wires

Magnet on side of motor

Spindle

Where do rainbow colours come from?

The colours of a rainbow are in light that comes from the Sun. This light is called white light. It is made up of lots of colours mixed together. We can see the colours if we send a beam of sunlight through a glass triangle called a prism, or when there's a rainbow in the sky.

Prism

Rainbow colours

Fast as light!

Light is the fastest thing in the Universe. It travels 300,000 kilometres every second. That means it could travel around the Earth seven times in less than a second!

Make

On a sunny day, stand with your back to the Sun. Spray water into the air and you should see a rainbow!

What is the loudest sound?

The roar of a jet engine is the loudest sound we normally hear. It is thousands of times louder than someone shouting. Sounds this loud can damage our ears if we are too close to them. The quietest sounds we can hear are things like rustling leaves.

Where is science in a city?

Everywhere! In a big city, almost every machine, building and vehicle is based on science. Cars, buses and trains help us move around the city. Scientists and engineers have also worked out how to build tall skyscrapers where people live and work.

City

Look

Look at the city picture. How many different forms of transport can you see?

Railway signals

Who works railway signals?

Nobody does! The signals work by themselves. Electronic parts on the track work out if a train is passing. Then a computer changes the signals to red, to stop another train moving onto the same piece of track.

How do skyscrapers stay up?

Skyscrapers stay up because they have a strong frame on the inside. The frame is made from steel and concrete. These are very strong materials. Normally you can't see the frame. It is hidden by the skyscraper's walls. The walls hang on the frame.

Plane spotters!

There's science at an airport, too. A radar machine uses radio waves to find aircraft in the sky. This helps people at the airport to guide the aircraft onto the runway.

How do you make magnets?

By using another magnet! Magnets are made from lumps of iron or steel. You can turn a piece of iron into a magnet by stroking it with another magnet. A magnet can also be made by sending electricity through a coil of wire. This is called an electromagnet. Some electromagnets are so strong, they can pick up cars.

Electromagnet picking up scrap cars

Count

Find a magnet at home (you can use a fridge magnet). How many paper clips can your magnet pick up?

VF 2314

Does a magnet have a field?

Yes – but it's not a field of grass! The area around a magnet is called a magnetic field. A magnetic field is shown by drawing lines around a magnet. The Earth has a magnetic field, too. It is as though there is a giant magnet inside the Earth.

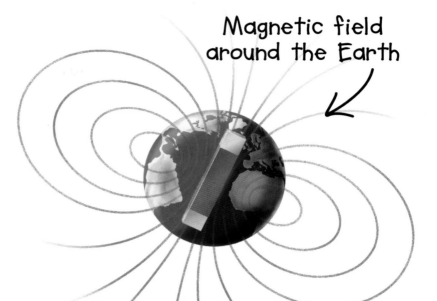

Magnetic field around the Earth

What are poles?

Every magnet has two poles. These are where the pull of a magnet is strongest. They are called the north pole and the south pole. A north pole and a south pole always pull towards each other. Two north poles always push each other away. So do two south poles.

Handy rock!

Some rocks act like magnets. Years ago, people used magnetic rocks to find their way. If they let the rock spin round, it always pointed in the same direction.

Where does electricity come from?

Battery →

Electricity comes to your home along cables from power stations. The cables are held off the ground by pylons. Around your home are holes in the wall called sockets. When a machine is plugged into a socket, electricity flows out to work the machine.

Electric!

Our homes are full of machines that work using electricity. If there was no electricity we wouldn't have televisions, lights, washing machines or computers!

Power station →

Remember

Mains electricity is very dangerous. It could kill you. Never play with mains sockets in your home.

What is a circuit?

A circuit is a loop that electricity moves around. This circuit is made up of a battery, a light bulb and a switch. If the switch is turned on, the loop would be broken. Then the electricity would stop moving and the light would go out.

Light bulb

Switch

When is electricity in the sky?

When there's a thunderstorm! During a storm, a kind of electricity called static electricity builds up. This can make a big flash, that lights up the sky. This is lightning. The hot lightning heats up the air around it and this makes a loud clap. This is thunder.

Pylon holds cables off the ground

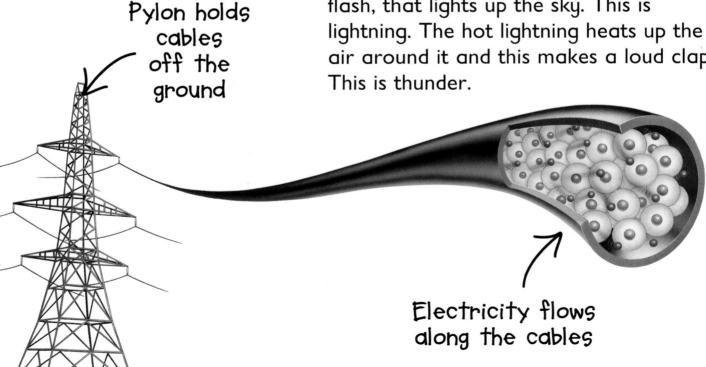

Electricity flows along the cables

What waves are invisible?

Radio waves are all around us, but we can't see them. We use radio waves to send sounds and pictures to radios and televisions. Some radio waves come from satellites in space. A radio set receives radio waves through a metal rod called an aerial. A dish-shaped aerial picks up radio waves for television programmes.

Satellite

Radio waves

Aerial

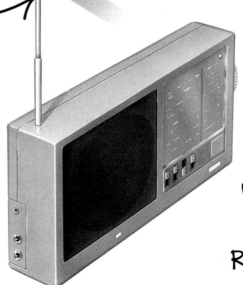

Radio

Remember

Which part of your body would stop an X-ray? Skin or bone?

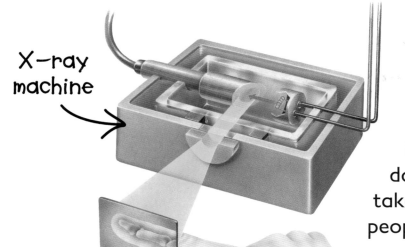

X-ray machine

Picture of bone

What is an X-ray?

An X-ray is like a radio wave. X-rays can go through the soft bits of your body. However, hard bones stop them. That's why doctors use X-ray machines to take pictures of the inside of people's bodies.

Dish-shaped aerial

Space radio!

Radio waves can travel through space. But they can't travel through water. So you can listen to a radio in a space station, but not in a submarine!

What waves can cook food?

Microwaves can. These are a kind of radio wave. They have lots of energy in them. A microwave uses this energy to cook food. Microwaves are fired into the oven. They make the particles in the food jiggle about. This makes the food hot.

Are computers clever?

Not really! Computers are amazing machines, but they can only do what they are told. They carry out computer programs written down by people. These are full of instructions that the computer follows. You can also tell a computer what to do by using its keyboard and mouse.

Typing on a keyboard

Mouse

Remember

Can you remember the name for a computer's electronic brain? Read these pages again to help you.

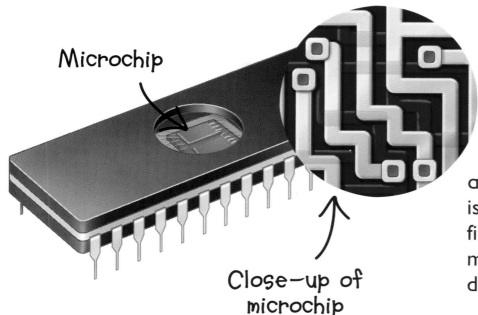

Microchip

Close-up of microchip

Does a computer have a brain?

A computer doesn't have a brain like yours. It has an electronic brain called a central processing unit. This is a microchip the size of your fingernail. This amazing mini machine can do millions of difficult sums in a split second.

Computer

Computer room!

The first computer was made 60 years ago. It was so big that it filled a whole room. A modern calculator can do sums much more quickly!

How does a computer remember?

A computer remembers with its electronic memory. This is made up of lots of tiny microchips. When you turn the computer off, everything in the memory is lost. So you have to save your work on a disc, otherwise you lose it when you switch off.

Is the Internet like a web?

The Internet is made up of millions of computers around the world. They are connected like a giant spider's web! A computer connects to a machine called a modem. This sends signals to a server. The server lets you connect to the Internet. People can send emails and open web pages.

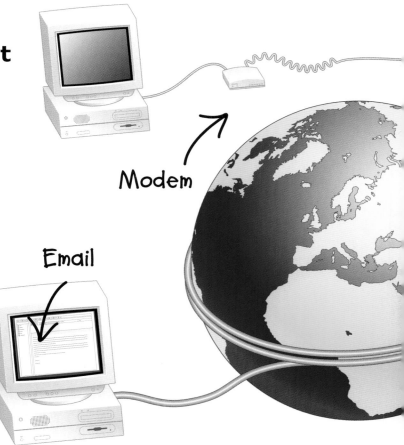

Modem

Email

Find out

Look at the main picture on these pages. See if you can find out what the word 'email' is short for.

What does www stand for?

The letters www are short for World Wide Web. The World Wide Web is like a giant library of information, stored on computers all over the world. There are also thousands of shops on the World Wide Web, where you can buy almost anything.

Can I use the Internet without a computer?

Yes. Other machines can link to the Internet, too. You can see simple information from the Internet on a mobile phone. You can send and get emails, too. A mobile phone connects to the Internet by radio.

Server

Mobile phone

Web page

Millions of pages!

The World Wide Web has more than 8000 million pages of information. That's two pages for every person on the planet!

The Internet

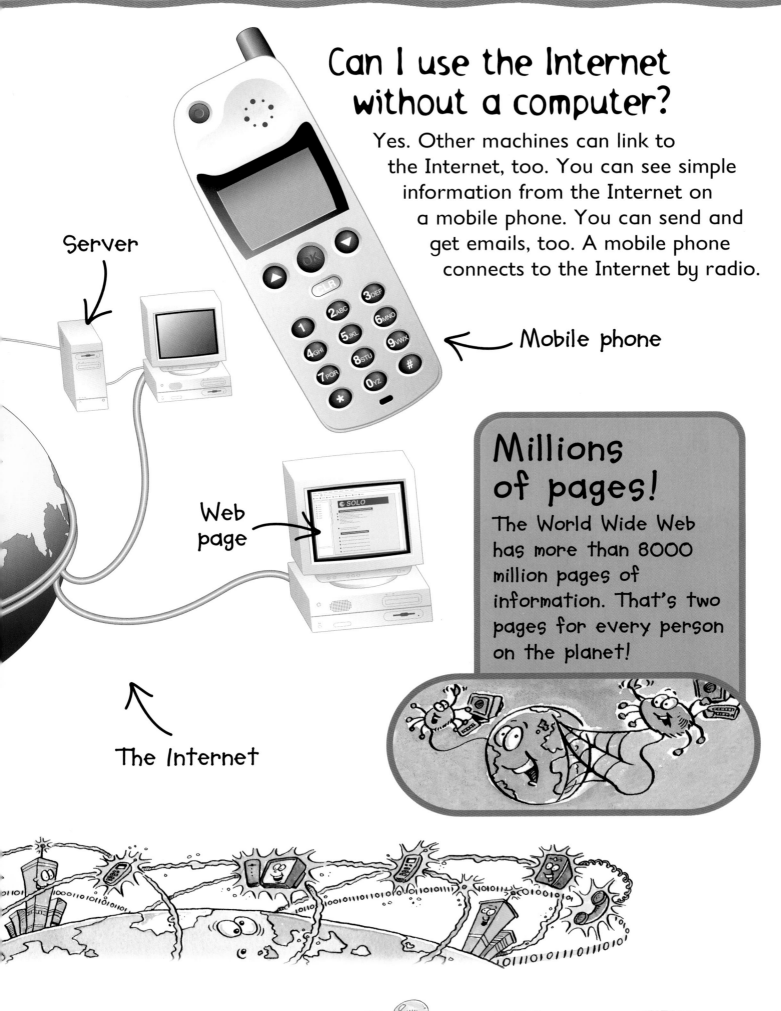

Can a car be made from card?

Yes, it can – but it would break if you sat inside it! It is always important to use the right material to make something. Cars are made from tough, long-lasting materials. Metal, plastic and rubber are all materials used to make cars.

A racing car is made up of hundreds of parts and different materials

Think
Think of three more materials from which things are made. If you get stuck, ask an adult.

Cotton plants make clothes

What materials grow?

Many of the materials we use every day come from plants. Wood comes from the trunks and branches of trees. Cotton is made from the seeds of cotton plants to make clothes such as T-shirts. Some rubber is made from a liquid (sap) from rubber trees.

Rubber tree makes tyres

Tree trunks and branches make wooden bats

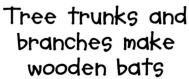

Does glass grow?

Glass doesn't grow! It is made from sand and two other materials called limestone and soda. These materials are mixed together and melted to make a gooey liquid. When the mixture cools down, it forms the hard glass that we use to makes windows, drinking glasses and other objects.

Bullet proof!

Some glass is extra-strong. Toughened glass is so hard that even a bullet from a gun bounces off it!

What do scientists do at work?

Some scientists try to find out about the world around us. Others find out about space, planets and stars. Some scientists discover useful materials that we can use. Scientists carry out experiments in laboratories to test their ideas.

Scientist in a laboratory

Who is the most famous scientist?

The most famous scientist is called Albert Einstein (1879–1955). He made many discoveries about time, space, the force of gravity and nuclear energy. The ideas that Einstein wrote down were so amazing that they made him famous across the world.

Albert Einstein

Do scientists help doctors?

Yes, they do. Many scientists make medicines that the doctor gives you when you are ill. They also help to make the complicated machines that doctors use in hospitals. Scientists also try to find out what makes us ill, and how we can stay healthy.

Are we harming the Earth?

Many of the things we do are harming the world around us. Machines such as cars put dangerous gases into the air. These gases can harm plants and make people ill. They are also making the weather change. Scientists are always looking for new ways to reduce damage to the Earth.

Pollution

Dirty cars!

Cars and other vehicles can produce so much pollution that in some cities it has become difficult for people to breathe.

What is recycling?

Recycling is using materials again, instead of throwing them away. This helps to make less waste. Ask your parents to take empty glass bottles to a bottle bank. The glass in the bottles is made into new bottles. Paper, metal and plastic are also recycled.

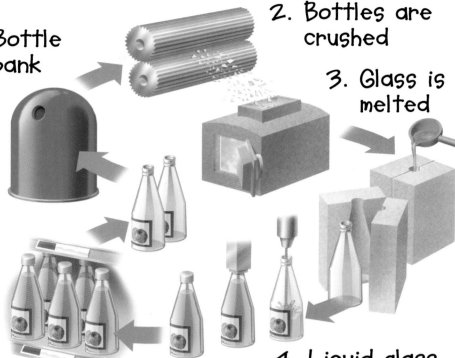

1. Bottle bank

2. Bottles are crushed

3. Glass is melted

4. Liquid glass is put in moulds

5. New bottles are ready

Glass recycling

Save

Ask your family to save electricity. Get them to switch off the lights when nobody is in the room.

Does electricity harm the Earth?

Yes, it does. Lots of coal, oil and gas are burned to make electricity. These make harmful gases that go into the air. You can help by turning things off to save electricity. Scientists are inventing new ways of making electricity from the wind, the Sun and water.

Quiz time

Do you remember what you have read about science? These questions will test your memory. The pictures will help you. If you get stuck, read the pages again.

1. Is science in the playground?

page 68

2. Do I need energy?

page 71

3. What is a thermometer?

page 71

4. What is in an electric motor?

page 72

5. How do skyscrapers stay up?

page 75

6. Does a magnet have a field?

page 77

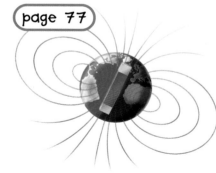

7. What is a circuit?

page 79

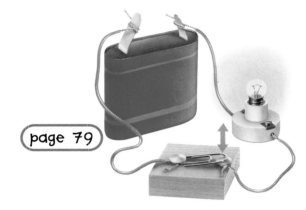

page 84

11. What does www stand for?

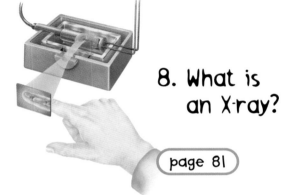

8. What is an X-ray?

page 81

12. Who is the most famous scientist?

page 89

13. Does electricity harm the Earth?

page 91

9. What waves can cook food?

page 81

page 82

10. Are computers clever?

Answers

1. Yes it is, in rides such as see—saws
2. Yes, you need energy for your body to work
3. A machine that measures heat
4. Magnets and wires
5. They have a strong frame that supports them
6. Yes, a magnetic field
7. A loop that electricity moves around
8. It is a radio wave
9. Microwaves
10. No, but they can follow instructions
11. World Wide Web
12. Albert Einstein
13. Yes, it can

Brainy questions about...

What does my skin do?   96
How thick is my skin?   97
Why do I sweat when I'm warm?   97

How much hair do I have?   98
What are nails made from?   99
Why do we have fingernails?   99

How many bones
do I have?   100
What are bones
made from?   101
How are bones
joined together?   101

How do muscles work?   102
What is my biggest muscle?   102
What makes my muscles move?   103

Why do I need to breathe?   104
Is my voice kept in a box?   105
What makes air go into
    my lungs?   105

What food is good for me?   106
Why do I need to eat food?   107
What happens when I swallow?   107

What are teeth made of?   108
How many sets of teeth do
    I have?   108
What happens to the food
    I swallow?   109

Your Body

Why does my heart beat?   110
What does blood do?   111
Does blood get dirty?   111

Are my eyes like a camera?   112
What is inside my ears?   113
How do I hear sounds?   113

Why can't I see smells?   114
How do I taste things?   115
How many smells can I sense?   115

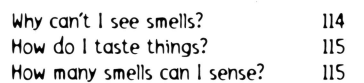

Is my brain really big?   116
Can my brain really wave?   117
How does my brain help
   me to play?   117

Quiz time   118

What does my skin do?

Skin protects you from bumps and scratches. It stops your body from drying out, and prevents germs from getting in. When you play on bikes or skateboards, you should wear gloves and knee pads to protect your skin.

Knee pads protect from cuts

Gloves protect from scrapes

Ouch! Ouch! Ouch!

There are millions of tiny touch sensors in your skin. They tell your brain when something touches your skin. Some sensors feel hot and cold. Others feel pain. Ouch!

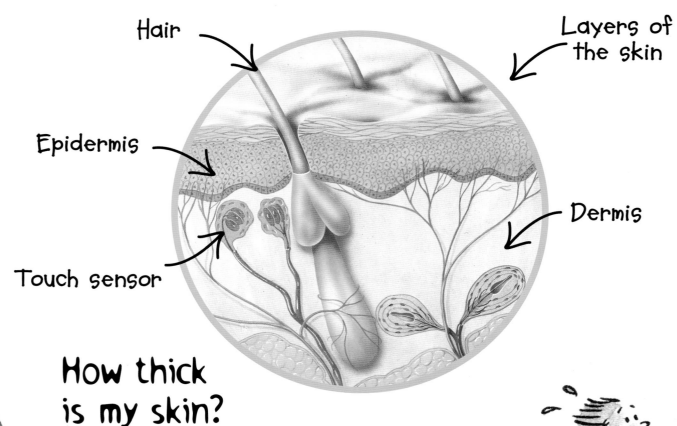

Hair

Layers of the skin

Epidermis

Dermis

Touch sensor

How thick is my skin?

Your skin is very thin. It is only 2 millimetres thick. On top is a layer of tough, dead cells called the epidermis. These cells gradually rub off. New cells grow underneath to replace them. Underneath is another layer of skin called the dermis. This contains areas that give you your sense of touch.

Think

If you are riding a bike or playing on a skateboard, what should you wear on your head, and why?

Why do I sweat when I'm warm?

To cool down again. Your body warms up on a hot day or when you run about. You sweat to get rid of the heat. Your body lets sweat out through your skin. As the sweat dries, it takes away heat. This cools you down.

How much hair do I have?

Your whole body is covered in about five million hairs!
You have about 100,000 hairs on your head. Hair grows out of tiny pits in your skin, called follicles. Hair grows in different colours and it can be wavy, curly or straight.

Blonde wavy hair

Red straight hair

Black curly hair

Black straight hair

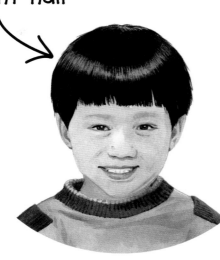

For the chop!

The hair on your head grows about 2 millimetres a week. If a hair is never cut, it reaches about one metre in length before it falls out. It is replaced by a new hair.

What are nails made from?

Fingernails and toenails are made from a hard material called keratin. It is the same material that hair is made from. Nails grow out of the nail root. In a week, a nail grows by about half a millimetre. They grow faster at night than in the day!

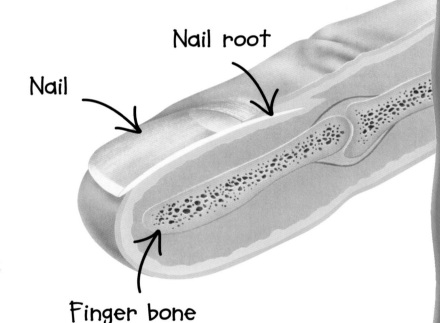

Nail root

Nail

Finger bone

Look

Have a look in the mirror. Is your hair straight, wavy or curly? Use the pictures on page 8 to help you.

Why do we have fingernails?

Fingernails protect your fingertips. The nail stops your fingertip bending back when you touch something. This helps your fingers to feel things. Nails are useful for picking up tiny objects.

How many bones do I have?

Most people have 206 bones. Half of them are in your hands and feet. All your bones together make up your skeleton. The skeleton is like a frame. It holds up the other parts of your body. It also protects the squashy bits inside.

Find

Can you find your collarbone? It starts at your shoulder and runs to the top of your rib cage.

Skeleton key

① Skull
② Collar bone
③ Shoulder blade
④ Ribs
⑤ Upper arm bone
⑥ Pelvis
⑦ Thigh bone
⑧ Kneecap
⑨ Calf bone
⑩ Shin bone

What are bones made from?

Bones are made from different materials mixed together. Some of the materials are very hard and some are tough and bendy. Together they make bones very strong. There is a kind of jelly called marrow inside some bones. This makes tiny parts for your blood, called red and white cells.

Marrow

Spongy bone

Hard bone

Strong bones!

Your bone is lightweight but super-strong. It is stronger than concrete or steel, which are used for making buildings and bridges! But bones can still break if they are bent too much.

How are bones joined together?

Your bones are connected by joints. They let your back, arms, legs, fingers and toes move. You have about 100 joints. The largest joints are in your hips and knees. The smallest joints are inside your ear.

How do muscles work?

Muscles are made from fibres that look like bits of string. The fibres get shorter to make the muscle pull. Many muscles make your bones move. They help you to run, jump, hold and lift things. Some muscles move your eyes, your heart and other body parts.

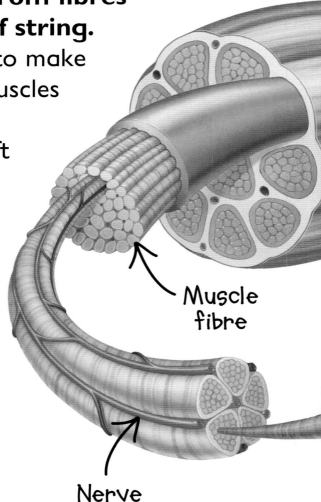

Muscle fibre

Nerve

What is my biggest muscle?

The biggest muscles in your body are the ones that you sit on — your bottom! You use them when you walk and run. The strongest muscle in your body is in your jaw. It scrunches your teeth together.

Cheeky muscles!

Your face is full of muscles. You use them to smile, to wrinkle your nose, or to cry. You use more muscles to frown than to smile!

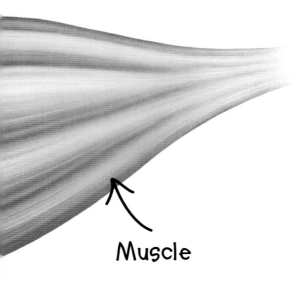

Muscle

What makes my muscles move?

Your brain does. It sends messages along nerves to your muscles. Lots of muscles are needed, even for small movements, like writing with a pen. Your brain controls other muscles without you thinking about it. For example, the muscles in your heart keep working even when you are asleep.

Feel

Bend and unbend your arm. Can you feel your arm muscles getting shorter and longer?

Why do I need to breathe?

You breathe to take air into your body. There is a gas in the air called oxygen that your body needs to work.

The air goes up your nose or into your mouth. Then it goes down a tube called the windpipe and into your lungs.

1. Air goes into your nose or mouth

2. Air goes down the windpipe

3. Air enters the lungs

Count

How many times do you breathe in and out in one minute?

Is my voice kept in a box?

Not quite! The real name for your voicebox is the larynx. It's at the top of the windpipe, and makes a bulge at the front of your neck. Air passing through the voicebox makes it shake, or vibrate. This is the sound of your voice. Your voice can make lots of sounds, and helps you to sing!

Singing

What makes air go into my lungs?

There is a big muscle under your lungs that moves down. More muscles make your ribs move out. This makes your lungs bigger. Air rushes into your lungs to fill the space. When your muscles relax, the air is pushed out again.

Fill 'em up!

When you are resting, you take in enough air to fill a can of fizzy drink in every breath. When you are running, you breathe in ten times as much air.

What food is good for me?

Lots of food is good for you! Different foods give your body the goodness it needs. Fruit and vegetables are very good for you. Bread and pasta give you energy. Small amounts of fat, such as cheese, keep your nerves healthy. Chicken and fish keep your muscles strong.

Fats keep nerves healthy

Vegetables help digestion

Fruit is full of goodness

Eating elephants!

You eat about one kilogram of food every day. During your life, you will eat about 30 tonnes of food. That's the same weight as six elephants!

Bread gives energy

Fish helps muscles to grow strong

Why do I need to eat food?

Food keeps your body working. It is like fuel for your body. It keeps your body going through the day and night, and works your muscles. Food also contains things your body needs to grow, repair itself and fight illness.

Your whole body needs food

What happens when I swallow?

The first thing you do with food is chew it. Then you swallow lumps of the chewed food. When you swallow, the food goes down a tube called the gullet. Muscles in the gullet push the food down into your stomach.

Draw

Look at some of the pictures on these pages. Can you draw a healthy meal that you would like to eat?

What are teeth made of?

Teeth are covered in a material called enamel. This is harder than most kinds of rock! Teeth are fixed into your jaw bones by roots. Sharp front teeth (incisors) bite food into small pieces. Tall, pointy teeth (canines) tear and pull food. Flat back teeth (molars) chew food to a mush.

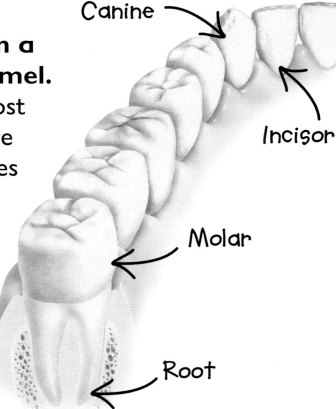

Canine

Incisor

Molar

Root

How many sets of teeth do I have?

You have two sets. A baby is born without teeth. The first set of teeth appears when a child is six months old. This set has 20 teeth. These teeth fall out at about seven years old. They are replaced by 32 adult teeth.

Discover

Do you still have your first set of teeth, or have your baby teeth begun to fall out?

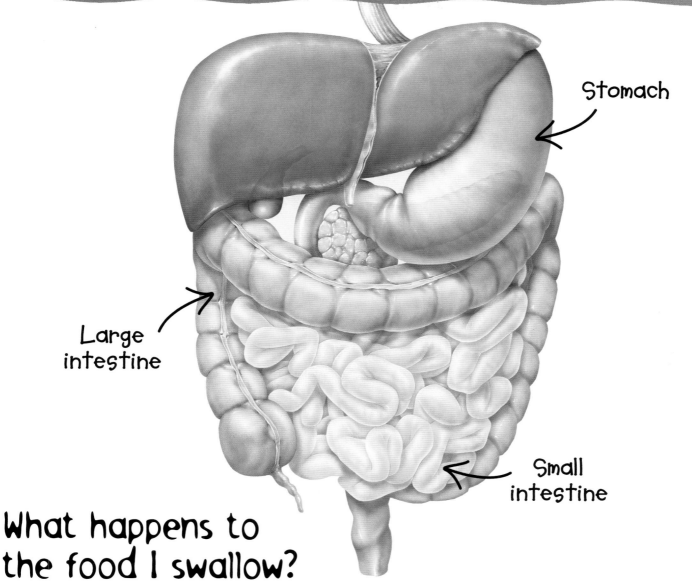

Stomach

Large intestine

Small intestine

What happens to the food I swallow?

The food you swallow goes into your stomach. Here, special juices and strong muscles break the food up into a thick mush. The mushy food then goes into a long tube called the intestines. Here, all the goodness from the food is taken out, to be used by our body.

All gone!

When you go to the toilet, you get rid of waste. This is leftover food. It is stored in your large intestine until you go to the toilet.

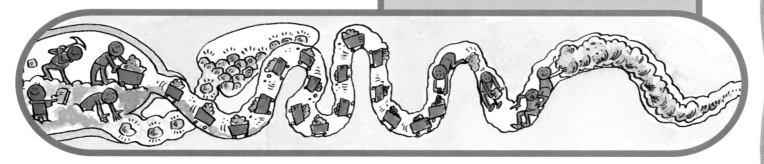

Why does my heart beat?

To pump blood and oxygen around your body. Your heart is about the size of your fist and is made of muscle. When it beats, your heart squeezes blood into tubes. These carry blood and oxygen around your body. The blood then comes back to the heart from the lungs, with more oxygen.

Blood to body

Blood from body

Blood to lungs

Blood from lung

Blood from lung

Blood from body

Heart muscles

Blood to body

Beat of life!

Your heart beats once a second for the whole of your life. That is 86,000 beats a day, and 31 million beats a year. In total, this is 2000 million beats in your life.

What does blood do?

Your whole body need oxygen to work. Blood carries oxygen to every part of your body in its red cells. Blood also contains white cells that fight germs. Tubes called arteries and veins carry blood around your body.

Artery

Red cell

White cell

Does blood get dirty?

Yes, it does. Because blood carries waste away from your body parts, it has to be cleaned. This is done by your kidneys. They take the waste out of the blood and make a liquid called urine. This liquid leaves your body when you go to the toilet.

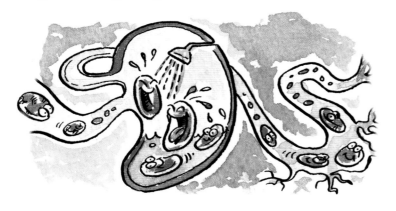

Feel

Touch your neck under your chin. Can you feel the blood flowing through an artery to your brain?

Are my eyes like a camera?

Your eyes work like a tiny camera. They collect light that bounces off the things you are looking at. This makes tiny pictures at the back of the eyes. Here, millions of sensors pick up the light. They send a picture to your brain along a nerve.

In a spin!

Inside your ear are loops full of liquid. They can tell when you move your head. This helps you to balance. If you spin around, the fluid keeps moving. This makes you feel dizzy!

Lens collects light

Pupil lets light into your eye

Nerve to brain

Muscles make eye move

What is inside my ears?

The flap on your head is only part of your ear. The hole in your ear goes to a tiny piece of tight skin, called an eardrum. Sounds enter your ear and make the eardrum move in and out. Tiny bones pass these movements to the cochlea, which is shaped like a snail. This is filled with liquid.

Look

Look in the mirror at your eye. Can you see the dark pupil where light goes in?

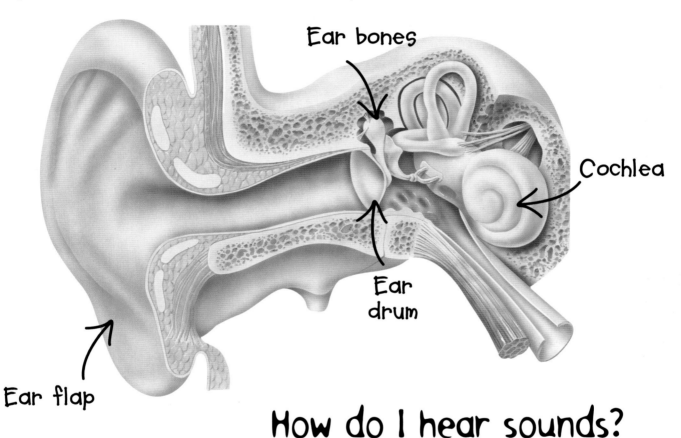

Ear bones

Cochlea

Ear drum

Ear flap

How do I hear sounds?

The cochlea in your ear contains thousands of tiny hairs. It is also is full of liquid. Sounds make the liquid move. This makes the hairs wave about. Tiny sensors pick up the waving, and send messages to your brain so you hear the sound.

Why can't I see smells?

Because they're invisible! Smells are tiny particles that float in the air. Inside the top of your nose are sticky smell sensors. When you sniff something, the sensors collect the smell particles. They send messages to your brain, which tell you what you can smell.

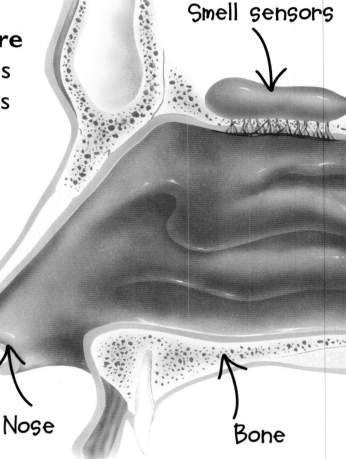

Smell sensors

Nose

Bone

A blocked dose!

Smell and taste work together when you eat. Your sense of smell helps you to taste flavours in food. When you have a cold, your smell sensors get blocked, so you cannot taste, either.

How do I taste things?

With your tongue. Your tongue is covered with tiny taste sensors. These are called taste buds. Buds on different parts of your tongue can sense different tastes, or flavours. Your tongue also moves food around your mouth and helps you to speak.

Salty flavours are tasted here

Sour flavours are tasted here

Sweet flavours are tasted here

How many smells can I sense?

Your nose can sense about 3000 different smells. You don't just have a sense of smell so you can smell nice things, such as flowers and perfumes! Your sense of smell warns you if food is rotten before you eat it.

Think

Look at the picture of the tongue. Can you think of three different things that taste sour, sweet and salty?

Is my brain really big?

Your brain is about the same size as your two fists put together. It is the place where you think, remember, feel happy or sad — and dream. Your brain also takes information from your senses and controls your body. The main part is called the cerebrum.

Cerebrum

Right and left!

The main part of your brain is divided into two halves. The left half helps you to play music and to draw. The right half is good at thinking.

Cerebellum controls muscles

Brain stem

Can my brain really wave?

Well, sort of! Your brain works using electricity. It has about 10,000 million tiny nerve cells. Tiny bursts of electricity are always jumping around between the cells. Doctors can see your brain working by looking at the electricity with a special machine called an EEG. It shows the electricity as waves on a screen.

Remember

Your brain controls the five senses – smelling, tasting, touching, hearing – can you remember your fifth sense?

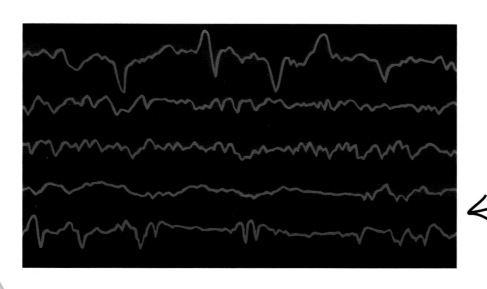

Brain waves from an EEG machine

How does my brain help me to play?

Different parts of your brain do different jobs. One part senses touch. Another part deals with thinking. Speaking is controlled by a different part. The cerebellum controls all your muscles. When you play and run, the cerebellum sends messages to your muscles to make them move.

Quiz time

Do you remember what you have read about your body? These questions will test your memory. The pictures will help you. If you get stuck, read the pages again.

1. What does my skin do?

page 96

2. Why do I sweat when I'm warm?

page 97

3. How much hair do I have?

page 98

4. How are bones joined together?

page 101

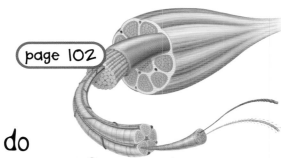

page 102

5. How do muscles work?

page 105

6. What makes air go into my lungs?

7. Why do I need to eat food?

page 107

11. How do I taste things?

page 115

8. How many sets of teeth do I have?

page 108

12. Is my brain really big?

page 116

9. What does blood do?

page 111

13. How does my brain help me to play?

page 117

page 113

10. How do I hear sounds?

Answers

1. It protects you
2. To help you cool down again
3. You have five million hairs on your body
4. They are connected by joints
5. The fibres inside get shorter and pull
6. Muscles
7. To keep your body working
8. Two sets
9. Carries oxygen around your body
10. With the parts that are inside your ear
11. With your tongue
12. It's as big as your fists put together
13. It tells your muscles to move

Prehistoric questions about...

What is a dinosaur? 122
When did dinosaurs live? 122
Where did the dinosaurs live? 123

Did any dinosaurs eat plants? 124
Why were dinosaurs so big? 125
Why did dinosaurs eat stones? 125

How big is a dinosaur tooth? 126
Did plant eaters need
    sharp teeth? 126
Did all dinosaurs have teeth? 127

What were the biggest dinos? 128
What was the biggest dinosaur
    that ever lived? 129
What did sauropods eat? 129

Why did dinosaurs have claws? 130
Were all claws sharp? 131
Which dinosaur had a spike
    on each hand? 131

What was the scariest dinosaur? 132
What was the biggest
    meat-eating dinosaur? 133
How did meat eaters get
    their food? 133

Which dinosaur had big eyes? 134
What were the noisiest
    dinosaurs? 135
Were dinosaurs clever or stupid? 135

Dinosaurs

How fast could dinosaurs move? 136
Could big dinosaurs move quickly? 137
Were some dinosaurs small? 137

Did dinosaurs wear armour? 138
Which dinosaur had a lumpy tail? 139
Which dinosaur had three horns? 139

How did dinosaurs have babies? 140
Did dinosaurs look after their babies? 141
How do we know about dinosaur babies? 141

Did dinosaurs live alone? 142
Could dinosaurs leap and jump? 143
Why are some dinosaurs like birds? 143

Why did the dinosaurs die? 144
What killed millions of animals? 145
Could the dinosaurs have died from a disease? 145

Can we find new dinosaurs? 146
How do scientists find dinosaur fossils? 147
Could dinosaurs ever come back to life? 147

Quiz time 148

What is a dinosaur?

Dinosaurs were animals that lived millions of years ago. There were lots of different types of dinosaur – little ones, big ones, fierce ones and shy ones. All dinosaurs lived on land – and they died out a long time ago. There are no dinosaurs living today.

Make

Use salt dough or plasticine to make some dinosaur models. Use a picture or a toy dinosaur as a guide.

When did dinosaurs live?

It is thought that the first dinosaurs lived around 230 million years ago. They roamed the Earth for the next 165 million years, before becoming extinct (dying out) about 65 million years ago. Humans haven't been around for two million years yet!

Herrerasaurus

Where did the dinosaurs live?

Dinosaurs lived all over the world. At that time, the weather was much hotter than it is today. There were plants such as ferns, mosses and large evergreen trees, but there were no flowers.

What a terror!

The word 'dinosaur' means 'terrible lizard', even though dinosaurs weren't lizards! Many of the plant–eating dinosaurs were about as terrible as today's sheep!

Did any dinosaurs eat plants?

Many dinosaurs ate plants. *Plateosaurus* grew up to 8 metres long. It had a long neck and could reach high up into trees by standing on its back legs. It grabbed branches with the hooks on its thumbs and nibbled at the tastiest leaves.

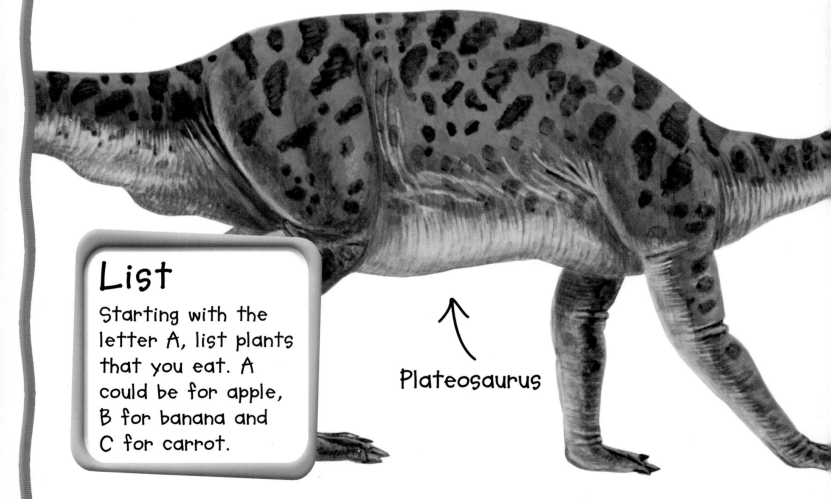

Plateosaurus

List

Starting with the letter A, list plants that you eat. A could be for apple, B for banana and C for carrot.

Why were dinosaurs so big?

Riojasaurus (ree-oh-ja-saw-rus) was a giant dinosaur that measured 10 metres from its nose to the tip of its tail. Being tall meant that it could reach high into trees for food. Big dinosaurs could fight off enemies, such as *Rutiodon*, a big crocodile that lived at the time.

Riojasaurus

Rutiodon

No fruit!

Early plant–eating dinosaurs did not eat fruit or grass — none had appeared yet! Instead, they ate plants called horsetails, ferns, cycads and conifer trees.

Why did dinosaurs eat stones?

Lots of plant-eating dinosaurs swallowed their food without chewing. Instead, they gobbled stones and pebbles, which stayed in their stomachs. When they swallowed food, the stones helped to mash the food up, turning it into a pulp.

How big is a dinosaur tooth?

Dinosaur teeth were different sizes. Meat eaters, such as *Tyrannosaurus rex*, needed large, sharp and pointed teeth for tearing flesh. Each tooth measured up to 15 centimetres! When scientists look at dinosaur teeth they can work out what type of food the dinosaur ate.

Toothy!

Baryonyx had small, pointed, cone-shaped teeth. These are like the teeth of a crocodile or dolphin today. They were good for grabbing slippery food such as fish.

Did plant eaters need sharp teeth?

Plant-eating dinosaurs, such as *Apatosaurus*, had long, thin teeth that were blunt, not sharp. They used these teeth to pull leaves off branches. Herds of these dinosaurs could strip all the plants clean in one area, before moving on.

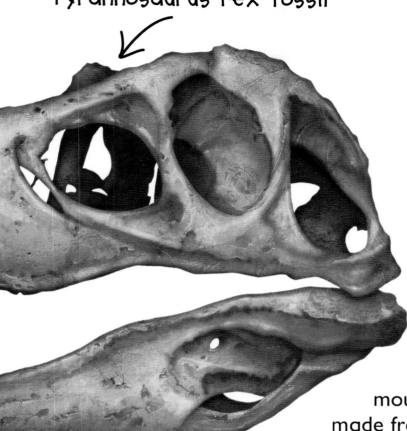

Tyrannosaurus rex fossil

Think

You have different types of teeth. Think about which ones you use to cut food, and which ones you use to chew.

Did all dinosaurs have teeth?

Not all dinosaurs needed teeth. *Ornithomimus* had a beak-shaped mouth without teeth. Its mouth was made from the same tough substance as our hair and nails. This bird-like dinosaur probably pecked at seeds, worms and bugs. Its large eyes helped it to find food.

Ornithomimus

What were the biggest dinos?

The biggest dinosaurs, called sauropods, were ENORMOUS! Each one could weigh as much as ten elephants. *Brachiosaurus* was one of the largest dinosaurs that ever lived and was 25 metres long. It was twice as tall as a giraffe and could reach the tops of the tallest trees.

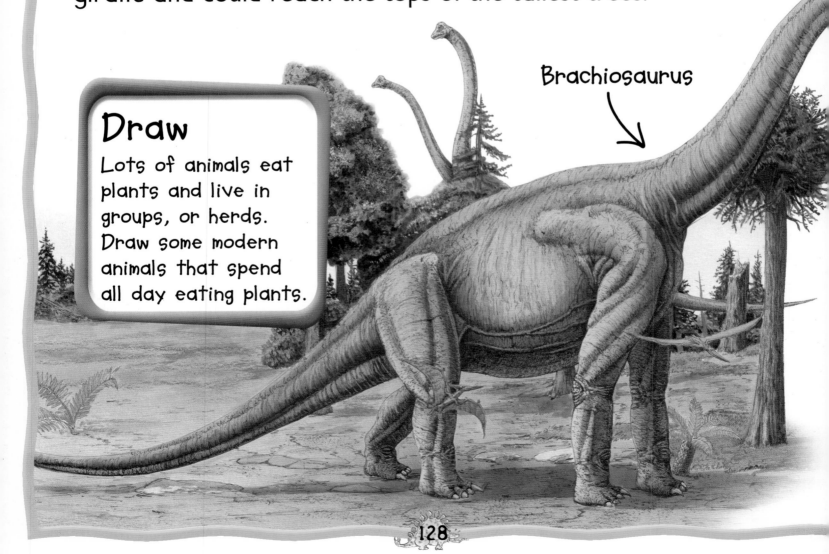

Brachiosaurus

Draw

Lots of animals eat plants and live in groups, or herds. Draw some modern animals that spend all day eating plants.

Argentinosaurus

What was the biggest dinosaur that ever lived?

The biggest dinosaur ever discovered is *Argentinosaurus*. Not much is known about this giant, but it is thought that it may have measured 40 metres from head to tail! *Argentinosaurus* had a huge body but a small head and brain.

Scary tail!

Diplodocus is also known as 'Old Whip–tail'! It could swish its tail so hard that it made a CRACK! like a whip. This would scare off enemies or even rip off their skin.

What did sauropods eat?

All sauropods ate plants. They probably had to spend most of the day eating, just to get enough energy for their enormous, heavy bodies. They may have spent 20 hours every day just grazing and nibbling at plants.

Why did dinosaurs have claws?

Most dinosaurs had claws on their fingers and toes. Meat-eating dinosaurs, such as *Deinonychus* (die-non-ee-kus) used their claws for catching and killing other animals. These dinosaurs were fast, clever and strong. Their claws could cut like knives and their teeth were razor-sharp.

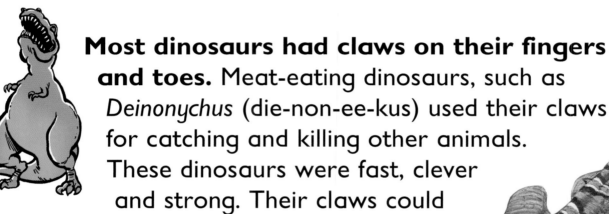

Deinonychus

Discover

Look at books to find pictures of elephants' feet. Do their toenails look like the claws of Apatosaurus?

Apatosaurus

Claws

Were all claws sharp?

Even plant-eating dinosaurs, such as sauropods, had claws. They didn't need claws to catch other animals, so they were flat and blunt rather than sharp. *Apatosaurus* had claws to protect its feet from stones, just like nails protect your fingertips and toes.

Thumb nose!

When scientists discovered remains of Iguanodon, they found a bone shaped like a horn. They put this on Iguanadon's nose. Now they think it is a thumb claw!

Which dinosaur had a spike on each hand?

Iguanodon was a plant-eating dinosaur. It didn't need spikes to kill other animals, but it could use them as weapons to defend itself. If meat-eating dinosaurs attacked *Iguanodon*, it could fight back with its strong arms, using its spikes like daggers.

What was the scariest dinosaur?

Tyrannosaurus rex – known as T-rex for short – is one of the scariest dinosaurs. This dinosaur was a large meat eater. It had powerful legs that helped it run fast and a huge mouth filled lots of sharp, pointed teeth.

Tyrannosaurus rex

Colour

No one knows what colour dinosaurs were. Draw your favourite dinosaur, then colour it in using spots, stripes and colours!

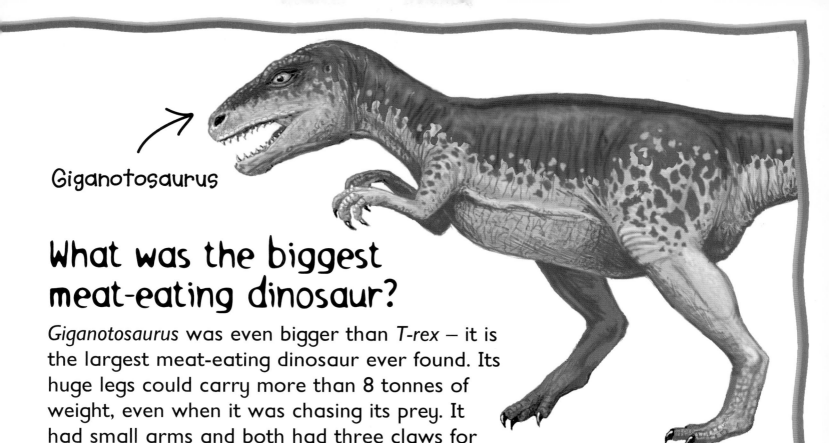

Giganotosaurus

What was the biggest meat-eating dinosaur?

Giganotosaurus was even bigger than *T-rex* – it is the largest meat-eating dinosaur ever found. Its huge legs could carry more than 8 tonnes of weight, even when it was chasing its prey. It had small arms and both had three claws for grabbing and stabbing.

How did meat eaters get their food?

Some meat eaters hunted and captured their prey using their powerful claws and sharp teeth. Others were scavengers. This means that they ate any dead animals that they found. It is thought that *T-rex* both hunted, and scavenged, for food.

Bite marks!

Some meat-eating dinosaurs not only bit their prey, but also each other! Remains of a T-rex had bite marks on its head. Perhaps the dinosaurs fought each other to become leader of the pack.

Which dinosaur had big eyes?

Dinosaurs used their senses to see, touch, hear, smell and taste. *Troodon* was a bird-like dinosaur that had HUGE eyes. Scientists think it may have hunted at night, and that its large eyes helped it to find food in the dark.

Troodon

Play

Play a game of hide and seek. Use your senses, such as seeing and hearing, to hunt your prey!

What were the noisiest dinosaurs?

We can't be sure what sounds dinosaurs made, but *Parasaurolophus* was probably one of the noisiest! It had a large crest on its head that was made of hollow bone. *Parasaurolophus* could have blown air through the crest to make a bellowing noise, like a giant trumpet.

Parasaurolophus

Were dinosaurs clever or stupid?

Animals with big brains are usually cleverer than those with small brains. *Apatosaurus* had a tiny brain. *Troodon* had a large brain, compared to the size of its body. It may have been one of the cleverest dinosaurs that ever lived.

Dino rap!

Small meat-eating dinosaurs are called 'raptors'. These dinos lived and hunted in packs. They were slim, clever and fast. Some even had feathers to keep them warm!

How fast could dinosaurs move?

Some dinosaurs could run very fast – up to 80 kilometres an hour. That is faster than a horse at full gallop! *Ornithomimus* could run this fast because it had a slim body, hollow bones and long, thin legs. It ran fast so it could chase other animals, and escape being eaten itself!

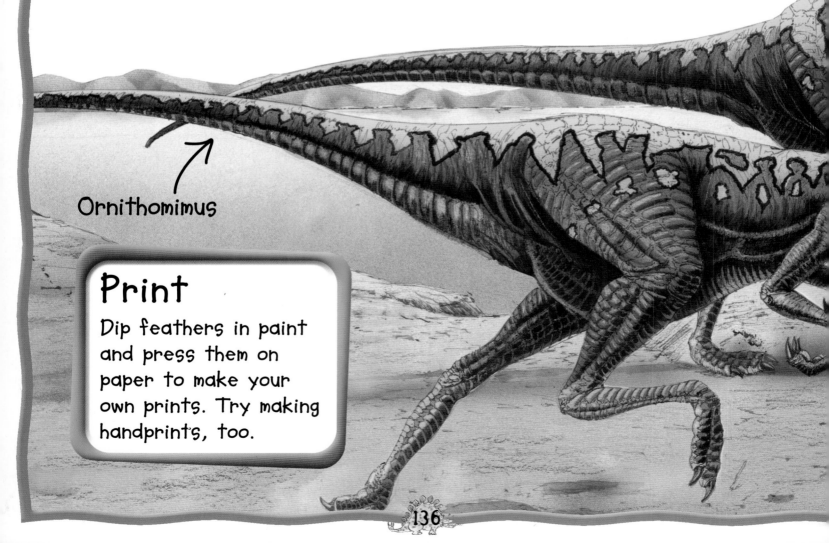

Ornithomimus

Print

Dip feathers in paint and press them on paper to make your own prints. Try making handprints, too.

Could big dinosaurs move quickly?

Large dinosaurs were often slower. Heavy bodies were harder to move! *Muttaburrasaurus* was a big dinosaur that may have run on its hind legs, holding its head up to look for enemies. Its long tail may have helped it to keep its balance.

Muttaburrasaurus

Speedy!

Coelophysis (co—el—off—ee—sis) could trot, jump and leap. It ran upright on its two back legs. It could also bound along on all four legs like a dog, at speeds of 30 kilometres an hour.

Were some dinosaurs small?

All dinosaurs were quite small when they first hatched from their eggs! Some fully-grown dinosaurs were not much bigger than a pet cat. *Compsognathus* was a small, light dinosaur that ate little creatures, such as lizards and bugs.

Did dinosaurs wear armour?

Dinosaurs needed to protect themselves from their enemies. Some of them did this by growing great pieces of bone over their bodies. These bony plates protected the dinosaurs' soft bodies underneath, like huge shields, or suits of armour.

Triceratops

Which dinosaur had a lumpy tail?

Euoplocephalus (you-o-plo-seff-a-lus) had a tail that was strengthened with lumps of bone. When this dinosaur swung its tail, it could hit an attacker with such force that it could break a leg!

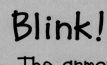
Which dinosaur had three horns?

Triceratops was a plant eater and it probably used its three horns to frighten away attackers. It would also have used them for fighting enemies. *Triceratops* looked scary, but it probably spent most of its time quietly eating plants.

Styracosarus

Euoplocephalus

Protoceratops

How did dinosaurs have babies?

Dinosaurs laid eggs, just like birds, lizards and crocodiles do today. *Protoceratops* was a small dinosaur, the size of a pig. It lived in the desert. The female made a bowl-shaped nest in the warm sand and then laid her eggs inside it.

Find out

Find out how much you weighed and how long you were when you were born. Ask how quickly you grew!

Did dinosaurs look after their babies?

Some dinosaurs did look after their babies, until they were old enough to look after themselves. *Maiasaura* collected food for its newly hatched young and fed it to them, rather like birds feed their chicks today. The parents probably guarded their babies, too.

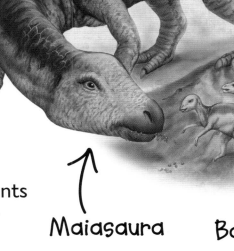

Maiasaura

Baby dinosaurs

Protoceratops

How do we know about dinosaur babies?

Scientists have found dinosaur eggs, and the remains of nests that have lasted for millions of years. They have even discovered large areas where many *Maiasaura* mothers came to lay their eggs, year after year.

Big baby!

Baby dinosaurs grew up to five times faster than human babies! A baby dinosaur, such as Diplodocus, was already one metre long and 30 kilograms in weight when it came out of its egg!

Did dinosaurs live alone?

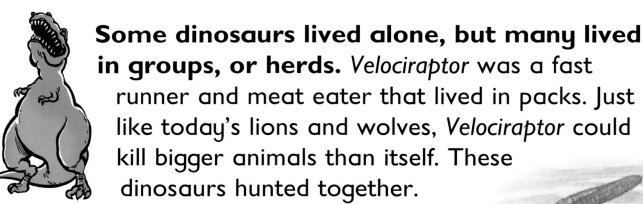

Some dinosaurs lived alone, but many lived in groups, or herds. *Velociraptor* was a fast runner and meat eater that lived in packs. Just like today's lions and wolves, *Velociraptor* could kill bigger animals than itself. These dinosaurs hunted together.

Velociraptor

Fossil poo!

Dinosaur droppings also form fossils! These have pieces of food inside such as bones or plants. Some fossil droppings are as big as TV sets!

Coelophysis

Could dinosaurs leap and jump?

Scientists work out how dinosaurs moved by looking at their bones. The bones of *Coelophysis* are small, hollow and light so it was probably able to dart about easily. The shapes of its teeth and jaw bones suggest that *Coelophysis* ate insects or fish.

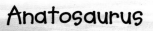

Anatosaurus

Look

Look at some pictures of birds such as ostriches. Do they remind you of any dinosaurs in this book?

Why are some dinosaurs like birds?

Some dinosaurs had feathers, large eyes and beaks. They even laid eggs and ate insects. It is believed that some changed (evolved) over time and became the very first birds on Earth.

Why did the dinosaurs die?

About 65 million years ago the dinosaurs suddenly died (became extinct). No one knows for sure why this happened, but something HUGE must have taken place to affect all life on the planet.

The dinosaurs may have been killed by a giant rock from space

Read

Go to the library to find out about animals today that are in danger of becoming extinct. Find out why.

What killed millions of animals?

Maybe volcanoes erupted, spitting out enormous clouds of ash and poisonous gas. Maybe a large lump of rock from space (a meteorite) smashed into the Earth. These things can change the weather, so perhaps the dinosaurs died because it got too cold for them.

Erupting volcanoes

Egg hunters!

Some dinosaurs might have become extinct because their eggs were eaten by other animals. Shrew—like creatures around at the time may have eaten the eggs at night as dinosaurs slept.

Could the dinosaurs have died from a disease?

This is unlikely because it wouldn't explain why so many millions of other animals died too. It is thought that more than two-thirds of all living things died at the same time as the dinosaurs, including sea creatures and plants.

Can we find new dinosaurs?

The remains of animals and plants that lived long ago are called fossils. These remains are bones, teeth, eggs and footprints — that have turned to rock over millions of years. Fossils of new dinosaurs such as *Jobaria* and *Janenschia* have been found in Africa.

Jobaria

Think

If you found fossils from a new dinosaur, think of what name you would give your own dinosaur.

Dino girl!
Leaellynasaura (lee—ell—in—oh—saw—ra) was named after the daughter of the scientists who found its fossils!

Leaellynasaura

How do scientists find dinosaur fossils?

Fossils are difficult to find because they are usually buried deep underground. Scientists look in places where layers of rock and soil have been removed by wind or water. At Dinosaur Cove the sea has washed away the rock, revealing the fossils of *Leaellynasaura*.

Janenschia

Could dinosaurs ever come back to life?

It is unlikely that dinosaurs will ever walk the Earth again. However, scientists are still finding fossils and using them to uncover new facts about the lives of these magnificent creatures. Dinosaurs live on, but only in our imaginations!

Quiz time

Do you remember what you have read about dinosaurs? These questions will test your memory. The pictures will help you. If you get stuck, read the pages again.

3. What were the biggest dinos?

page 128

4. What was the scariest dinosaur?

page 132

page 125

1. Why did dinosaurs eat stones?

5. What was the biggest meat-eating dinosaur?

page 133

2. How big is a dinosaur tooth?

page 126

6. Which dinosaur had big eyes?

page 134

7. Were some dinosaurs small?

page 137

page 144

11. Why did the dinosaurs die?

12. How do scientists find dinosaur fossils?

page 147

8. Which dinosaur had a lumpy tail?

page 139

13. Could dinosaurs ever come back to life?

page 147

9. Did dinosaurs look after their babies?

page 141

10. Could dinosaurs leap and jump?

page 143

Answers

1. To mash food up in their stomachs
2. Different sizes
3. Sauropods
4. Tyrannosaurus rex
5. Giganotosaurus
6. Troodon
7. Yes, some were not much bigger than pet cats
8. Euoplocephalus
9. Yes, some did
10. Yes, Coelophysis could
11. Volcanoes may have erupted, or a meteorite may have smashed into the Earth
12. In rocks
13. No

Chirpy questions about...

What is special about birds?   152
Do birds have teeth?   152
Why do birds lay eggs?   153

How do birds fly?   154
How far can a bird fly?   154
Do all birds fly?   155

Why are some birds colourful?   156
Which birds strut around
    and coo?   157
Why do birds sing?   157

Birds

Why do birds lay eggs in nests?   158
Why are cuckoos lazy?   159
How do birds build nests?   159

How does a bird eat a snail?   164
Which bird has a
   scissor-shaped beak?   165
Why do flamingos have
   long necks?   165

Quiz time   166

What is a bird of prey?   160
How does a sea eagle catch fish?   161
Do hunting birds live
   in towns?   161

Why do woodpeckers peck?   162
How do honeyguides find
   their food?   163
Do antbirds eat ants?   163

What is special about birds?

Birds can fly, walk, run and even swim! Because they have wings, birds are able to fly to all parts of the world, from steamy rainforests to the icy Arctic. There are about 9000 different types of bird, from beautiful barn owls to giant ostriches.

Do birds have teeth?

Birds don't have teeth. Instead, they have really strong mouths that are called beaks, or bills. Sharp, pointed beaks are good for grabbing bugs and short, strong beaks are great for cracking nuts open!

Discover

Beaks and feathers are made of a special tough material. See if you can you discover what it's called.

Barn owl

The early bird!

The oldest-known bird lived about 150 million years ago. Archaeopteryx (ark—ee—op—ter—ix) had feathers and wings, but it had teeth instead of a beak.

Why do birds lay eggs?

Birds lay eggs so that their babies can grow. Baby birds are called chicks and they begin life in an egg. The eggs are kept safe in a nest until they hatch.

Song thrush

Eggs in a nest

How do birds fly?

Peregrine falcon

 **Birds can fly because they have wings, powerful muscles and very light bones.** Feathers also help birds move smoothly through the air. This peregrine falcon is the fastest of all animals. It can reach top speeds of 180 kilometres an hour as it swoops and dives.

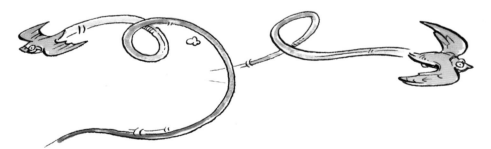

How far can a bird fly?

Birds can fly very long distances. Swifts are super fliers and even eat and mate while they swoop through the clouds. When young swifts leave the nest they may fly for the next two years and travel more than 500,000 kilometres!

Count

If a bird beats its wings ten times in one second, how many times would it beat its wings in two seconds?

Do all birds fly?

All birds have wings, but not all of them fly. This speedy roadrunner lives in the desert. It can fly, but it prefers to walk or run as it looks for lizards, snakes and bugs in the sand.

Roadrunner

Swift

Hum that tune!

Hummingbirds beat their wings 50 times a second. As the wings slice through the air they make the humming noise that gives the birds their name.

Why are some birds colourful?

Birds can be big show-offs and they use bright colours to make themselves look attractive. Male birds are usually more colourful than females. When this peacock sees a female (a peahen) he displays his fine tail and shakes it, so she can admire his great beauty.

Love birds!

Great crested grebes are water birds that dance for each other. During the dance they offer each other gifts – beakfuls of water weed. Lovely!

Peacock

Which birds strut around and coo?

Male birds puff up their feathers, strut around and make cooing noises to impress the females. These cocks-of-the-rocks also dance and spread their wings to show off to the female birds. They live in the South American rainforest.

Cocks-of-the-rocks

Why do birds sing?

Birds sing to get the attention of other birds. Like their colourful feathers, they may use songs to attract mates. Some birds squawk loudly if they are being attacked. Most baby birds learn to sing by copying their parents.

Dress-up

A bird's feathers are called its plumage. Put on some bright clothes and see if anyone notices your plumage!

157

Why do birds lay eggs in nests?

Birds lay their eggs in a nest to keep them safe. Once the eggs have hatched, the little chicks stay in the nest until they have grown enough to be able to fly. These bald eagles build giant nests up to 2.5 metres across.

Bald eagle

Chicks

Why are cuckoos lazy?

Cuckoos don't bother making their own nests. Instead, they lay their eggs in other birds' nests. This way cuckoos do not have all the hard work of looking after their own chicks – other birds do it for them!

How do birds build nests?

Birds build their nests in different ways, but most of them use twigs and sticks. African weaver birds make their delicate nests using strips of leaves and grass. They knot and weave the strips together to make a cosy, safe home.

Make it

Use sticks and twigs to make a nest. Make a soft lining with grass or straw. Pop some chocolate eggs in the middle.

1. The weaver bird twists strips of leaves

2. The roof is made

3. The finished nest

Watch the birdie!

Most birds take minutes to lay an egg. The mother cuckoo can lay an egg in 9 seconds! This allows her to quickly pop it in the nest of another bird.

What is a bird of prey?

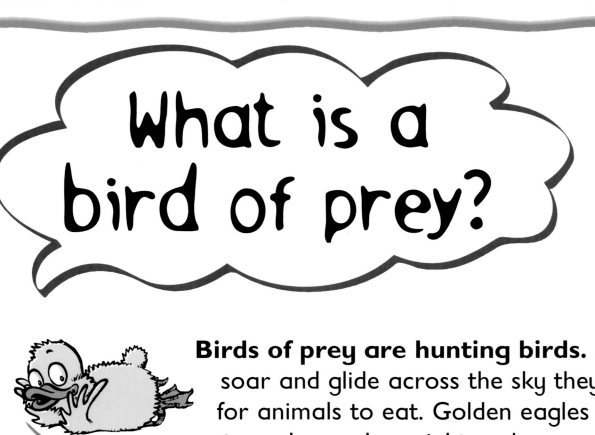

Birds of prey are hunting birds. As they soar and glide across the sky they search for animals to eat. Golden eagles have extremely good eyesight and can spot food far away. They swoop to the ground and grab rabbits and mice with their sharp claws.

Golden eagle

Top bird!

Eagles like to build their nests in high places. One pair of sea eagles made their nest on top of a light-tower by the coast in Norway!

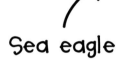

How does a sea eagle catch fish?

Sea eagles need good eyes and strong claws to catch a swimming fish. Each foot has a pointed hook for holding onto a slippery fish. Sea eagles take their fish to a cliff or rocky ledge where they can eat in comfort.

Sea eagle

Do hunting birds live in towns?

It's unusual to see big hunting birds such as eagles in towns. But you might see smaller ones, such as ravens. These black birds are very clever animals. They hunt mice and rats but they will eat almost any food that they can find.

Try it

Eagles use their feet to grab their food. See if you can pick up anything using just your feet.

Why do woodpeckers peck?

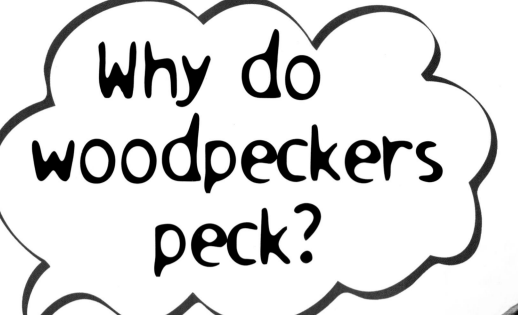

Woodpeckers peck at trees to disturb the little insects that live in the bark. They then gobble them up. These birds can also use their strong, pointed beaks to hammer at the tree until they have made a hole big enough for a nest.

Hummm, I'm hungry!

Bee hummingbirds beat their wings 200 times a second. If we used up the same amount of energy we would need to eat three times our own weight in potatoes each day!

How do honeyguides find their food?

Honeyguide birds follow honey badgers to find their favourite food — delicious bee grubs! The clever birds follow the badgers when they go in search of a bee's nest. When the badger opens the nest it feeds on the honey, while the birds eat the grubs and beeswax.

Honeyguide

Make it

Ask an adult to help you make a bird feeder. You can then hang it upside down from a tree.

Do antbirds eat ants?

Antbirds follow army ants as they march through the forest, but they don't usually eat them. The birds perch on trees as the army ants pass by, then they pounce on the other small animals and insects that come to feed on the ants.

How does a bird eat a snail?

Birds that eat snails need to get the soft body out of the hard shell. Some birds smash snails against rocks. This snail kite uses its sharp beak to cut the slimy snail away from its shell and hook it out.

Knobbly knees!

Flamingos look as if they have got back-to-front legs. Actually, what appear to be their knees are really their ankles!

Snail kite

Which bird has a scissor-shaped beak?

The beak of a skimmer is shaped like scissors. This is because the lower beak is much longer and flatter than the top beak. As it flies over water, the skimmer dips its lower beak below the surface. When it touches a fish it snaps its beak shut.

Flamingo

Why do flamingos have long necks?

Flamingos have long necks so that they can reach underwater to find their food. They use their beaks to catch tiny pink creatures called shrimps that float past. Flamingos turn pink after eating lots of these shrimps!

Remember

Can you remember what a skimmer's beak is shaped like? If you can't, read this page again to find out.

Quiz time

3. Do all birds fly?

page 155

Do you remember what you have read about birds? These questions will test your memory. The pictures will help you. If you get stuck, read the pages again.

4. Why do birds sing?

page 157

page 153

1. Why do birds lay eggs?

5. How do birds build nests?

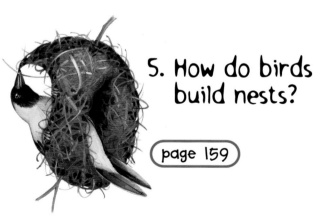

page 159

page 154

2. How far can a bird fly?

6. Why are cuckoos lazy?

page 159

166

7. What is a bird of prey?

page 160

11. How does a bird eat a snail?

page 164

12. Which bird has a scissor-shaped beak?

page 165

page 161

8. Do hunting birds live in towns?

page 162

page 165

9. Why do woodpeckers peck?

13. Why do flamingos have long necks?

10. Do antbirds eat ants?

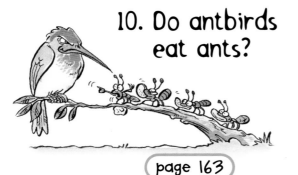

page 163

Answers

1. So their babies can grow
2. Very long distances
3. Not all birds can fly
4. To get the attention of other birds
5. With twigs and sticks
6. Because they don't make their own nests
7. A hunting bird
8. Smaller ones do
9. To disturb insects that live in the bark
10. Yes, they eat army ants
11. The snail kite hooks it out with it's beak
12. The skimmer
13. So they can reach underwater to find their food

Fur-raising questions about...

Why are some animals furry? 170
What is a joey? 171
Why do some mammals sniff
  the air? 171

What is the biggest mammal? 172
How big is an elephant? 173
What is the smallest mammal? 173

How do cheetahs run so fast? 174
Why do hares kick? 175
Which mammal is very bouncy? 175

Are mammals good swimmers? 176
Can seals breathe underwater? 176
What does a killer whale kill? 177

Mammals

Are polar bears cuddly? 178
Why are some animals white? 179
How do seals stay warm? 179

Why do wolves live in packs? 180
How many meerkats live
    together? 181
What is a group of whales
    called? 181

How big is a baby panda? 182
What are baby elephants called? 183
Which mammal has the most
    babies at a time? 183

How do tigers catch their food? 184
What do bears eat? 185
Why do dogs hunt in packs? 185

Are rhinos dangerous? 186
Why do some mammals
    have scales? 187
What is the stinkiest mammal? 187

Quiz time 188

Why are some animals furry?

Fur or hair keeps some animals warm. Animals that have fur or hair are called mammals. Fur also protects from the weather. This hairy orang-utan lives in the rainforest. She picks fruit and leaves to eat. She feeds her baby on milk.

Orang-utan

What is a joey?

A joey is a baby kangaroo. When a joey is born it is smaller than your big toe! Even though it is tiny and blind, the joey crawls all the way to its mother's pouch and climbs in. It feeds on milk from its mother.

Joey

Egg-citing news!

Most mammals give birth. This means that they have babies, cubs or kittens. Some strange mammals, such as the duck-billed platypus, lay eggs.

Find out

Were you a beautiful baby, or did you hatch from an egg? Look at old photos of yourself to find out.

Why do some mammals sniff the air?

Many mammals use their noses to get information about the world around them. Their noses are very sensitive to smells. Wild animals, such as deer and rabbits, sniff the air around them to check for signs of danger.

What is the biggest mammal?

The blue whale is – and it's enormous! In fact, it is the biggest animal that has ever lived. Even a baby blue whale is huge – it measures 7 metres in length. All whales are mammals and give birth to their babies, which are called calves.

What a hooter!

African elephants have the longest noses! Their noses are called trunks and they can be 2.5 metres long. Trunks are used for smelling, picking up food and drinking.

How big is an elephant?

One African elephant can weigh more than 100 people put together. Elephants are the biggest animals that live on land and they can reach 4 metres in height. They spend most of their day eating to keep themselves that huge!

← African elephant

Measure

Using a measuring tape, see if you can mark out how long a blue whale calf is.

Blue whale

What is the smallest mammal?

The tiny hog-nosed bat is not much bigger than your thumb! Bats are the only mammals that can fly. They usually sleep during the day and come out at night to look for food.

How do cheetahs run so fast?

Cheetahs have big muscles in their legs and they can run faster than any other animal. These speedy cats run out of breath quickly. This means that the animals they're chasing, such as gazelles, often manage to escape. Cheetahs can reach speeds of 100 kilometres an hour!

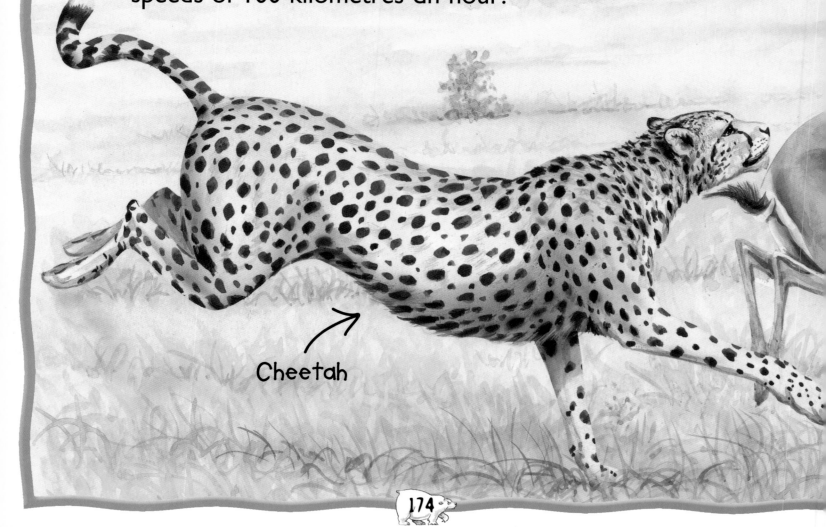

Cheetah

Why do hares kick?

Hares sometimes kick out at their enemies. Other animals such as foxes try to catch hares to eat them. If the hare sees, smells or hears an enemy, it can run fast to get away, or kick out with its back legs.

Hare

Run

How fast can you run? Ask an adult to time you next time you are in the park or garden.

Gazelle

Whoosh!

The pronghorn deer is one of the fastest mammals in North America. It runs fast to escape from wolves, which hunt it for food.

Which mammal is very bouncy?

Kangaroos bounce instead of running. The red kangaroo is a champion jumper and it leaps across the dry deserts of its Australian home. It travels quickly to search for water and food, which are hard to find in a desert.

Are mammals good swimmers?

Some mammals are super swimmers! Whales, dolphins and seals have bodies that are perfectly shaped for moving through water smoothly and quickly. They have fins and tails instead of arms and legs. Whales and dolphins spend their whole lives in water.

Harp seal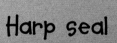

Can seals breathe underwater?

No mammals can breathe underwater — not even seals, whales and dolphins. Instead, they have to take in all the air they need when they are at the surface of the water, then hold their breath. Some seals can stay underwater for an hour at a time!

Bowhead whale

Diving deep!

The Weddell seal is a daring diver. It plunges down to the deep, dark, cold water of the oceans as it hunts for fish to eat.

What does a killer whale kill?

Killer whales kill squid, fish, seals and even birds. They are strong swimmers and have sharp, pointed teeth. Killer whales can be friendly. They live in family groups and calves stay with their mothers all their lives!

Swim

You are a mammal and you can learn to swim too! Visit your local pool for some watery fun!

Are polar bears cuddly?

Polar bears may look cuddly with their thick, white fur, but they are fierce hunters. These bears live in the ice-covered lands near the North Pole. Their fur keeps them warm — they even have fur on the soles of their feet so that their toes don't get frost bite!

Polar bear →

Lots of lemmings!

A female lemming can have her first babies when she is only 14 days old. From then on, she can have as many as 12 babies every single month!

Why are some animals white?

White animals usually live in places that are covered with snow in winter. A white Arctic hare blends into the snow and hides from enemies. In summer, the snow melts and the hare grows brown fur.

Paint

Paint a snowy scene showing some animals that live in cold places, such as polar bears, seals and penguins.

How do seals stay warm?

Seals spend a lot of their time underwater in cold parts of the world. They can keep warm because they have thick layers of fat, called blubber, under their skin. Seals also have waterproof fur that stops water getting through to their skin.

Mother seal

Seal pup

Why do wolves live in packs?

Wolves live in packs because they hunt together and look after one another. A mother wolf takes good care of her cubs. As the cubs grow, they are brought food from their father and other members of the wolf pack.

Wolves

Cool cats!

Lions may be fierce, but they are also very lazy. They sleep or doze for more than 20 hours a day, keeping cool in the shade!

How many meerkats live together?

Meerkats live in groups of up to 30 animals. A group is called a colony and each colony is made up of several families. While some meerkats search for food, others stand guard and look for enemies, such as hawks.

Meerkats →

What is a group of whales called?

A group of whales is called a pod. Pilot whales live in pods of 20 or more animals that swim and hunt together. Some dolphins live in pods that may have more than 1000 members.

Count

How many people can you count in your family? Include all your grandparents, aunts, uncles and cousins.

How big is a baby panda?

Pandas give birth to tiny babies, or cubs. Each cub could fit inside your hand and weighs the same as an apple. Newborn pandas are blind and helpless. They do not open their eyes until they are two or three months old.

Panda cub

Panda

What are baby elephants called?

Baby elephants are called calves. Soon after they are born, elephant calves are able to stand up. Within a few days, they can run around. Elephants live in groups called herds. The adult elephants protect the young from lions and hyenas.

Elephant calf

Big baby!

The baby blue whale is bigger than any other mammal baby. It weighs more than 30 people put together and drinks up to 500 litres of milk every day.

Measure

How much milk do you drink every day? Use a measuring jug to see how much milk fills up a glass.

Which mammal has the most babies at a time?

The Virginia opossum can have up to 21 babies at a time – more than any other mammal. Each baby opossum is no bigger than a fingertip! If it is attacked, a Virginia opossum lies down and pretends to be dead.

How do tigers catch their food?

Tigers are hunters. Their bodies are perfect for finding, chasing and killing other animals. Stripy fur helps the tiger blend in with tall grass so they are difficult to spot. When a tiger sees a meal, it runs and pounces. It uses its claws and teeth to kill.

Tiger

Deer

What do bears eat?

Bears eat all kinds of food. Some bears hunt other animals but most eat insects, fruit and leaves. Sloth bears love to eat termites. They have long claws for digging out termite nests. The bears suck the termites up one at a time!

Sloth bear

Why do dogs hunt in packs?

Wild dogs hunt in packs because they are more likely to get something to eat. By working together they can surround an animal. They may catch a bigger animal than one dog alone could catch.

Are rhinos dangerous?

A rhinoceros is one of the most dangerous mammals. Mother rhinos may attack people, or other animals, to protect their babies. They can run fast and they have sharp horns for attacking. Male rhinos also use their horns to fight one another.

Bee-eaters!

Smelly skunks sometimes feed on bees. They roll the bees on the ground to remove the stings before eating them.

Why do some mammals have scales?

Some mammals have scales to protect themselves, rather like a suit of armour. Pangolins are strange ant-eating mammals that live in Africa and Asia. Their bodies are covered in overlapping scales that protect them from other animals — and the stinging bites of ants.

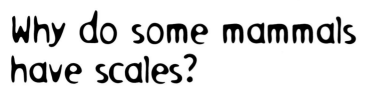

Pangolin

Rhinoceros

What is the stinkiest mammal?

Skunks are very stinky mammals! These stripy creatures shake their tails at an enemy to warn it to stay away. If that doesn't work, the skunk raises its tail and sprays a smelly liquid in its enemy's face!

Make it

Ask an adult to help you make a cardboard suit of armour. How easy is it to move wearing the armour?

Quiz time

Do you remember what you have read about mammals? These questions will test your memory. The pictures will help you. If you get stuck, read the pages again.

1. What is a joey?

page 171

2. What is the biggest mammal?

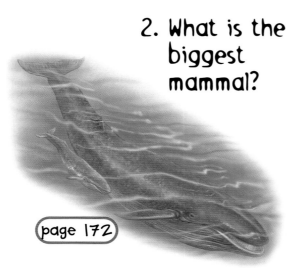

page 172

3. Which mammal is very bouncy?

page 175

4. Can seals breathe underwater?

page 176

5. Are polar bears cuddly?

page 178

6. Why are some animals white?

page 179

7. Why do wolves live in packs?

page 180

page 185

11. What do bears eat?

8. How many meerkats live together?

page 181

page 185

12. Why do dogs hunt in packs?

13. Are rhinos dangerous?

9. How big is a baby panda?

page 182

page 186

page 183

10. What are baby elephants called?

Ancient questions about...

Why were the pyramids built? 192

What guards the Great Pyramid? 193

What was inside the Great
    Pyramid? 193

Who was the top god? 194

Why were cats important? 195

Who took care of the temples? 195

Which queen found a
    magical land? 196

Who was the boy king? 197

What did tomb robbers find? 197

Ancient Egypt

How do you make a mummy?   198
What did the priest do?   199
What were mummies kept in?   199

Did Egypt have an army?   200
Who defeated Egypt?   200
Who were the Sea People?   201

Did food grow in the desert?   202
How did the Egyptians farm?   202
What did farmers grow?   203

Who had the biggest houses?   206
How did the Egyptians cook?   206
Were houses built with bricks?   207

Who shaved their hair off?   208
Did Egyptians ever wear wigs?   209
What was the fashion?   209

Who had the best jobs?   204
Who was head of the family?   204
What did children play with?   205

Quiz time   210

Why were the pyramids built?

Pyramids were tombs (burial places) for Egyptian rulers, called pharaohs. The three great pyramids of Khufu, Khafre and Menkaure were built in Giza, Egypt, 4500 years ago. The Great Pyramid of Khufu is the biggest. It took 20 years and 4000 workers to build it!

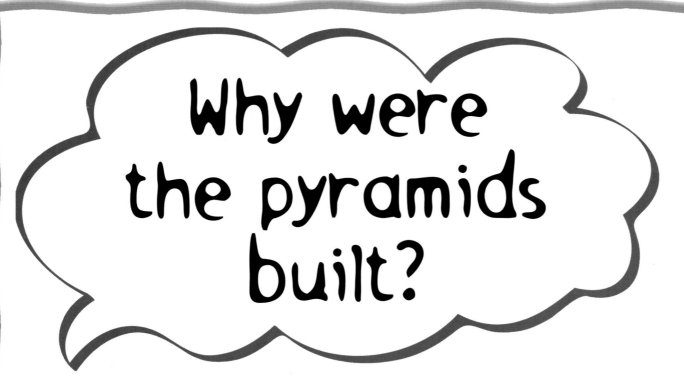

Great Pyramid of Pharaoh Khufu

Pyramid of Pharaoh Khafre

Pyramid of Pharaoh Menkaure

What guards the Great Pyramid?

The pyramids were full of treasures. A stone statue was built to guard the Great Pyramid at Giza. It was carved in the shape of a sphinx. A sphinx has the body of a lion and the head of a man. The sphinx at the Great Pyramid has the face of Pharaoh Khafre.

The sphinx

Tomb robbers!

'The Book of Buried Pearls' told robbers all about the treasures inside the tombs. It also showed them how to get past spirits that guarded the dead.

What was inside the Great Pyramid?

The Great Pyramid had two huge burial chambers. They were built for the pharaoh and his queen. A corridor called the Grand Gallery led to the pharaoh's chamber. The corridor's ceiling was 8 metres tall!

Map

Draw a plan of a pyramid. Include secret tunnels and hidden rooms to stop the robbers.

Who was the top god?

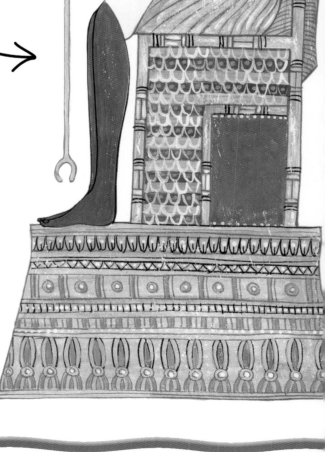

Ra

Ancient Egyptians worshipped more than 1000 gods. The most important was Ra, the Sun god. Every evening, Ra was swallowed by Nut, the sky goddess. At night, Ra travelled through the land of the dead. He was born again each morning. Later, Ra became Amun Ra, king of the gods.

Dead body god!

Anubis was the god in charge of dead bodies. He looked like a jackal, a kind of dog. People who wrapped bodies for burial often wore Anubis masks!

Why were cats important?

Cats were sacred (holy) animals in ancient Egypt. The goddess for cats, musicians and dancers was called Bastet. When a pet cat died it was wrapped up carefully and placed in a special cat-shaped coffin. Then the cat was buried in a cat cemetery!

Who took care of the temples?

Fabulous temples were built for the gods. Many temples were built for Amun Ra, king of the gods. Priests looked after the temples, their riches and the lands around them. These massive statues of Pharaoh Ramses II guard the temple at Abu Simbel.

Draw

Draw a picture of Ra travelling through the night in the land of the dead. He travelled in a boat.

Temple at Abu Simbel

Which queen found a magical land?

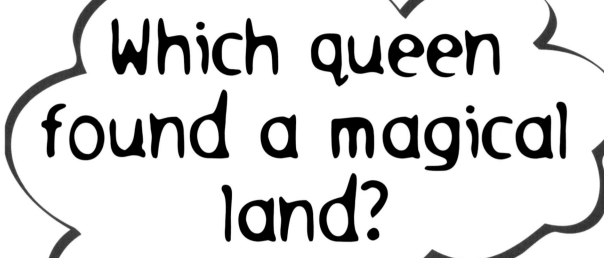

Queen Hatshepsut sent explorers to look for Punt, a magical land she had heard about. Punt was said to be filled with treasure and animals. The explorers returned with gold, ivory, perfumes and special oils. In fact, Punt was probably part of present-day Somalia in Africa.

Shaving for the gods!

Ancient Egyptians could only visit temples for the gods if they shaved off their hair and eyebrows!

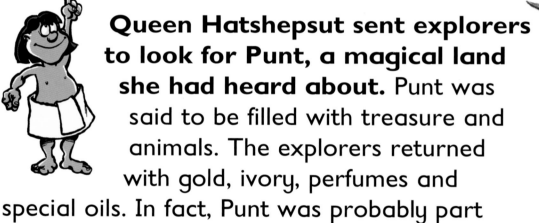

Who was the boy king?

Tutankhamun became king of Egypt when he was just nine years old. He was just 18 years old when he died. His tomb was discovered in 1922. Inside was a solid gold death mask of the king.

Death mask of Tutankhamun

Queen Hatshepsut

Make

Find six boxes that fit inside each other. Decorate them with things a pharaoh might use in the next world.

What did tomb robbers find?

Ancient Egyptian kings were buried with all the things they might need in the world of the dead. These included gold, silver, jewels, furniture and even cooking pots. Robbers stole the lot – even the bodies! But robbers did not find King Tutankhamun's tomb.

How do you make a mummy?

Ancient Egyptians mummified their dead. First, the inside parts such as the brain, but not the heart, were removed. Then the body was salted and dried. Cloth was stuffed inside the body to help it keep its shape. Then the body was oiled and wrapped in lots of bandages.

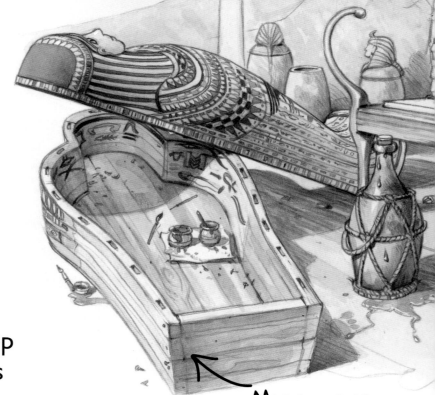

Mummy case

All wrapped up!

The mummy was wrapped in tight bandages. This helped to stop the body from rotting away.

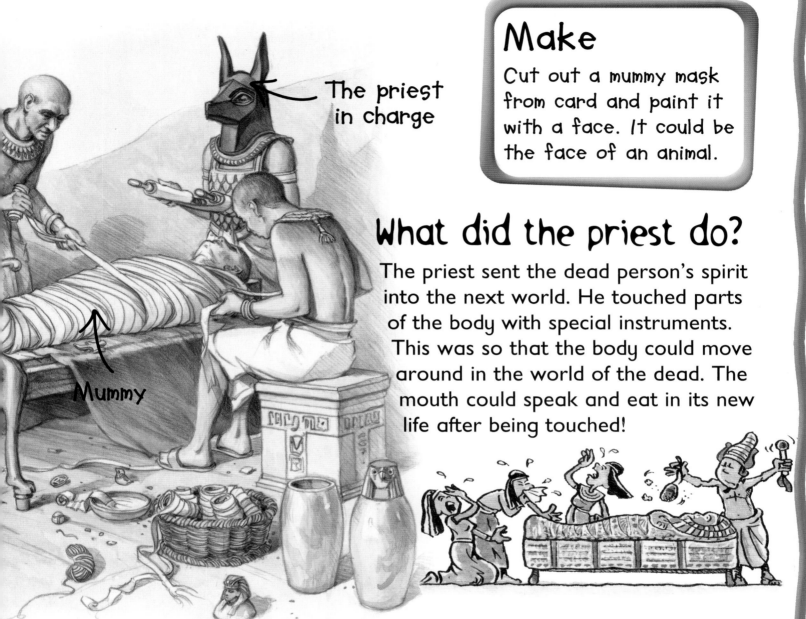

The priest in charge

Mummy

What did the priest do?

The priest sent the dead person's spirit into the next world. He touched parts of the body with special instruments. This was so that the body could move around in the world of the dead. The mouth could speak and eat in its new life after being touched!

What were mummies kept in?

The mummy was placed in a case. Some cases were just wooden boxes. Others were beautifully decorated. An important person, such as a pharaoh, was placed in a stone coffin called a sarcophagus (sarc-off-a-gus).

Sarcophagus (sarc-off-a-gus)

Did Egypt have an army?

Ancient Egypt had a powerful army that won many battles. About 3500 years ago, the Egyptians made a new weapon. It was a chariot pulled by two horses and driven by two soldiers. They drove very fast at the enemy and fired arrows at them.

Chariot

Who defeated Egypt?

General Ptolemy defeated Egypt over 2300 years ago. The rulers who followed him were called the Ptolemies. They built a new city called Alexandria. It was guarded by a massive lighthouse. The city also had a museum and a huge library with thousands of books.

Buzz off!

Egyptian soldiers were given golden fly medals! Perhaps it's because the soldiers annoyed the enemy so much!

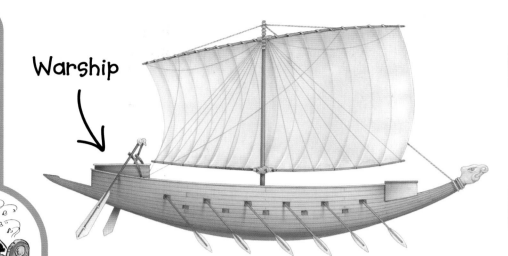

Warship

Who were the Sea People?

The Sea People attacked Egypt and tried to take over the country. Pharaoh Ramses III sent lots of warships to try to defeat them. The ships had sails and oars for travelling quickly at sea. The Sea People were beaten back by the Egyptians.

Read

Can you remember what new weapon the Egyptians made? Read the pages again to remind you.

Did food grow in the desert?

Most of Egypt was in the hot desert.
However, every year in July, the great
river Nile flooded the dry fields. The water
brought rich, black soil with it. This soil
spread in wide strips on each side of the
river. Farmers sowed their seed in this good soil.

Cattle were counted

How did the Egyptians farm?

Farmers used oxen and wooden ploughs to dig
the soil. They weeded and dug channels with
hoes. Then they planted seed, mostly by
hand. Farmers also kept goats, sheep, ducks
and geese. They kept bees to make honey.

Farmers' crops

What did farmers grow?

Farmers grew barley for beer and grapes for wine. Dates, figs, melons, cucumbers, onions, leeks and lettuces grew well in the rich soil. Wheat was also grown to make bread.

Farm workers

Water from the river Nile

Draw

Draw a basket full of crops grown by Egyptian farmers. You can see an Egyptian basket in this picture.

Who had the best jobs?

Doctors, high priests or priestesses and government officers had the best jobs.

So did viziers. A vizier helped the pharaoh to rule the land. Next came the traders and craftsmen, such as carpenters and jewellers. Labourers and farmhands had the poorest jobs.

Who was head of the family?

In ancient Egypt the man was the head of the family. The eldest son was given all the land, property and riches when his father died. Women could also own land and property and get good jobs.

Little monkey!
Pet baboons were sometimes trained to climb fig trees and pick the ripe fruit!

Children playing

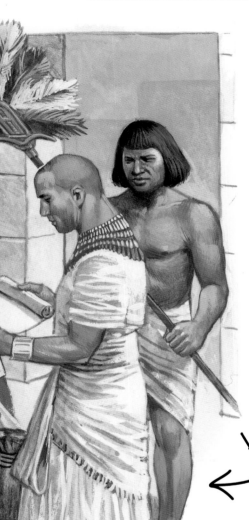

Vizier checking grain

Imagine
Imagine you are an Egyptian worker. Which job would you choose to do and why?

What did children play with?
Children played with toys made from clay and wood. They had carved animals with legs and heads that could move. They also had spinning tops, clay balls, toy horses and dolls. Children played games such as leapfrog and tug-of-war, too.

Who had the biggest houses?

Rich family

Rich Egyptians lived in large country houses called villas.

Villas often had several storeys. Some had walled gardens with fruit orchards and a fish pond. Poor families often lived in one room. Many lived on crowded streets in the towns and cities.

How did the Egyptians cook?

Some ancient Egyptians cooked their food in a clay oven. Others cooked on an open fire. Clay ovens were made from baked clay bricks. Wood or charcoal were burned as fuel. Cooks used pottery saucepans with two handles.

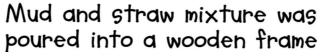

Mud and straw mixture was poured into a wooden frame

Finished bricks

Were houses built with bricks?

Egyptian houses were built with bricks. Mud from the river Nile was mixed with straw and pebbles. The mixture was shaped into brick shapes and dried in the hot sun. Trunks from palm trees held up the flat roofs. Inside walls were plastered and painted.

Make

Mix clay with dried grass and pebbles. Put the mixture in an ice-cube tray. Let your bricks dry in the sun.

Sticky fingers!

Ancient Egyptians ate with their fingers. Rich people washed their hands between each dish. Their servants brought jugs of washing water for them.

Who shaved their hair off?

Both men and women shaved their hair off. They believed that this kept them clean. Men and women also wore make-up such as black kohl, which lined their eyes. Fingernail paint and face powder were also used. Red colouring was worn on lips and cheeks.

Egyptian lady

Cosy toes!

Rich people wore shoes made with padded leather. Sandals were made of the grass–like papyrus plant. Poor people went barefoot.

Did Egyptians ever wear wigs?

Rich Egyptians wore wigs made from human hair or sheep's wool. The wigs were kept in boxes held on stands. Egyptians also used hair dye. Girls plaited their hair into pigtails. Some boys wore a pigtail on one side.

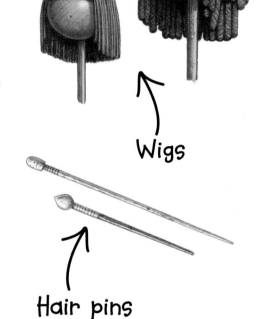

Wigs

Wooden comb

Ivory comb

Hair pins

What was the fashion?

Rich women wore the best linen cloth with beads sewn onto it. The cloth was dyed in pale colours. It was made into long dresses and cloaks. Men wore long robes. They also wore cloths wrapped around the waist. These were tied in a knot.

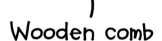

Make

Draw an Egyptian wearing clothes and make–up. Use wool to make a wig. Glue this to the person's head.

Quiz time

Do you remember what you have read about Egypt? These questions will test your memory. The pictures will help you. If you get stuck, read the pages again.

3. Who was the boy king?

page 197

4. Which queen found a magical land?

page 196

page 193

1. What guards the Great Pyramid?

5. What were mummies kept in?

page 199

page 195

2. Why were cats important?

6. Who defeated Egypt?

page 200

7. What did farmers grow?

page 203

11. Who shaved their hair off?

page 208

page 204

8. Who was head of the family?

12. What was the fashion?

page 209

13. Did Egyptians ever wear wigs?

page 205

9. What did children play with?

page 209

10. How did the Egyptians cook?

page 206

Answers

1. The sphinx
2. Because they were holy
3. Tutankhamun
4. Hatshepsut
5. Mummy case or sarcophagus
6. General Ptolemy
7. Barley, grapes, dates, figs, melons, cucumbers, onions, leeks and lettuces
8. The man
9. Wooden or clay toys, spinning tops, clay balls, toy horses and dolls
10. With clay ovens or open fires
11. Men and women
12. Dresses, cloaks and long robes
13. Yes they did

Medieval questions about...

Why were castles built on hills?   214
Were all castles made from wood?   215
What was a moat?   215

What was inside the castle?   216
Where was the safest place?   217
How did people get bread
    and water?   217

What happened at knight school?   218
Who had the best horses?   219
What was dubbing?   219

Knights and Castles

Did knights fight with a ball? 220
Did knights wear woolly jumpers? 221
How long was the Hundred
  Years War? 221

Did knights have fun? 224
Did knights only fight on
  horseback? 224
How did knights find a wife? 225

How were knights told apart? 222
What was a herald? 223
Where did soldiers meet? 223

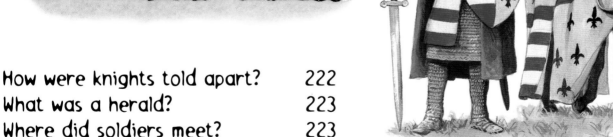

What was a siege? 226
How did the castle crumble? 227
How did enemies get inside
  a castle? 227

Quiz time 228

Why were castles built on hills?

People began building castles over 1000 years ago. They were built on a hill so that people could see the enemy better. The hill was made from a huge mound of mud and stones. It was called a motte.

Motte

Were all castles made from wood?

Early castles were made from wood. They were not very strong and they caught fire easily. People began to build stone castles. These were much stronger. They lasted longer and did not burn.

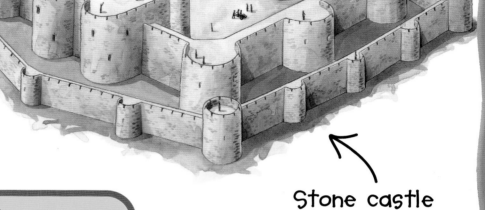

Stone castle

Slimy walls!

Builders often covered wooden castles with wet, slippery leather. This stopped them from burning so easily.

What was a moat?

Builders dug a big ditch around the castle. Then they filled it with water. This watery ditch was called a moat. Enemy soldiers got wet and cold if they attacked the castle from the moat. It was hard to fight from the bottom of it, too!

Think

Stone castles were a lot warmer in winter than wooden ones. Why do you think this was so?

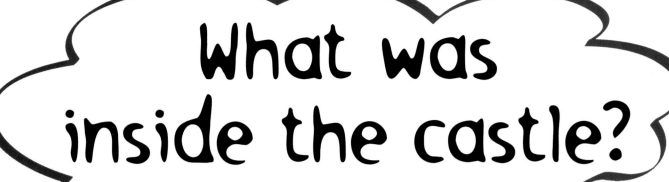

What was inside the castle?

A big courtyard was inside the castle. This was called a bailey. A thick wall was built all around it. Smaller buildings were put up inside the bailey. Sometimes there were gardens. There were often animals and chickens, too!

Thick wall

Where was the safest place?

The safest place in the castle was a tall, strong tower. This tower was called a keep. The lord of the castle lived there with his family. In later times they slept on the top floor. There were big rooms downstairs to hold feasts for visitors.

Keep

Thick walls!

The walls of the keep were at least 3.5 metres thick! This meant that building a castle took a long time. It was also a very expensive job.

Water wheel

How did people get bread and water?

A castle often had its own mill and bakery. Many castles got water from a well. The well was dug inside the bailey. A massive wheel drew water up into the castle. Later castles had piped water with taps.

Measure

The walls of the keep were 3.5 metres thick. Use a tape measure to see how thick this is.

What happened at knight school?

A knight had to train for 14 years! First, he went to a lord's house when he was seven years old. There, he was taught how to ride and to shoot with a bow. Then he became a squire and was taught how to fight with a sword.

Teacher

Count

A nobleman's son went to knight school when he was seven. He studied for 14 years. How old was he when he became a knight?

Who had the best horses?

Rich knights owned three horses. The heaviest horse was used for fighting and in tournaments. The quickest was used for long journeys. The third carried the bags!

Knight and his horse

Dying for love!

Jaufre Rudel was a French knight. He sent love letters to the beautiful Countess of Tripoli, even though had never seen her! When he finally met her he fell into her arms and died!

Squire

What was dubbing?

A new knight was given a special ceremony called a dubbing. First, he had to spend a whole night in church, praying on his knees. Then the new knight was tapped on the shoulder with a sword.

Did knights fight with a ball?

Morning star

Knights hit the enemy with a spiked ball on a long chain. This was called a 'morning star'.

Knights used swords, too. Foot knights from Switzerland used a halberd. This was an axe with a hook on the back. It was good for getting a knight off his horse!

Sword

Get to the point!

Soldiers called 'retrievers' fetched all the fallen arrows. They had to run through the battle to get them!

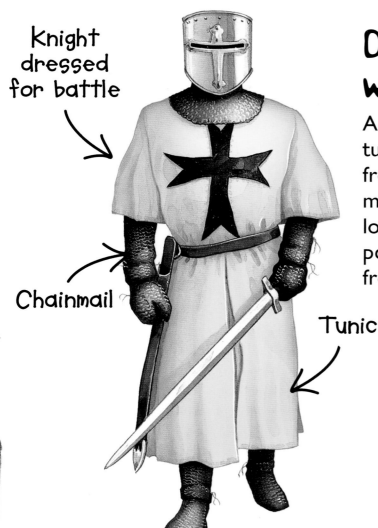

Knight dressed for battle

Chainmail

Tunic

Did knights wear woolly jumpers?

A knight in early times wore a bright tunic with long sleeves. It was made from wool or linen. He also wore metal armour called chainmail. It looked and felt like knitted wire! A padded jacket stopped the chainmail from scratching the skin.

Design

In later times, knights wore steel armour. They even wore metal shoes! Design your own suit of armour to protect a knight.

How long was the Hundred Years War?

The Hundred Years War was fought between the English and the French. It actually lasted for 116 years, between 1337 and 1453. English and Welsh soldiers used longbows against the French. The bowmen could fire 12 arrows every minute!

How were knights told apart?

A knight wore a helmet that covered his head. Even his soldiers could not recognize him! Each knight put a special symbol on his shield and robes. The symbols and colours were called a 'coat of arms'.

Don't shoot the messenger!

Using a coat of arms was called 'heraldry'. This is because the lord's messenger was called a 'herald'. The herald wore his lord's coat of arms as he crossed the battlefield.

Knight wearing coat of arms

What was a herald?

A herald was a messenger. He carried messages for knights during battles. The herald had to be able recognize each knight by his coat of arms. The heralds were very good at recognizing coats of arms. This eventually came to be known as heraldry.

Herald →

← Horse wearing coat of arms

Where did soldiers meet?

Each lord had a banner with his coat of arms on it. Knights and soldiers gathered around the banner on the battlefield. The lord could then explain his battle plans. The winner of a battle often stole the enemy's banner from him.

Make

Draw and cut out a shield from cardboard. Paint your own symbol on it.

Did knights have fun?

Yes they did! Knights took part in competitions called tournaments. These helped them to improve their fighting. The knights formed two teams that fought each other in pretend battles.

Did knights only fight on horseback?

At a tournament, knights also fought on the ground. They wore heavy armour. Skill and speed were much more important than strength.

Make

Write and design a programme for a tournament. You can include fighting competitions and entertainment.

224

Rotten cheat!

Some knights tried to cheat in a jousting competition. They wore special armour that was fixed to the horse's saddle!

Knight taking part in a tournament

Jousting knight

How did knights find a wife?

Ladies from the king's court went to tournaments. The knights showed off their bravery to their favourite lady. Each knight tried to push another knight off his horse with a long pole called a lance. This was called jousting.

What was a siege?

People sometimes became trapped inside a castle if the enemy surrounded it. This was called a siege. The people inside could not get food supplies. So they had a terrible choice. They could either starve to death or surrender to the enemy.

Castle under attack

Think

Try to think of ways to get into a castle without being seen. Look at the castle on page 216 to help you find a way in. Draw a map of your route.

How did the castle crumble?

Sometimes the enemy bashed down the castle gates with battering rams. These were thick tree trunks capped with iron. The enemy also tried to climb the walls with giant ladders. Huge catapults hurled burning wood and stones.

Battering ram

Siege

Hairy weapons!

Giant catapults were wound up with ropes made of human hair! The hair was made into plaits and was very strong.

How did enemies get inside a castle?

Sometimes enemy soldiers dug tunnels underneath the castle. They then popped up inside the castle walls. The enemy also pushed wooden towers against the castle walls. Soldiers hiding in the towers leapt out and climbed into the castle.

Quiz time

3. Where was the safest place?

page 217

4. What happened at knight school?

page 218

Do you remember what you have read about knights and castles? These questions will test your memory. The pictures will help you. If you get stuck, read the pages again.

1. Why were castles built on hills?

page 214

5. What was dubbing?

page 219

2. What was a moat?

page 215

6. Did knights fight with a ball?

page 220

7. Did knights wear woolly jumpers?

page 221

11. How did a knight find a wife?

page 225

8. How were knights told apart?

page 222

12. How did the castle crumble?

page 227

13. How did enemies get inside a castle?

page 227

9. What did people die from?

page 223

10. Did knights only fight on horseback?

page 224

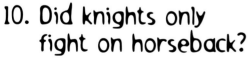

Answers

1. So people could see the enemy
2. A watery ditch around a castle
3. The keep
4. Boys were trained to be knights
5. A special ceremony for a new knight
6. They fought with a spiked ball on a chain
7. No, they wore chainmail and tunics
8. By coats of arms
9. From disease, the Black Death
10. No, they also fought on the ground
11. When he was jousting
12. The walls were bashed with battering rams
13. They dug tunnels under the castle

Plundering questions about...

What is a pirate?   232

Who was afraid of the
    Barbarossas?   233

Did all pirates want treasure?   233

Who stole the Spanish gold?   234

When were pirates not pirates?   235

Can you be a pirate with
    one leg?   235

Could women be pirates?   238

Whose prisoners ate caterpillars?   239

Who said she was sorry?   239

What were the best ships?   240

Where did pirates sleep?   240

What did pirates eat?   241

Did sailors fight the pirates?   236

What did pirates do with
    their money?   236

Where was there a pirate
    paradise?   237

Who was afraid of a flag?   242

Were buccaneers heroes?   242

Where was the treasure?   243

Pirates

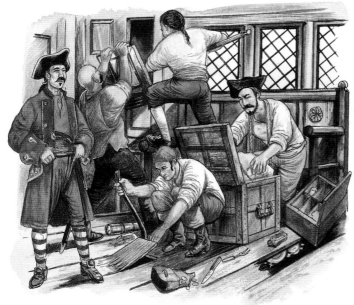

What were pirates scared of?	246
How did pirates find their way?	247
How did pirates save a sinking ship?	247

What was the best treasure?	244
Was the treasure shared?	245
Where were all the jewels?	245

Who is Long John Silver?	248
What ate Captain Hook's hand?	249
Did pirates sing?	249
Quiz time	250

What is a pirate?

A pirate attack

Pirates are people who steal from ships and ports. As soon as the first ships began to carry goods, pirates began to attack them. About 600 years ago, there were many pirates sailing on the seas and oceans around the world.

Hairy pirates!

'Barbarossa' was a nickname for two pirate brothers. 'Barbarossa' means 'Redbeard' – because they both had red beards!

Who was afraid of the Barbarossas?

Every sailor was afraid of the two Barbarossa brothers! They were pirates who attacked ships about 500 years ago. One of the brothers captured the town of Algiers in North Africa. The other attacked ships that belonged to the Pope, who was the leader of the Christian church.

Make

Make your own Barbarossa mask. Draw your pirate's face on card. Use red wool to make a big red beard.

Did all pirates want treasure?

Pirates from the Mediterranean were called corsairs. They didn't want treasure. Instead, they took people from ships and ports and sold them as slaves. Corsairs also captured rich people. They were paid a lot of money to release them.

Corsairs and their ships

Who stole the Spanish gold?

About 500 years ago, Spanish captains sailed to the Americas. There they found gold, silver and jewels. The Spanish stole it from the American people and took it back to Spain. Pirates often attacked the Spanish ships before they got home and took the treasure from them.

Spanish captains and their treasure

234

When were pirates not pirates?

English captains such as John Hawkins raided Spanish treasure ships. England and Spain were enemies at this time, so the English thought it was okay to steal from the Spanish. The captains wanted to be called 'privateers' instead of 'pirates'.

Act
Try to act out your own story about Spanish and English captains. One is trying to steal treasure from the other.

Pirate queen!
Queen Elizabeth I of England encouraged her sea captains to be privateers. However, the privateers were often robbed before they reached England!

Can you be a pirate with one leg?

Francois Le Clerc

Yes! Francois Le Clerc was a dangerous pirate with just one leg. In the 1550s, he raided Caribbean islands owned by Spain. He captured the port of Havana on the island of Cuba. No one would pay Le Clerc to give up the port, so he burned it to the ground.

Did sailors fight the pirates?

Sailors fought hard against pirates when they were attacked. But they didn't try to fight Francis L'Ollonais in the 1660s. He was very cruel and tortured his prisoners. When Francis attacked a ship, the captain and sailors usually gave up without a fight.

Captain surrendering

What did pirates do with their money?

Pirates sold their treasure to people at the docks. They usually made lots of money. Most of the money was spent in public houses!

Francis L'Ollonais

Where was there a pirate paradise?

Port Royal was a harbour on the island of Jamaica. A strong fort guarded the harbour. Pirates could even mend their ships in the docks. Jamaica was ruled by the English, who left the pirates alone.

Paint

Paint a pirate scene with ships and a port. There might be lots of ships, with the pirates carrying their treasure onto dry land.

Pirates in Port Royal

Could women be pirates?

Yes, they could! Mary Read dressed up as a man and became a sailor in the 1700s. Her ship was raided by pirates and Mary decided to join them. Her ship was raided by 'Calico Jack' and his wife, Anne Bonney. Mary made friends with Anne and they fought against the navy.

Mary Read and Anne Bonney

Make

Make a plate of food for a pirate's prisoner! Take a paper plate and stick on cut-out food — such as caterpillars!

Whose prisoners ate caterpillars?

Ching Shih was a Chinese pirate. In 1807, she controlled many ships that raided China's coast. Ching Shih was a great leader. She had very strict rules for her sailors. Her prisoners had to eat caterpillars in boiled rice!

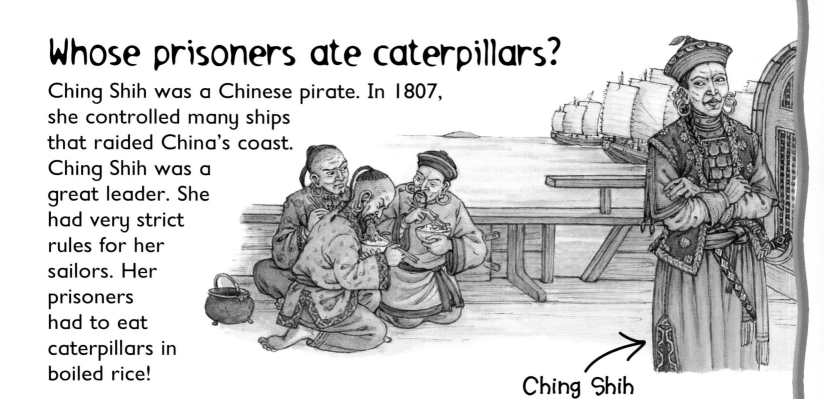

Ching Shih

Baldy!

Grace O'Malley shaved her head to look more like her sailors. She was given the nickname 'Baldy'!

Who said she was sorry?

Grace O'Malley went to sea when she was a young girl. She ended up controlling pirate ships off the coast of Ireland. Grace had 20 ships under her command. In 1593 Grace asked Queen Elizabeth I of England to forgive her for being a pirate.

What were the best ships?

A galley ship

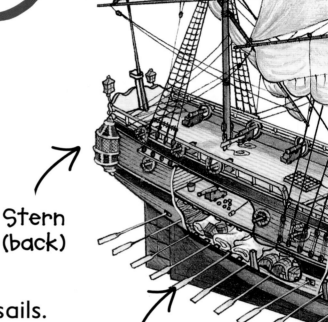

Pirate ships had to be very fast! Many were small and easy to sail. Schooners were ships that had two masts. Corsairs sailed in galleys – ships that had oars as well as sails. The captain had a cabin in the stern (back of the ship). Treasure, gunpowder and food were stored in the hold, beneath the deck.

Stern (back)

Oars

Water and stores (middle)

Where did pirates sleep?

Most pirates slept on the deck unless the weather was bad. Some put up hammocks below deck in the middle of the ship. It was cramped, smelly and noisy. This made some pirates ill. So did their food. They didn't eat enough fruit and vegetables!

Recycling!

Pirates even stole their prisoners' clothes! They usually sold them, but sometimes kept the best items for themselves.

Sails

Write

Look at the picture of the galley. Write a guided tour of the ship. Describe how the pirates lived on it, too.

Bow (front)

What did pirates eat?

Pirates mostly ate dry biscuits and pickled meat when on board ship. They hunted for fresh meat when they landed on islands. They also collected fresh water and fruit. Pirate cooks often had only one arm or leg. They couldn't fight, so they cooked!

Who was afraid of a flag?

Merchant seamen were terrified when they saw the flag of a pirate ship. Early flags were bright red. By the 1700s, pirates flew black flags. Each pirate captain added his or her own symbol. Sometimes this was the famous white skull-and-crossbones.

Were buccaneers heroes?

Buccaneers were violent thieves. Some people thought they were heroes. Bartholomew Roberts was a buccaneer. His nickname was Black Bart. He was handsome and bold, yet he never drank anything stronger than tea! In the 1720s, he captured 400 ships.

Pirate flag

Duck!

When pirates attacked a ship, they shot at sailors working on the sails. They also shot at the helm, the steering area of the ship.

Where was the treasure?

Sailors often hid their treasure. Pirates had to break down walls and doors to find it. They threatened their prisoners until they revealed the treasure. Pirates had frightening weapons such as knives, daggers and pistols.

Design

Design your own pirate flag. Choose a bold colour. You could draw your own frightening symbol on it.

Pirates looking for treasure

What was the best treasure?

Gold and silver was the best pirate treasure. It could be gold or silver coins, plain bars or made into fine ornaments. Silk cloth and hardwoods such as ebony were also valuable. So was ivory. But pirates were not so happy with cotton, coal or iron.

Pirates and their stolen treasure →

Spicy sands!

Spices from India and Sri Lanka were very valuable, but they were difficult to sell. Pirates often dumped them overboard. These spices piled up on the beaches.

Was the treasure shared?

The captain was in charge of sharing out the treasure. Officers got more than ordinary sailors. The cook and the carpenter got less because they didn't fight. Captains tried to divide everything fairly. Unhappy pirates might attack the captain and take over the ship!

Make

Make a mini treasure chest. Take a small box and paint it to look like wood. Then fill it with painted cut-out jewels.

Where were all the jewels?

Pirates stole jewels from ships all over the world. Diamonds came from Africa. Red rubies and blue sapphires came from Burma. Green emeralds were mined in Colombia. Divers scooped up shiny pearls from the Persian Gulf.

Treasure chest →

What were pirates scared of?

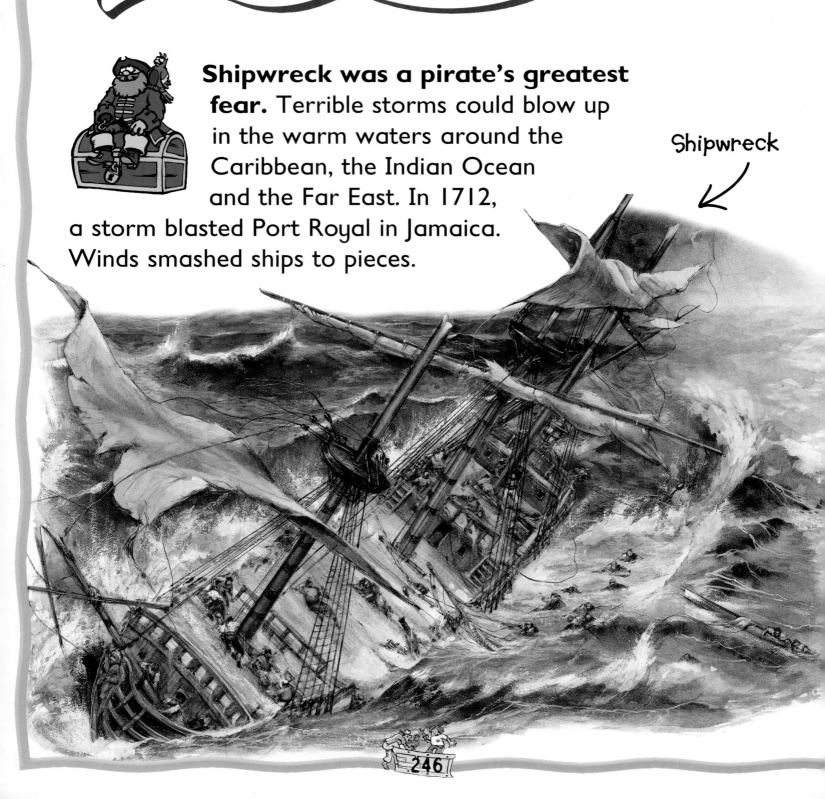

Shipwreck was a pirate's greatest fear. Terrible storms could blow up in the warm waters around the Caribbean, the Indian Ocean and the Far East. In 1712, a storm blasted Port Royal in Jamaica. Winds smashed ships to pieces.

Shipwreck

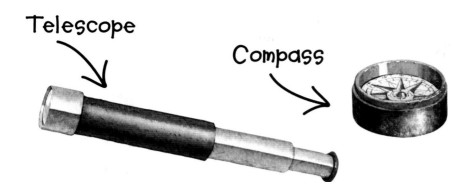

Telescope

Compass

Map

How did pirates find their way?

Pirates used the position of the Sun and stars to guide them in the right direction. They also used a compass to help them. A telescope helped pirates to see landmarks and work out their position. Pirates used maps to find their way on land.

Write

Pretend you are captain of a pirate ship. Write down all the jobs that are carried out on board every day.

Round and round!

Captain William Dampier was a brilliant navigator. This means he knew where he was going! In the 1680s he sailed around the world three times.

How did pirates save a sinking ship?

Pirates tried to pump out water if the ship was leaking. Sometimes ships 'ran aground'. This means they got stuck in shallow water. The pirates had to throw out anything heavy. This helped the ship to refloat. Sometimes they threw out food barrels and cannons.

Who is Long John Silver?

Long John Silver is a one-legged pirate. But he isn't real! He appears in a book called *Treasure Island*. This adventure story is all about pirates and buried treasure. It was written by Robert Louis Stevenson in 1883.

Long John Silver

Dancing pirates!

Blackbeard was a real and dangerous pirate. In 1798, his story was made into a ballet!

What ate Captain Hook's hand?

Captain Hook is a fierce pirate in a story called *Peter Pan*. It was written as a book and a play by J.M. Barrie in 1904. Peter Pan is the hero. He cut off Captain Hook's hand and fed it to a crocodile. That's why the Captain needed a hook.

Captain Hook →

Did pirates sing?

Gilbert and Sullivan were famous songwriters. They wrote a musical about pirates in 1879, called *Pirates of Penzance*. But the pirates were softies! They wouldn't steal from orphans — children who had no parents — so everyone pretended to be an orphan!

Write

Write your own pirate story. Your pirates can be kind or cruel. They could be modern pirates. What would treasure be like today?

Quiz time

Do you remember what you have read about pirates? These questions will test your memory. The pictures will help you. If you get stuck, read the pages again.

1. What is a pirate?

page 232

2. Who was afraid of the Barbarossas?

page 233

3. When were pirates not pirates?

page 235

4. Did sailors fight the pirates?

page 236

5. What did pirates do with their money?

page 236

6. Could women be pirates?

page 238

7. Whose prisoners ate caterpillars?

page 239

8. Where did pirates sleep?

page 240

9. What did pirates eat?

page 241

page 242

10. Who was afraid of a flag?

11. Where were all the jewels?

page 245

12. How did pirates find their way?

page 247

13. What ate Captain Hook's hand?

page 249

Index

A

Abu Simbel, temple 195
aerials 80, 81
Africa 40, 56, 146, 172, 173, 187, 233, 245
air 30, 31, 41, 42, 43, 44, 45, 55, 59, 60, 62, 104, 105, 114
aircraft 75
Alexandria, Egypt 200
Algiers 233
Americas 234
Amun Ra, god 194, 195
Anatosaurus 142–143
animals 12, 40, 58, 128, 133, 145, 160, 161, 163, 202, 205, 216
Antarctica 48
antbirds 163
antelopes 185
ants 187
Anubis, god 194
Apatosaurus 126, 130, 131, 135
apes 185
Archaeopteryx 153
Arctic 152
Arctic hares 178
Argentinosaurus 129
armour 138, 139, 221, 224, 225
army 200–201
army ants 163
arrows 220, 221
arteries 111
Asia 187
asteroids 11, 23, 60
astronauts 30–31

spacesuits 17, 31
Athens, Greece 63
Atlantic Ocean 51, 63
atmosphere 42–43, 63
atoms 89
auroras 55
Australia 175
autumn 39
avalanches 49
axes 220

B

babies 108, 140–141, 170, 171, 172, 182, 186
blue whales 183
lemmings 178
opossums 183
baboons 205
baileys 216
balance 112
bald eagles 158
balloons 61
banners 223
Barbarossa brothers 232–233
barn owls 152–153
Barrie, J. M. 249
Baryonyx 126
Bastet, goddess 195
bats 173
batteries 72, 78, 79
battering rams 227
battles 220, 221, 222, 223
beads 209
beaks 127, 143, 152
skimmers 165
woodpeckers 162
beards 232
bears 178, 185
Beaufort Scale 51
bee hummingbirds 162
bees 163, 186, 202
Bible 47
bills *see also* beaks
birds 140, 143, 152–153, 177, 181, 184, 202, 203

birds cont.
bird feeders 163
birds of prey 160–161
earliest 153
fastest 154
Black Bart (Bartholomew Roberts) 242
Blackbeard (Edward Teach) 248
blood 101, 110–111
blubber 179
blue whales 172–173, 183
boats 74
bones 81, 99, 100–101, 102, 113, 143, 146, 154
Bonney, Anne 238
'Book of Buried Pearls' 193
bottle banks 91
bowhead whales 176–177
bows 218, 221
Brachiosaurus 128–129
brains 103, 112, 113, 114, 116–117, 129, 135
bread 106, 107, 203
breathing 104–105
breezes 51
bricks 206, 207
Britain 238
buccaneers 242
bugs 127, 137, 142, 143, 152, 155, 162, 163
bullet-proof glass 87

C

cables 79
calculators 83
calves 172, 177, 183
cameras 60
canines 108
cannons 247
canyons 15
captains 236, 245, 247
carbon dioxide 63
Caribbean 235, 246
carpenters 204, 245
cars 69, 70, 74, 76, 86, 90
castles 214–215
sieges 226–227
catapults 227
caterpillars 239
cats 174, 195
cattle 202
cells 97, 101, 111, 117

central processing units 83
cerebellum 116, 117
cerebrum 116
chainmail 221
charcoal 207
chariots 200–201
Charon 16
cheese 106
cheetahs 174
chemicals 70, 71
chewing 107
chicken 106
chicks 153, 158
cuckoos 159
children 205
chimpanzees 185
chin 111
China 56, 239
churches 219
cities 74–75, 90
claws 130–131, 133
clay 205, 206, 207
clothes 87, 241
clothing 209
clouds 21, 44–45, 55, 60
clusters 25
coal 91, 244
coats of arms 222, 223
cochlea 113
cocks-of-the-rocks 157
Coelophysis 137, 143
coffins 199
cold 17, 31, 48, 57, 62, 63, 96, 97
collar bones 100
Colombia 245
colour 15, 21, 25, 54, 55, 156–157, 165
colours 73
combs 209
comets 22–23
compasses 247
Compsognathus 137
computers 78, 82
electronic brains 83
Internet 84–85
railway signals 75
concrete 75, 101
conifers 125
cookers 70, 81
cooking pots 197, 206
cooks 241, 245
corsairs 233, 240

cotton 87, 244
courtyards 216
cows 57
craftworkers 204
craters 13, 15, 17
crests 135
crocodiles 125, 126, 140
crops 41, 203
Cuba (Hispaniola) 235
cubs 171, 180, 181, 182
cuckoos 159
cycads 125
cyclones 51

D

daggers 243
Dampier, William 247
day 9, 13, 38, 39, 42
death masks 197
deer 171, 175, 184
Deinonychus 130–131
dermis 97
deserts 40–41, 47, 202
diamonds 245
Dinosaur Cove 147
dinosaurs 62, 122–123
    armoured 138–139
    babies 140–141
    biggest 128–129
    cleverest 135
    death 122, 144–145
    eyes 127, 134, 143
    fastest 136–137
    fossils 142, 146–147
    meat-eating 130, 131,
        132–133
    noisiest 135
    plant-eating 124–125, 129
    senses 134
    smallest 137
    teeth 126–127, 132, 133,
        146
Diplodocus 129
disease 145
doctors 81, 89, 117, 204
dogs 185
dolls 205
dolphins 126, 176, 181
droppings 142
drought 40, 41
dubbing 219
duck-billed platypus 171
dust 11, 15, 22, 24, 25, 62

E

eagles 158, 160, 161
ears 101, 112, 113
Earth 10, 11, 12, 13, 15,
        17, 18, 22, 29, 38, 48,
        61, 62, 73, 77, 90–91,
        122, 123, 145, 147
    atmosphere 42–43, 63
    day and night 13
    inside Earth 12–13
    probes 32–33
    Sun 8–9
eating 106–107
ebony 244
eclipses 9
EEG machines 117
eggs 140, 141, 145, 146,
        153, 171
    cuckoos 159
Egypt 46
Einstein, Albert 89
El Niño 40
electricity 52, 53, 72, 76,
        91, 117
    circuits 79
    mains electricity 78
elephants 128, 130, 172,
        173, 183
Elizabeth I 235, 239
emails 84, 85
emeralds 245
enamel 108
enemies 214, 215, 226, 227
energy 70–71, 89
engineers 74
engines 70, 73, 74
England 221, 234–235, 237
epidermis 97
Euoplocephalus 139
Europe 63
experiments 88
extinction 122, 144–145
eyelids 139
eyes 9, 102, 112, 113, 127,
        134, 143, 182
eyesight 160

F

face 103
Fahrenheit, Gabriel Daniel
        59
Far East 246
farming 63, 202–203, 204

fat 106
feathers 135, 143, 152,
        154, 157
feet 100, 160, 161
ferns 123, 125
fighting 133
fingers 99, 101
fire 215
fireworks 70
fish 106, 107, 126, 142,
        161, 177
fish-eating dinosaurs
    Baryonyx 126
    Coelophysis 137, 143
flags 242
flamingos 164, 165
flavours 114, 115
flies 201
floods 46–47, 51, 202
flowers 123
flying 152, 154–155
fogbows 55
follicles 98
food 30, 70–71, 81,
        106–107, 108, 109, 114,
        115, 226, 238, 239, 240,
        241, 247
    animals 160, 161, 163
    fish 161
    insects 152, 155, 162,
        163
    nuts 152
    shrimps 165
    slugs and snails 164
forces 69, 89
fossils 142, 146–147
foxes 175
France 221
friction 69
frost 57
fruit 106, 125, 170, 185
fuel 28, 207
fur 170, 179
furniture 197

G

galaxies 26–27
galleys 240–241
gardens 206, 216
gas 8, 14, 18, 24, 25, 28,
        90, 91
    Jupiter 11, 19
    Neptune 11

gas cont.
    Saturn 11, 19
    Uranus 11
gazelles 174
germs 111
Giganotosaurus 133
giraffes 128
Giza, Egypt 192, 193
glass 87, 91
gloves 96
goats 202
gods 194–195
gold 197, 244
golden eagles 160
government officers 204
Grand Gallery, Great
        Pyramid 193
grass 125
gravity 69, 89
great crested grebes 156
Great Dark Spot 21
Great Pyramid 192–193
Greece 63
Greenland 63
Groundhog Day 58
growing 96, 107
gullet 107
gunpowder 240

H

hailstones 52
hair 97, 98–99, 113, 170,
        209
halberds 220
hammocks 240
hands 100
hares 175, 178
harp seals 176
hatching 153
Hatshepsut, Queen
        196–197
Havana 235
Hawkins, John 235
head 97
hearing 113, 117, 134
heart 102, 103, 110–111
heat 8, 14, 17, 24, 25, 31,
        41, 59, 63, 70, 71, 81,
        96, 97
heaters 70
helium 61
helmets 222
heralds 222–223

herds 128, 142, 183
Herrerasaurus 122–123
hips 101
Hispaniola (Cuba) 235
hoes 202
hog-nosed bats 173
honey 202
honey badgers 163
honeyguides 163
Hook, Captain 249
horns 139
horses 136, 218, 219, 220, 223, 225
horsetails 125
houses 50, 206–207
humans 122
hummingbirds 155, 162
Hundred Years War 221
hunters 133, 134, 135
hurricanes 51, 61
hyenas 183

I

ice 11, 48, 49, 52, 55, 63
  comets 22
  Saturn's rings 19
Iguanodon 131
illness 107
incisors 108
India 43, 244
Indian Ocean 51, 246
insect-eating dinosaurs
  Coelophysis 137, 143
  Compsognathus 137
insects 127, 137, 142, 152, 155, 162, 163, 185, 186, 187
Internet 84–85
intestines 109
Io 18
Ireland 239
iron 76, 244
Isis 47
ivory 244

J

Jamaica 237
Janenschia 146–147
jaw 102, 108
jets 73
jewellers 204
jewellery 197
jewels 245

Jobaria 146
jobs 204–205
joeys 171
joints 101
jousting 225
Jupiter 18–19
  biggest planet 18
  gas 11, 19
  moons 11, 18
  Voyager 1 33

K

kangaroos 171, 175
keeps 217
keratin 99
Khafre, Pharaoh 192, 193
Khufu, Pharaoh 192
kidneys 111
killer whales 177
kittens 171
knee pads 96
knees 100, 101
knights 225
  fighting 220–221
  heraldry 22–223
  tournaments 219, 224–225
  training 218–219
knives 243
kohl 208

L

L'Ollonais, Francis 236
laboratories 88
labourers 204
ladders 227
ladies 225
lances 225
larynx 105
Le Clerc, François 235
Leaellynasaura 146–147
leather 209, 215
leaves 39, 170, 185
legs 101
lemmings 178
lens 112
levers 68
life 12
light 8, 24, 25, 38, 41, 54, 55, 70, 73, 80, 112
lightning 52, 53, 79
lights 78, 79
limestone 87

linen 221
lions 142, 181, 183
liquid 11, 18, 19
lizards 137, 140, 155
longbows 221
loot 244–245
lords 217, 218
lungs 104–105, 110

M

machines 68–69, 75, 78, 83, 89, 90
magnets 72, 76–77
  electromagnets 76
  magnetic fields 77
Maiasaura 141
make-up 208
mammals 170–171
  biggest 172–173
  dangerous 186
  families 180–181, 184
  fastest 174–175
  flying 173
  hunters 184
  smallest 173
  stinkiest 187
  swimmers 176–177
maps 247
marrow 101
Mars 14
  moons 11
  probes 33
  red planet 15
materials 75, 86, 87, 88, 91
mating 154, 157
meat 241
meat-eating dinosaurs 130, 131, 132–133
  Deinonychus 130–131
  Giganotosaurus 133
  Rutiodon 125
  Tyrannosaurus rex 126–127, 132, 133
  Velociraptor 142
medals 201
medicines 89
Mediterranean 233
meerkats 181
melons 203
Menkaure, Pharaoh 192
Mercury 10
  hot and cold 17
  no moons 11

messengers 222, 223
metal 86, 91
meteorites 62, 144, 145
mice 160, 161
microchips 83
microwaves 81
milk 170, 171, 183
Milky Way 26–27
mills 217
mirages 41
moats 215
mobile telephones 80, 85
mock suns 55
molars 108
money 233, 236, 237
monkeys 185
monsoon 43
Moon 9, 11, 16, 57, 80
  shape changes 13
  wind and rain 17
moons 11, 16, 18, 20
morning star 220
mosses 123
motors 72
mottes 214
Mount Everest 15
mountains 43, 45, 49
mouth 104, 115
mud 207
mummies 198–199
muscles 102–103, 105, 106, 107, 109, 110, 112, 117, 154
Muttaburrasaurus 137

N

nails 99
navigation 247
neck 105, 111
Neptune 10
  clouds 21
  gas 11
  Pluto 21
  Voyager 2 32
nerves 103, 112, 117
nests 153, 158–159
night 9, 13, 38, 39, 42
Nile river 46, 202, 207
Noah's ark 47
North America 175
North Pole 39, 178
Northern Lights 55
nose 104, 114, 115, 171, 172

nuclear energy 89
nuts 152

O

O'Malley, Grace 'Baldy'
239
oil 91
Olympus Mons 15
onions 203
opossums 183
orang-utans 170
orchards 206
Ornithomimus 127, 136–137
ostriches 152
ovens 206
owls 152–153
oxen 202
oxygen 104, 110, 111

P

Pacific Ocean 40, 51
packs 133, 142, 185
pain 96
pandas 182
pangolins 187
paper 91
papyrus 209
Parasaurolophus 135
Pathfinder 33
peacocks 156–157
pearls 245
pebbles 125
pelvis 100
people 12, 40, 41, 43, 45,
49, 56, 58
peregrine falcon 154–155
Persian Gulf 245
Peter Pan 249
pharaohs 192, 195, 199,
201, 204
photographs 32, 60, 61
pilot whales 181
pirates 232–233
flags 242
loot 244–245
ships 240–241, 246–247
women pirates 238–239
pistols 243
pivots 68
planes 51, 60–61
planets 10–11
biggest 18
coldest 17

planets cont.
hottest 14
red planet 15
smallest 16
plant-eating dinosaurs 124,
129
Apatosaurus 126, 130,
131, 135
Argentinosaurus 129
Brachiosaurus 128–129
Diplodocus 129
Iguanodon 131
Plateosaurus 124–125
Riojasaurus 125
Triceratops 138, 139
plants 12, 40, 42, 44, 87,
90, 123, 126, 139, 145
plastic 86, 91
Plateosaurus 124–125
playgrounds 68–69
playing 96, 117
ploughs 202
plugs 78
plumage 157
Pluto 10
coldest planet 17
ice 11
Neptune 21
smallest planet 16
pods 181
polar bears 178
poles 77
pollution 90
Port Royal 237, 246
power stations 78
praying 219
priests and priestesses 199,
204
prisms 73
privateers 235
probes 32, 33
pronghorn deer 175
Protoceratops 139, 140–141
Ptolemy, General 200
Punt 196
pupils 112, 113
pups 179
pylons 79
pyramids 192

R

Ra, Sun god 194
rabbits 160, 171

Rackham, 'Calico Jack'
238
radar 75
radio 61, 80, 81
radio waves 75, 80–81
railway signals 75
rain 17, 40, 41, 42, 43,
44–45, 48, 59
floods 51, 46–47
rain dances 56, 57
rainbows 54–55, 73
rainforests 42, 152, 157,
170
ramps 68
Ramses II, pharaoh 195
Ramses III, pharaoh
201
raptors 135
rats 161
ravens 161
Read, Mary 238
recycling 91
red kangaroos 175
remembering 116
retrievers 220
rhinoceroses 186–187
ribs 100, 105
rings
Neptune 21
Saturn 19
Uranus 21
Riojasaurus 125
rivers 44, 46, 47
roadrunners 155
Roberts, Bartholomew
'Black Bart' 242
robes 222
robots 32–33
rock 13, 17, 23, 77, 144,
145, 146, 147
Earth 11, 12–13
Mars 11, 15, 33
Mercury 11
shooting stars 22
Venus 11
rockets 28, 29
roots 99, 108
rope 227
Royal Navy 238
rubber 86, 87
rubies 245
Rudel, Jaufre 219
Rutiodon 125

S

Sahara Desert 40
sand 87
sandals 209
sapphires 245
sarcophagus 199
satellites 61, 80
Saturn 10, 33
gas 11, 19
moons 11
rings 19
sauropods 128, 129, 131
scales 187
scavengers 133
schooners 240
science 68, 74, 75
scientists 69, 74, 88, 89, 90,
91, 147
Scooter 21
sea 40, 44, 147
sea creatures 145
sea eagles 161
Sea People 201
seals 176, 177, 179
see-saws 68–69
senses 116, 117
sensors 96, 97, 112, 113,
114, 115
servants 207
shaving 196
sheep 202
shields 222
Shih, Ching 239
shins 100
ships 240–241, 246–247
shoes 209, 221
shooting stars 22
shops 85
shoulder blades 100
shrews 145
shrimps 165
shuttles 28–29
sieges 226–227
sight 112, 134
signals 75
silk 244
silver 197, 237, 244
Silver, Long John 248
singing 105, 157
skateboards 96, 97
skeleton 100–101
skimmers 165
skin 96–97, 98, 113

skull 100
skull-and-crossbones 242
skunks 186, 187
skyscrapers 74, 75
slaves 233
sleeping 31, 240
sloth bears 185
smell 114, 115, 117, 134, 171, 175, 187
snail kites 164–165
snails 164
snakes 155
snow 48–49, 56
snowflakes 48, 49
sockets 78
soil 25, 147, 202, 203
Sojourner 33
Solar System 10, 14, 18, 23, 33
soldiers 200–201, 215, 220, 221, 222, 223, 227
Somalia 196
song thrushes 153
sound 70, 73, 105, 113
South Pole 39
space 62, 81, 89, 144, 145
space travel 14, 17, 19
  astronauts 30–31
  robots 32–33
  shuttles 28–29
  spacecraft 8, 14, 19, 30–31, 60
  spacesuits 17, 31
Spain 234–235
speaking 115, 117
speed 73, 80
sphinx 193
spices 244
spindles 72
spinning tops 205
spring 38
squid 177
squires 218, 219
Sri Lanka 244
stars 8, 22
  galaxies 26–27
  how stars are made 24–25
steel 75, 76, 101
Stevenson, Robert Louis 248
stomach 107, 109
stone 215, 227
stones 125

storms 50, 51, 246
  Jupiter 18
  Mars 15
  Neptune 21
Styracosaurus 139
submarines 81
summer 38, 39
sums 83
Sun 8–9, 10, 11, 13, 17, 21, 22, 38, 39, 42, 47, 55, 62, 63, 73, 91, 247
  asteroid belt 23
  star 24, 25
  sunspots 9
sun dogs 55
swallowing 107, 109
sweat 97
Sweden 38
swifts 154, 155
swimming 152
switches 79
Switzerland 220
swords 218, 219, 220

T
tails 129, 139
taste 114, 115, 117, 134
taste buds 115
Teach, Edward 'Blackbeard' 248
teachers 218
teeth 102, 108, 126–127, 132, 133, 146, 152
telescopes 247
televisions 78, 80, 81
temperatures 48, 59, 60, 71
temples 195, 196
termites 185
thermometers 59, 71
thinking 116, 117
thunderstorms 50, 52–53, 79
tigers 184
time 89
toes 99, 101
tombs 192, 197
  tomb robbers 193, 197
tongue 115
tornadoes 50
tortoiseshell 56
touch 96, 97, 117, 134
tournaments 219, 224–225
Tower of Winds 63

towers 217
towns 49
toys 205
trade 204
trains 69, 74, 75
treasure 233, 240, 243, 245
Treasure Island 248
trees 39, 50, 63, 87, 123, 125
Triceratops 138, 139
Tripoli, Countess of 219
Troodon 134–135
tropics 42
trunks 173
tunics 221
tunnels 227
Tutankhamun 197
typhoons 51
Tyrannosaurus rex 126–127, 132, 133

U
United States 41, 58
Uranus 10, 20–21
  gas 11
  moons 20
  Voyager 2 32
urine 111

V
vegetables 106
veins 111
Velociraptor 142
Venus 10, 15
  hottest planet 14
  no moons 11
Vikings 32, 63
villas 206
Virginia opossums 183
viziers 204, 205
voice 105
volcanoes 12, 144, 145
  biggest 15
  Io 18
Voyager 1 33
Voyager 2 32

W
Wales 221
walls 207, 215, 216, 217, 227
washing 31
washing machines 78

waste 91, 109, 111
water 8, 12, 30, 31, 45, 48, 52, 55, 60, 71, 81, 91, 202–203, 207, 217, 240, 241
  water cycle 44
weapons 227, 243
weather 42, 56, 90, 123, 145
  changing 63
  dinosaurs 62
  drought 40, 41
  floods 51, 46–47
  forecasting 60–61
  monsoon 43
  rain 40, 41, 42, 43, 44–45, 48, 59
  rainbows 54–55
  sayings 57
  snow 48–49, 56
  thunderstorms 50, 52–53
  wind 50–51, 56, 58, 60, 63
weather houses 59
weather vanes 58–59, 63
weaver birds 159
web pages 84
Weddell seals 177
weight 30, 69
whales 172–173, 176–177, 181
wheat 203
wheels 69
wigs 209
wild dogs 185
wind 17, 50–51, 56, 58, 60, 63, 91
windows 87
windpipe 104, 105
wings 152, 154, 159
winter 38, 39
wires 72, 76
wolves 175, 180–181
women 204, 208, 209
women pirates 238–239
wood 87, 205, 207, 215, 227
woodpeckers 162
wool 221
World Wide Web 84, 85
wrecks 246

X
X-rays 81

T H E
ESSENTIAL
MICROWAVE
HANDBOOK

T H E
ESSENTIAL
MICROWAVE
HANDBOOK

THE COMPLETE GUIDE TO
MICROWAVE COOKING

Carol Bowen

LORENZ BOOKS

This paperback edition published by Lorenz Books
an imprint of
Anness Publishing Limited
Hermes House
88-89 Blackfriars Road
London SE1 8HA

Published in the USA by Lorenz Books
Anness Publishing Inc., 27 West 20th Street, New York, NY 10011;
(800) 354-9657

This edition distributed in Canada by Raincoast Books
9050 Shaughnessy Street, Vancouver, British Columbia V69 6E5

A CIP catalogue record for this book is available from the British Library

Publisher: Joanna Lorenz
Senior Editor: Linda Fraser
Editor: Bridget Jones
Designer: William Mason
Illustrator: Madeleine David

© Anness Publishing Limited 1998
Updated © 2001
1 3 5 7 9 10 8 6 4 2

NOTES
For all recipes, quantities are given in both metric and imperial measures and, where
appropriate, measures are also given in standard cups and spoons. Follow one set, but
not a mixture, because they are not interchangeable.

Standard spoon and cup measures are level.
1 tsp = 5ml, 1tbsp = 15ml, 1 cup = 250ml/8fl oz

Australian standard tablespoons are 20ml. Australian readers should use 3 tsp in place
of 1 tbsp for measuring small quantities of gelatine, cornflour, salt etc.

Size 3 (medium) eggs are used unless otherwise stated.

CONTENTS

~

INTRODUCTION
6

SOUPS AND STARTERS
32

FISH AND SEAFOOD
42

MEAT AND POULTRY
54

PULSES, PASTA AND GRAINS
62

VEGETABLES AND SALADS
72

DESSERTS
80

BAKING
88

COOKING AND DEFROSTING CHARTS
96

INDEX
127

Introduction

Undeniably, speed is the main advantage of microwave cooking; however, it is not this in isolation that has made microwaves the success story they are. Not only do microwaves make light work of cooking many staple dishes and family favourites, but they also cook them to perfection. With a microwave cooker, limp, soggy greens, over-sticky rice, nutritionally poor fruit-based desserts and labour- and time-intensive meat, fish and poultry dishes are things of the past; these emerge from the microwave fresh, colourful, nutritionally rich and, moreover, most appetizing. The time-saving aspect may be great, as when cooking a jacket potato in about 6 minutes, or minimal, for example in the case of rice and pasta, but the additional benefit is being able to cook foods with the minimum attention and to just the right degree, be it *al dente*, tender-crisp, fork-tender or succulently moist.

ADVANTAGES OF MICROWAVE COOKING

Speed
You can reduce normal cooking times by up to 75 per cent by using a microwave oven.

Nutrient Retention
Nutrient loss from food is often associated with other cooking methods. With microwave cooking, since timings are short and so precise, and additional cooking liquid is minimal, there is less likely to be a loss of nutrients during cooking or by seepage as when boiling.

Economy
Since microwave cooking does not involve a lengthy preheating period and cooks for a shorter period of time, this method requires less energy and therefore saves money on energy bills.

Few Cooking Smells
Cooking odours are usually contained within the microwave oven cavity, so kitchen odours are kept to an absolute minimum.

Cool Kitchen
Because of the mechanics of microwave cooking, the microwave oven, dishes and the kitchen all stay cool, while only the food becomes piping hot. Also, in kitchens where there is a problem with ventilation, the microwave is a great improvement on the conventional hob, which creates a lot of steam during boiling or other moist cooking methods.

Less Risk of Burns
Since dishes do not become red hot, but only heat up by the conduction of heat from the food, there is less risk of getting a nasty

burn from dishes or from the oven itself. This makes the microwave one of the safest cooking machines for the very young and for the elderly or infirm to use.

Less Cleaning and Washing Up
It is possible to cook and serve in the same container with microwave cooking, thereby reducing the amount of washing up. Cleaning the cooker is also easier as food does not bake on or splatter as found in conventional ovens and on hobs.

An End to Dried-out Dinners
With a microwave oven, dried-out dinners can become a thing of the past. Individual members of the family can eat when they want and late-comers can have a meal reheated in minutes to just-cooked perfection.

SELECTING FOOD FOR
MICROWAVE COOKING

Apart from a few restrictions, virtually any food can be cooked in the microwave, but there are some foods that cook better than others. When planning a meal or choosing a recipe consider the following:

Fish and Shellfish
Whether fresh or frozen, whole or filleted, plain cooked or in a fancy sauce, microwave-cooked fish and shellfish are hard to beat for texture, flavour, appearance and ease of preparation. With little fear of drying out, these delicate foods stay succulently moist. Often, the only additional ingredients required are a tablespoon or two of water, lemon juice or stock, or a little butter, so fish and seafood are favourites with those following a healthy diet regime or watching their weight.

Whole Fish Slit the skin in two or three places on whole fish, such as salmon, trout and mackerel, to prevent it from bursting during cooking. (Boil-in-the-bag prepared fish should also have the pouch pierced.) The narrow end of the tail may need protecting for half the cooking time by shielding with a little foil.

Fillets, Steaks and Portions For best results when cooking fillets, roll them up into an even shape and secure each one with a wooden cocktail stick. Brush with lemon

juice or melted butter and cover tightly during cooking. Fish steaks and pieces should be cooked so that the thicker portions are to the outer edge of the dish and the thinner pieces to the centre, where they receive the least microwave energy.

Coated Portions Breadcrumb-coated and battered fish can be cooked in the microwave, but the result will not be as crisp as when cooked conventionally. A microwave browning dish may help appreciably with these products.

Shellfish Prawns, shrimps, lobster and scallops cook superbly, but always start with the minimum time when cooking these items as they cook very quickly; also remember to take the standing time into account as part of the overall cooking process. Mussels and clams can also be steamed and cooked in the microwave with unbelievable ease.

Poultry and Game

Whole birds; quarters; breast, thigh and drumstick portions; stir-fry strips; and medallions of poultry and game can be cooked in the microwave with good results. Those dishes that require little browning, with portions cooked in a sauce, are most successful.

Whole Birds Truss well to hold the wings and legs close to the body to give a neat, compact shape. The narrow wing tips and drumstick bone ends may have to be protected with small pieces of foil for part of the cooking time. Start cooking whole birds breast-side down and turn over halfway through cooking. Place on a special microwaveproof roasting rack or on an upturned saucer so that the bird is lifted above the cooking juices.

With large birds and longer cooking times, browning is usually sufficient, but smaller birds and portions may need a little help. In all cases, whether cooking a whole bird or portions, these can be browned under a preheated hot grill after microwave cooking – the time savings are still considerable and warrant microwave cooking.

When cooking birds that have been stuffed, add an extra 1 minute per 450g/1lb to the times recommended in cooking charts. After cooking, leave to stand, covered in a tent of foil, to make best use of the residual heat; you will also find that the bird is easier to carve.

Small Birds and Portions Small birds, chicken quarters and small poultry joints should be cooked skin-side up, with the thicker parts towards the outside of the dish. Many will brown and crisp more readily if placed in a roasting bag.

If you are unsure of timings, then consider investing in a microwave thermometer, which takes the guesswork out of roasting and cooking times by indicating the internal temperature of the food.

Meat

With careful consideration of the quality and cut, meat cooked in the microwave is a great success. Cheaper, longer-cooking cuts can be microwaved with a measure of success, but the microwave performs better with prime-quality cuts. With the exception of roast pork, do not salt meat before microwave cooking as this draws out the moisture and toughens the meat.

Joints Ideally, choose joints that are symmetrically shaped; in other words, bone and roll joints like legs and shoulders for perfect results.

Minced Meat Minced beef, lamb and pork cook magnificently, whether as burgers or in moist dishes, like chilli con carne or Bolognese sauce. Meatloaves should be made in a ring mould for faster cooking.

Cubed Meat Cubes of meat for dishes such as casseroles, hot pots and curries, should be cut into pieces of the same size to ensure even cooking. Reduce the liquid required for such dishes by up to a third as there is very little evaporation in microwave cooking. Vegetables in casserole-type dishes tend to retain their shape and do not break down to thicken the liquid.

Sausages, Bacon and Kebabs Sausages, bacon and other fatty meats cook quickly with some degree of browning, but cover them with a sheet of absorbent kitchen paper during cooking to prevent fat from splattering on the oven walls. Wooden skewers should be used for kebabs which should, ideally, be cooked on a microwave roasting rack or placed across a shallow microwaveproof dish for success.

Vegetables

Whether freshly harvested from your garden, bought in the market, plucked from the supermarket shelf or taken from the freezer or store cupboard, the microwave will cook your vegetable selection to perfection. Only the minimum amount of water is used for most vegetables, so results are temptingly colourful and tender-crisp. Season with salt after cooking, as salt sprinkled directly on to vegetables can cause them to dehydrate and toughen.

Whole Vegetables Potatoes, aubergines and tomatoes need pricking before cooking to prevent them from bursting. Jacket potatoes will also have a crisper, drier skin if cooked on a sheet of absorbent kitchen paper. Whole vegetables or items which are not cut into small pieces should be positioned so that thicker parts are towards the outer edge of the dish, where they receive the most energy.

Cut Vegetables Most vegetables should be cut into uniformly sized pieces and placed in a cook bag or covered dish. Stir, rearrange or shake the vegetables halfway through the cooking time to ensure even results.

Fruit

From the basic apple to the exotic mango, fruit can be cooked in the microwave to retain its glorious characteristics. Most fruits can be prepared, sprinkled with sugar and cooked in a roasting bag or dish in the same way as fresh vegetables. Other items can be baked whole, poached in wine, cider or syrup, or stuffed with a sweetened filling.

Whole Fruit These must be scored or pricked if they are not peeled, so that the skin does not burst during cooking. Careful timing is important as fruit cooks surprisingly quickly.

Dried Fruit Dried fruit mixtures can also be cooked quickly to make fruit salads, compôtes and crumbles. Try mixtures of dried apple, pear, mango, peach, apricot and prune, and cook them in fruit juice and water for mouth-watering puddings at any time of the year.

Frozen Fruit The microwave is also useful for preparing fruit for the freezer when there is a glut, good price at the market or windfall of tree fruit. Use the microwave for cooking the fruit or for speedily making the sugar syrup in which to freeze fruit for long-term storage.

Pasta, Rice, Grains and Pulses

Any healthy diet should have its fair share of pasta, rice, grains and pulses; but, so often, it is the lengthy preparation of the latter that prevents us from serving them more often. The microwave makes light work of rehydrating beans and pulses, reducing what was once a long, overnight process of soaking to about 1½ hours.

The time savings with cooking pasta, rice, grains and pulses are virtually negligible but the bonuses are that little or no attention is required during cooking; the results are superb; there is no sticky, tacky saucepan to wash afterwards; no steamy kitchen and boil-over spills; and the food can be cooked ahead and reheated to perfection later.

All About Microwaves

For centuries people have cooked food to make it more palatable, easier to digest and safe to eat. From the smoky fire of prehistoric times through to today's high-tech microwave ovens, the principle of heating food to cook it has remained the same; the difference is in the speed of cooking and the methods employed. Traditional methods of cooking food in the fire, in the gas or electric oven and under or over the charcoal grill use conduction as the prime method of introducing heat, but what are microwaves and how do they cook?

MICROWAVE COOKING MADE SIMPLE

The mechanics of microwave cooking are no more magical than a television or radio. Inside the microwave is a magnetron vacuum tube, the "heart" or "brains" of the microwave, which converts ordinary household electrical energy into high-frequency electro-magnetic waves, called microwaves. The microwaves are then directed into the oven cavity, through a wave guide, and stirred by a fan for even distribution.

MICROWAVES IN ACTION

The waves are either reflected, pass through some materials or are absorbed by other materials. Metals reflect them (so cooking utensils must be non-metallic); glass, pottery, china, paper and most plastics allow them to pass through (so they make ideal cooking utensils); and foods absorb them.

The microwaves are absorbed by the moisture in food, causing the food molecules to vibrate rapidly, thus producing heat to cook food.

Imagine the boy scout rubbing two twigs together to light a fire and you have the general idea. However, the speed at which the microwaves cause the molecules to vibrate is millions of times per second, producing remarkably intense heat that cooks super fast.

This is completely different from conventional methods, where heat is passed along a chain from one molecule to the next until the whole becomes hot and cooked. It is especially different in that dishes remain cool, metals cannot be used and timings are fast, calling for different cooking procedures and techniques.

FACTORS WHICH AFFECT MICROWAVE COOKING

Starting Temperature of Food
Foods that are cooked from room temperature will take less time to cook than foods that are frozen or chilled. Cooking times in the recipes that follow are based on starting temperatures at which the foods are normally stored, unless otherwise stated.

Density of Food
The denser the food, the longer it takes to cook. Heavy, dense foods, like potatoes, will take longer to cook than light porous foods, like sponge cakes. For the same reason a solid, dense mass of food, like a whole cauliflower, will take longer to cook than the same food divided into pieces (in the case of cauliflower, cut into small florets) and spread out for cooking.

Composition of Food
Foods which are high in fats and sugars will cook faster than foods high in liquid because fats and sugars absorb microwave energy more readily. They also reach higher temperatures during the cooking process than water-based foods. It therefore takes longer to cook foods that are high in moisture, like vegetables, than it does to cook those with little moisture, such as breads and cakes.

Quantity of Food
As the volume or quantity of food being cooked in the microwave increases, the cooking time increases. If you double the amount of food, the time will increase by about half as much again.

Size and Shape of Food
Smaller pieces of food will cook more quickly than larger pieces and uniformly shaped pieces cook more evenly than irregular-shaped items. Cutting foods into regular pieces, fingers or rounds and slicing meat across the grain prior to cooking will all help to ensure even cooking. With unevenly shaped pieces that cannot be cut, the thinner parts will cook faster than the thicker areas and they should be placed towards the centre of the dish where they can be grouped together to receive less energy. Ideally, portions of food that are of the same size and shape cook most evenly.

It is also important to remember that round and ring shapes cook more evenly than square, oval or rectangular shapes. With the latter, there is a concentration of energy in the corners and at the ends that can cause charring; to avoid this, protect the corners with small pieces of smooth foil to shield them from the microwave energy.

Bones in Meat

Bones in meat conduct heat, therefore meat next to the bone in a joint will cook first. Wherever possible, it is wise to bone and roll meat for even cooking. If not, then remember to shield thin areas of meat next to the bone halfway through the cooking time to prevent overcooking.

Height in the Oven

Areas that are closest to any source of energy cook faster than those further away, and the microwave is no exception to this rule. Depending on its design, your microwave may cook faster near the floor or the roof, where the energy source is located. Rotating, turning over and stirring foods will minimize this effect.

THE MICROWAVE COOKER

All basic models are much the same in design: they consist of a cabinet, magnetron, wave guide, wave stirrer, power supply, power cord and controls. Some have special extra features such as automatic defrost, variable power control, turntable, integral thermometer or temperature probe, browning or crisping elements and stay-hot devices.

The microwaves are safely contained in the cavity by the metal lining inside the base and walls, which reflects the microwaves into the food. All cooker doors and frames are fitted with special seals as an extra safety measure to ensure that the microwaves stay in the cooker. In addition, all microwave cookers have one or more cut-out devices so that the flow of microwaves stops automatically whenever the door is opened or if the door has not been shut properly or is damaged.

Many portable microwave cookers have a turntable, which means that foods, such as fish, do not need turning.

Portable Microwave Cookers

These are undoubtedly the most popular. Almost as light and certainly as portable as a television, they require a 13 or 15 amp plug for use, making such cooking machines popular choices for students, flat-dwellers and the elderly. They are also good for use in a boat, caravan or second home.

A portable microwave may be sited conveniently on a work top, trolley or other firm, stable surface. Some models, with very basic controls, have been developed for the 'simplistic cooking and reheating' market, and are usually short in height, designed to fit under the work surface. Often budget-priced, this type of microwave will accommodate a chicken or a couple of stacked plated meals, but it is not suitable for those who require a flexible oven arrangement or sophisticated cooking.

Double Oven Cooker

A few microwave models are available in the same unit as a conventional cooker, with the microwave acting as a second or double oven. Most models are built-in, but a few free-standing models are available.

Combination Cookers

This is an expanding section of the microwave market and one that is likely to attract second-time buyers. These cookers have the facility to cook by both microwave and conventional means in one single operation and in one unit. The conventional and microwave powers can operate separately, simultaneously or in sequence, as required. Some models also offer further choice, with fan-assisted ovens, grills or automatic cooking sequence controls for microwave, combination and conventional cooking. In the chapters that follow, look out for recipes that can be cooked using combination controls, but follow the timings given in your manufacturer's instruction booklet.

INSTALLING THE MICROWAVE

All that is required to install a portable microwave cooker is a fused power socket. Manufacturers also recommend that you place the microwave on a stable surface and have adequate ventilation. It is therefore possible to site the microwave in a multitude of places – the kitchen work surface is typical, but also consider a trolley that can be wheeled between rooms or even out on to the terrace or patio for outdoor dining, providing wonderful flexibility when preparing accompaniments for barbecues.

  If you plan to build-in your microwave, then ensure that you buy the correct fixing kit or housing unit, with adequate venting, and always check your microwave handbook for any special instructions.

CLEANING THE MICROWAVE

This is something of a bonus! Since the walls in the microwave oven cavity remain cool during cooking, cleaning is often just a quick-wipe operation. Food does not have the opportunity to bake-on, so wiping the inside at regular intervals, or when spills occur, with a damp, soapy cloth is sufficient. Remember always to disconnect the oven from the electrical supply before wiping or cleaning. Remove and wash oven trays, shelving and bases according to the manufacturer's instructions.

  Wipe the outside surfaces and door regularly, but do not allow water to seep into the vents. If necessary, also clean any air filters or the stirrer fan guard according to the manufacturer's instructions.

  Stale cooking smells can be removed by boiling a solution of 1 part lemon juice to 3 parts water in a microwaveproof bowl in the microwave for about 5 minutes on HIGH. Then wipe the oven cavity dry with a clean cloth.

SERVICING

Remember to have the microwave checked by a qualified engineer every 12 months, or as recommended by the manufacturer.

NOTE
Do not operate the microwave oven when it is empty. For safety, especially when young children are around, place a cup of water in the cooker when it is not in use. If the cooker is accidentally switched on, the water will absorb the energy, then there is negligible risk of damaging the magnetron, something that can occur if the oven is operated when empty.

A sophisticated microwave cooker with combination cooking facility.

Microwave Dishes and Utensils

Without doubt, the range of dishes and utensils that can be used in the microwave is wider than that for cooking conventionally.

GLASS, POTTERY AND CHINA

Ovenproof and plain glass, pottery and china are all suitable for microwave cooking. Be sure to check that they do not have any metallic trim, screws or handles and, if using a pottery dish, that it is non-porous.

Clear glass dishes, such as Pyrex, are particularly useful since you can actually see the food being cooked and check its progress during cooking.

Glass measuring jugs are also superb and allow you to measure, mix, cook and, sometimes, serve from the same container. Ovenproof glass and glass-ceramic dishes are invaluable for use in one operation from the freezer to the microwave and vice versa (once the food has cooled completely).

The only type of glass to avoid for microwave cooking is the leaded type most often found as decorative drinking glassware.

PAPER

Paper is a good utensil for low heat and short cooking times, such as thawing, reheating or very short cooking, and for foods with a low fat, sugar or water content. Napkins, absorbent kitchen paper, cups, cartons, paper freezer wrap and the paper pulp board often used for supermarket packaging are all suitable. Absorbent kitchen paper or paper towels are especially useful for cooking fatty foods, since they absorb excess fats and oils and can be used to prevent splattering on the oven walls.

Avoid using metal in any form, including dishes wth metal decoration or trims; porous pottery and mugs or cups with glued-on handles; crystal glass; and polystyrene trays or non-dishwasher-safe plastics.

Wax-coated paper cups and plates should be avoided since the high temperature of the food will cause the wax to melt; they can be used for thawing items to be served cold, like frozen cakes and desserts.

PLASTICS

Whether these are dishwasher safe or not provides a useful indication as to whether or not a plastic item is suitable for microwave use. Unless made of a thermoplastic material, plastic dishes and containers should not be used for cooking foods with a high fat or sugar content, since the heat of the food may cause the plastic to melt and lose its shape.

Plastic or clear film for microwave use and items like bags suitable for boil-in-the-bag cooking work well.

Pierce a bag or film before cooking to allow steam to escape or fold back a corner to vent the film and prevent it from ballooning during cooking. Also take extra special care when removing clear film or opening plastic bags in case any trapped steam escapes and burns the hand or forearm.

Roasting bags provide a clean, convenient way of cooking many foods, from vegetables to roasts. Roasts particularly benefit from their use since browning seems to take place more readily in a roasting bag. Either tie loosely with room for steam to escape or snip a couple of holes in the bag to aid the escape of steam and replace the metal ties with elastic, string or a non-metal tie.

Do not attempt to microwave in thin polythene bags as they will not withstand the heat of the food. Thicker storage or freezer bags are acceptable. Use elastic bands, string or non-metal ties to secure the bags loosely before cooking.

Melamine is not recommended for microwave cooking as it absorbs enough microwave energy to cause charring.

COTTON AND LINEN

Napkins are ideal for short warming or reheating procedures, such as reheating bread rolls for serving. It is important to use only cotton or linen, as synthetic fibres, or fabrics containing a proportion of them, will be damaged.

WOODEN BOWLS AND BAKEWARE

These are suitable only for short periods of reheating, otherwise the wood or wicker will tend to dry out, crack or char.

SPECIAL MICROWAVE EQUIPMENT

With the increased popularity of microwave cooking, there are many specialist innovations in microwave cookware. Several ranges manufactured from polythene, polystyrene and

A selection of everyday items that are useful for microwave cooking.

thermoplastics are now widely available and come in a comprehensive range of shapes and sizes. If you are an enthusiastic microwave cook then you might consider investing in some of the more useful items such as a microwave baking tray, roasting rack, bun or muffin tray, ring mould and whisk.

If the microwave is your only form of cooker, you may well be interested in some other very special items of cookware, developed to broaden the options when cooking in a microwave. These include a special popcorn cooker, a microwave pressure cooker, special kebab and burger or chop cooker, and a range of microwaveproof saucepans.

Thermometers
Thermometers made specially for microwave ovens are available but can be used in an oven only when specified by the oven's manufacturer. Their main use is for checking the internal temperature of a meat roast to ensure it is cooked to your requirements. They can also be used to check that, after cooking for the recommended time, the internal

temperature of ready-made meals is sufficiently high to destroy microorganisms which may be present and could cause food poisoning. Some newer ovens have an automatic cooking control based on a temperature-sensing probe that can be inserted into the food while in the oven. When the food reaches a precise temperature, the oven turns itself off automatically.

Browning Dishes
Available from most microwave dealers and large kitchenware stores, these duplicate the browning and searing processes of conventional cooking. Especially useful for prebrowning burgers, chops, sausages and steaks, they can also be used to 'fry' eggs and sandwiches, and to brown vegetables.

The browning dish is made of a glass ceramic substance with a special coating that absorbs microwave energy. It is preheated in the microwave until the base coating changes colour, usually for about 8 minutes on HIGH. Always follow specific manufacturer's instructions as dishes, coatings and timings vary.

Examples of special microwave cookware.

The food is then placed on the dish to brown and turned to sear both sides. Preheating times and browning or searing times differ according to the food being cooked and the power output of the oven. Always follow the manufacturer's instructions for best results.

CHECKING SUITABILITY FOR MICROWAVE COOKING

If you intend to cook food in both the microwave and the conventional oven in a continuous operation, be sure to use a dish that is ovenproof as well as microwaveproof. The following is a simple test to check microwave suitability.

Fill a heatproof cup with cold water and stand it in the utensil being checked. Place the utensil in the microwave and microwave on HIGH for 1¼ minutes. If the water is warm in the cup and the utensil is cool, go ahead and use the utensil. If the utensil is warm or even hot and the water is still cool, or barely lukewarm, do not use the utensil for microwave cooking.

THE SHAPE AND SIZE OF DISH TO USE

After checking the material, consider the shape and size of the dish or utensil. Ideally, the more regular the shape the better for microwave cooking. For example, a round shape is much better than an oval; a straight-sided container is better than a curved one as the microwaves can penetrate more evenly; and a large shallow dish is better than a small deep one as the food is spread over a greater surface area and therefore exposed to more microwave energy.

A Few Ideas
The following novel pieces of cookware can be used in the microwave successfully:
• scallop shells
• glass or plastic baby bottles for warming milk and juice
• wooden toothpicks for securing foods and wooden kebab skewers for brochettes and kebabs
• paper bun cases for buns and muffins – support them in teacups or ramekin dishes.

MATERIAL TO AVOID – METALS

Most manufacturers object to the use of metal. Even small amounts in the oven will reflect the microwaves so that they do not penetrate the food to be cooked.

Therefore, avoid metal dishes, baking trays and metal baking tins, foil dishes, cast-iron cookware, plates and china trimmed with a metallic design, metal kebab skewers, any dish with a metal screw or attachment and the paper-coated metal ties often found with freezer and cook bags.

Microwave Techniques

PREPARING INGREDIENTS

When cutting ingredients, prepare even-sized pieces so that they cook at the same rate.

• Slim strips of vegetables, such as carrots, cook more quickly and evenly than large, irregular pieces or different-sized whole vegetables.

• Even cubes or dice cook well. Large vegetables, such as swede, turnip, potato or pumpkin can all be cut into neat cubes to promote quick, even cooking.

• Slicing meat across the grain into thin pieces helps to tenderize it.

SCORING OR PRICKING FOODS

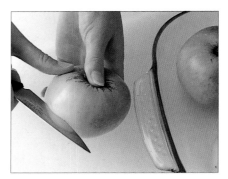

Foods with tight skins or membranes, such as sausages, kidneys, giblets, whole fish, jacket potatoes, egg yolks and apples must be lightly pricked or scored prior to cooking or they are liable to burst or explode. This is because of the tremendous amount of pressure that develops within foods that cook very quickly.

STIRRING

Stirring is important when cooking conventionally, and it is also necessary when cooking by microwave. Conventionally, we stir to redistribute heat from the bottom of the pan to the top, but with a microwave the aim is to redistribute heat and cooked areas from the outside to the centre of a dish for even cooking. Precise stirring instructions will be given in a recipe if it is important; if not, stirring halfway through cooking is usually sufficient.

ROTATING

If your microwave has a turntable, then this cooking technique becomes redundant. In models without a turntable, a quarter or half turn of the dish at regular intervals during the cooking period will ensure even results when food cannot be stirred or turned over.

TURNING OVER

Many large or dense items of food, such as potatoes or chicken drumsticks, should be turned over about halfway through cooking to ensure good results.

COOK'S TIP

A pair of food tongs is useful for turning firm foods, such as chicken portions, chops and sausages, for example.

ARRANGING FOOD

Arranging foods carefully in a dish for microwave cooking can mean that an ingredient is perfectly cooked rather than merely adequately cooked. For success, follow these guidelines.

• Try to cook foods of an even or similar size together and, if possible, arrange them in a ring pattern in a dish, leaving the centre empty.

• If foods are of an irregular shape, like chicken drumsticks or spears of broccoli, then arrange the thicker sections to the outside of the dish in a spoke-like arrangement so that the thick areas will receive the most energy and cook more quickly than the thin areas that are grouped together.

• Arrange whole fish in pairs, head to tail, to form an even area that will cook uniformly. Thin areas cook more quickly than thick or large areas, which are not penetrated as quickly by microwaves.

• When reheating plated meals, ensure food is spread out evenly. Thicker vegetables should be arranged towards the edge to receive the most energy.

• When heating more than one plated meal at a time, special plastic microwave stacking rings can be placed between plates. These rings ensure plates are positioned so that they all receive an equal amount of energy and therefore the meals reheat at the same rate.

• Try to ensure that the depth of food is even; if it is not, stir or rearrange ingredients.

• Foods cooked in a ring pattern or mould make the most of the microwave. Cakes cook particularly well in a ring mould. If you don't have one, then improvise: place a glass tumbler in a round microwaveproof dish, and hold it in place while adding the mixture.

REARRANGING FOODS

Even with a turntable, rearranging foods (usually once) will ensure even results. Move foods from the outside of the dish to the centre and vice versa.

• Rearrange foods cooked in a bag by gently shaking the bag. Remember that scalding-hot steam can escape as the contents of the bag are shuffled, so protect your hand and forearm with a folded dish towel or oven glove.

SHIELDING

As with conventional baking, some parts of foods are more vulnerable to overcooking than others. In such cases, it is acceptable to use small smooth strips of foil to protect thin or vulnerable areas.

This is the only time when metal may be introduced into a typical microwave oven, and it is important to make sure it does not touch the oven walls. Position the foil on the food for about half the cooking time, securing small patches with wooden cocktail sticks, if necessary.

Check the manufacturer's handbook to ensure that this is permissible in your particular model of microwave oven.

• Fish heads and tails should be protected to prevent eyes from bursting and thin areas from overcooking.

• Wing tips on poultry and the thinner tail-ends on ducks should be shielded to prevent them from overcooking and drying out.

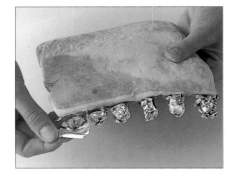

• Protruding bones, for example as on a rack of lamb, should be shielded to prevent scorching.

• Narrow ends of joints of meat, such as at the end of a leg of lamb or pork, should be shielded.

COVERING AND WRAPPING

Problems of surfaces drying out, splattering of food on the cavity walls and slower-than-optimum cooking times can all be eliminated by covering or wrapping foods. This locks in moisture, retains juices and speeds up cooking by trapping heat-retaining steam.

• Use double-strength plastic cooking bags, suitable for boiling

(sometimes referred to as "boil-in-the-bag" bags or "cook bags") or roasting bags for vegetables, meat and poultry. Replace metal ties with elastic bands.

• Some bags come with special, microwaveproof plastic clips.

• String can be used to loosely tie bags closed.

C O O K ' S   T I P

Remember to ensure that a cooking bag is not too hot to hold before picking it up; protect your hand with a folded dish towel, if necessary, and be aware that scalding-hot steam may escape from any small opening at the top of the bag as the contents move when lifted or as they are being rearranged.

• Use a tight-fitting purpose-made lid or improvise by using a saucer or plate instead.

• Cover bowls with a tight membrane of microwave-safe clear film. Puncture the top to allow some steam to escape during cooking.

• Turn back a small area of clear film to provide a vent to prevent a ballooning effect during cooking. Take care when removing clear film, as it will trap a significant amount of scalding-hot steam even when it is vented.

• Greaseproof paper may be used to cover small bowls, for example as when cooking steamed puddings. The paper may be secured with a large elastic band.

• Use absorbent kitchen paper as a base on which to stand food.

• Absorbent kitchen paper can also be used as a cover for some foods. It is especially good for absorbing excess moisture given off by foods like potatoes and bread.

• Covering bacon with absorbent kitchen paper prevents spattering as well as ensuring that moisture that is given off is absorbed.

• Absorbent kitchen paper is also invaluable for drying herbs.

• When dampened, absorbent kitchen paper can be used for reheating and steaming pancakes and shellfish.

COOK'S TIP

Even though microwave cooking is a moist method, foods can dry out because of the speed with which moisture evaporates from them. Microwave-safe clear film is often the most practical choice of covering, allowing you to see what's happening in the dish. When folded back at one corner, the contents can be stirred during cooking without discarding the film. Always remove the film starting at the side furthest away from you to avoid scalding your hands or forearms.

Removing Excess Cooking Juices

Any juices that seep from food will absorb microwave energy. If these juices are considerable, and the cooking time is longer than about 5 minutes on HIGH, it is advisable to remove some liquid regularly during cooking. Excess juices can prolong the cooking time appreciably. The juices can always be replaced towards the end of the cooking time if the food starts to dry out too much. Examples include cooking a chicken, duck or turkey.

Observing Standing Times

Food continues to cook by conduction after the microwave energy has been turned off. This is not solely a feature of microwave cooking – the same applies to a lesser degree with conventional cooking. With microwave cooking there is greater residual heat, so it is important to err on the side of safety and undercook rather than overcook food. Whereas there is no rescue package for overcooked food, additional cooking time can always be given if the dish is still inadequately cooked after observing the standing time.

Browning Foods

As a result of little applied surface heat during rapid cooking, foods cooked in the microwave do not readily brown. Try the following tips to encourage browning or disguise any pale results.

• Grill foods like gratins and roasts before or after microwave cooking.

• Use a specialist microwave browning dish, especially for foods like chops, steaks, fried eggs, toasted sandwiches, stir-fries and chicken portions.

• Buy or make a browning mix to coat foods – paprika, toasted breadcrumbs, crushed crisps, soy sauce, Worcestershire sauce and soup mixes all work well.

• Due to its high fat content, bacon browns readily, so it can be laid over poultry or roast meat.

• Baked items, such as cakes, biscuits, breads and muffins, can be sprinkled or coated with toasted coconut, chocolate vermicelli, chopped nuts, chopped glacé fruits, poppy seeds, toasted seeds and dark-coloured spices.

• Glaze ham, poultry or game with fruit preserve, particularly redcurrant jelly or citrus marmalade, before cooking to add colour.

• Add icing or frosting to a pale cake or other baked items after cooking.

Herby Baked Tomatoes are cooked in the microwave, then browned under the grill.

The Microwave and Freezer

During its introductory years, the domestic microwave was often referred to as "the unfreezer" due to its ability to defrost food both quickly and efficiently, and this is still one of the major advantages of microwave ownership.

Capitalizing on this effect, almost all microwave manufacturers have introduced a special DEFROST control or button to ensure optimum defrosting microwave action. This control programmes the microwave to introduce just the right amount of energy to defrost food without cooking it. This is done by pulsing the power on and off at regular intervals over a period of time.

When a defrost setting is not built in, it is possible to simulate the action of the setting by turning the microwave on and off manually at regular intervals, allowing rest periods in between; but this is rarely as successful as using a pre-programmed setting and it can be time-consuming.

DEFROSTING TIPS

Refer to your own manufacturer's handbook for a guide to defrosting times, but always err on the side of safety by heating for too short a period, rather than too long, until you can readily judge the defrosting speed of your own particular type of microwave.

• Open all cartons and remove any metal lids, ties or fastenings before defrosting food.

• Defrost foods slowly. Never try to hurry the process as there is the danger of overcooking the food or drying it out unnecessarily.

• Frozen foods wrapped in foil or placed in foil containers should have all foil removed, and they should be placed in a suitable dish for the microwave.

• Turn foods over during defrosting, about halfway through the recommended time.

• If it is not possible to turn food over during defrosting (for example, as with a decorated cake), then rotate the item or container regularly for even defrosting.

• Flex any pouches of food that cannot be broken up or stirred during the defrosting time and rotate on a regular basis.

• Place foods like cakes, bread rolls and pastry items on a double sheet of absorbent kitchen paper to absorb excess moisture that could cause the food to become soggy.

• Blocks of frozen food should be broken up with a fork during defrosting so that frozen chunks receive the maximum amount of microwave energy.

• Separate any blocks of frozen meat items, such as hamburgers, steaks, chops and sausages, as they defrost.

• Remove any giblets from the cavity of a chicken and other poultry or game birds as soon as they have defrosted.

• Remove any juices or drips from frozen foods during the defrosting time with a bulb baster or spoon as these will only continue to absorb microwave energy, leaving less to defrost the main food.

• Items like meat joints, whole birds and whole fish should be defrosted until icy, then left to defrost completely at room temperature before cooking.

• If any parts of the food start to defrost too fast (or even begin to become warm or cook), shield or protect these areas with small strips of smooth foil. These can be attached with wooden cocktail sticks where necessary. Check that this is acceptable for your model of microwave by reading the manufacturer's instructions.

• Always observe standing times as foods will continue to thaw by means of conduction from the small level of internal heat that is produced. Allow foods to defrost until they are just icy.

• Before defrosting, prick, slash or vent membranes and skins. Also, pierce clear film, pouches or similar wrappings in the same way as when cooking food in a skin.

• If you intend to defrost and cook in one operation, then follow all the guidelines on stirring, turning, rotating and rearranging foods, not forgetting to allow standing time before serving.

COOK'S TIP
~

If a member of your household is not a confident cook, but has to reheat an occasional meal, freeze suitable portions with a label giving brief instructions for defrosting and reheating the food in the microwave.

FREEZER TO MICROWAVE REMINDERS

The microwave and freezer are a terrific twosome to ease the life of the regular home cook, working mother, busy hostess and anyone with a prolific vegetable garden. When freezing home-made food that will later be defrosted or cooked in the microwave, the following hints are worth remembering.

• Freeze food in a microwaveproof container, so it can be defrosted, reheated or cooked straight from the freezer.

• Single portions are very useful in the freezer, allowing any member of the family to quickly and easily defrost and cook an individual meal at any time.

• Before freezing a conventionally made pizza, pie, flan or quiche, cut it into portions so that the required number of servings can be removed from the freezer as required, rather than having to defrost the whole item.

• Complete cooked main courses can be plated on microwaveproof plates and frozen for almost instant dinners. Remember to follow the advice on arranging food for microwave cooking and reheating when preparing complete meals. Adding a sauce of some kind helps to keep the meal succulent and moist during defrosting and reheating.

• When cooking a main course, consider doubling the quantities and freezing the second meal for future use.

• Save time and effort in the future by freezing soups, casseroles and hot pots in freezerproof bags that are also suitable for microwave defrosting. Use large bags and knot the tops firmly to prevent the contents from leaking, and avoid using metal ties. The unopened bags can be placed in the microwave until the contents are slightly defrosted and free of the plastic, then the food is ready to be transferred to a suitable microwaveproof serving dish for the final reheating.

• Consider freezing home-grown or bargain vegetable produce in freezer and microwaveproof boil-in-the-bags. These will serve as freezing, defrosting and cooking containers, without the need to transfer the contents at all before serving.

FREEZING FOOD TO FIT A DISH

1 If you do not want to lose the use of the dish while the food is in the freezer, line it with freezer film or foil, arrange the food in the dish and then freeze.

2 Once frozen, turn the food out of the container, wrap it tightly, label and return to the freezer.

3 To defrost or reheat the food, remove the freezer film or foil and return the food to the original container before placing in the microwave.

COOKING AND FREEZING IN ONE BAG

1 Fruits like apples and pears can be cooked in a roasting bag or boilable bag.

2 When cooked, the fruit can be crushed in the bag to make a purée and sealed while still hot. As the mixture cools it will form a vacuum pack that is ideal for freezing and ready for defrosting or reheating in the microwave.

> #### COOK'S TIP
> ∾
> Make a note of the weight of vegetables or fruit on freezer labels so you can calculate the microwave cooking time easily for the whole bag.

FREEZING AND DEFROSTING BABY FOOD

• Leftovers from suitable meals can easily be puréed and frozen in ice cube trays ready for baby and toddler meals. To defrost and reheat 2 cubes (about 60ml/4 tbsp food), place in a microwaveproof bowl. Place a small glass or cup of water in the microwave at the same time to absorb some energy and prevent the baby food from over-heating. Microwave on HIGH for 1–1¼ minutes until thawed and hot, stirring once to break up. Leave to stand and check the temperature before serving.

> #### COOK'S TIP
> ∾
> Once the trays of baby food are frozen, release the hard cubes of purée and store them in an airtight polythene bag. This way you will not have all your ice cube trays in use.

REHEATING FOODS IN THE MICROWAVE

Most foods will reheat successfully in the microwave without loss of quality, flavour and colour, and with maximum nutrient retention compared to alternative reheating methods. For best results follow these guidelines.

• Arrange foods on a plate with the thicker portions to the outer edge where they will receive the most energy.

• When plating meals for reheating, try to arrange the food in an even layer.

• Cover foods with clear film if a lid is not used to retain moisture.

• Observe the standing time to make maximum use of the microwave energy and to prevent the food overcooking.

• When reheating potatoes, pastry items and other moist baked foods, place them on a double sheet of absorbent kitchen paper to absorb the excess moisture and prevent sogginess.

• If possible, stir foods regularly during reheating; if this is not possible, then turn foods over or rearrange them, or at least rotate the dish for even reheating.

Basic Recipes

The microwave is invaluable for cooking a host of dishes, as you will see from the recipes that follow in this book, and it is also indispensable for cooking a range of basic recipes that form the basis for more complicated dishes and meals. The following are a few of the most useful basic recipes.

GIBLET STOCK FOR GRAVY

1 Place the contents of a bag of giblets from a chicken, turkey or duck in a microwaveproof bowl with 300ml/½ pint/1¼ cups boiling water and a few sliced seasoning vegetables, such as carrots, celery and onion.

2 Microwave on HIGH for 7–10 minutes. Strain and use the gravy as required.

WHITE POURING SAUCE

1 Place 25g/1oz/2 tbsp butter in a microwaveproof jug and microwave on HIGH for 30–60 seconds, until melted.

2 Stir in 25g/1oz/2 tbsp plain flour and 300ml/½ pint/ 1¼ cups milk. Microwave on HIGH for 3½–4 minutes, stirring or whisking once every minute, until smooth, boiling and thickened. Season to taste and serve. Makes 300ml/½ pint/1¼ cups.

VARIATIONS

One-stage Sauce: Place the flour and butter in a microwaveproof jug, then add the milk and whisk lightly. The ingredients will not combine thoroughly at this stage as the butter does not mix in, but it will break into small pieces. Continue as above.

Caper Sauce: Add 15ml/1 tbsp drained capers and 5ml/1 tsp vinegar from the jar of capers or lemon juice to the cooked sauce. Good with cooked lamb.

Cheese Sauce: Add 50–115g/2–4oz grated cheese, a pinch of dry mustard powder and a pinch of cayenne pepper to the cooked sauce. Whisk or stir well. Serve with vegetables, eggs, fish or pasta.

Parsley Sauce: Add 15–30ml/ 1–2 tbsp chopped fresh parsley and a squeeze of lemon juice (optional) to the cooked sauce and whisk or stir well. Serve with fish, ham or bacon and vegetables.

SCRAMBLED EGGS

1 Place 15g/½oz/1 tbsp butter in a microwaveproof jug or bowl and microwave on HIGH for about 30 seconds to melt.

2 Beat 4 eggs with 30ml/2 tbsp milk and salt and pepper to taste. Add to the butter and microwave on HIGH for 1¼ minutes. Stir or whisk the set pieces of egg from the outside of the bowl or jug to the centre.

3 Microwave on HIGH for a further 1¼–1¾ minutes, stirring or whisking twice. When about three-quarters cooked, there is still a significant amount of runny egg, as shown here. When cooked, the eggs are moist, not completely set. Leave to stand for 1–2 minutes, by which time the eggs will be set ready for serving. Serves 2.

JACKET POTATOES

1 Scrub and prick the potatoes. Place on a double thickness of absorbent kitchen paper. If cooking more than two potatoes, arrange them in a ring pattern.

2 Microwave on HIGH for the time given, turning over halfway through cooking. Leave to stand for 3–4 minutes before serving.

3 The potatoes may be cut in half and the flesh forked up or mashed, then replaced in the shells, topped with cheese or butter and heated for a few seconds in the microwave to melt the butter or cheese before serving.

COOKING TIMES FOR JACKET POTATOES

1 x 175g/6oz	potato	4–6 minutes
2 x 175g/6oz	potatoes	6–8 minutes
3 x 175g/6oz	potatoes	8–12 minutes
4 x 175g/6oz	potatoes	12-15 minutes

CORN-ON-THE-COB

These can either be cooked husked or unhusked.

1 For fresh unhusked corn-on-the-cob, fold back the husk and discard the silk.

2 Replace the husk to cover the corn and arrange the cobs, evenly spaced, on the base of the cooker or turntable. Microwave on HIGH for the time given, rotating and rearranging once halfway through cooking. Leave to stand for 5 minutes before removing the husk and cutting off the woody base with a sharp knife.

3 Alternatively, wrap fresh husked cobs individually in clear film or place in a microwave-proof dish with 60ml/4 tbsp water and cover. Microwave on HIGH for the time given, rotating and rearranging once halfway through cooking. Leave to stand for 3–5 minutes before serving.

COOKING TIMES FOR CORN-ON-THE-COB

Cooking Times for Corn Cobs in Husks

1 x 175–225g/6–8oz cob	3–5 minutes
2 x 175–225g/6–8oz cobs	6–8 minutes
3 x 175–225g/6–8oz cobs	8–10 minutes
4 x 175–225g/6–8oz cobs	10–12 minutes

Cooking Times for Husked Corn Cobs

1 x 175–225g/6–8oz cob	3–4 minutes
2 x 175–225g/6–8oz cobs	5–6 minutes
3 x 175–225g/6–8oz cobs	7–8 minutes
4 x 175–225g/6–8oz cobs	9–10 minutes

HOLLANDAISE SAUCE

1 Place 115g/4oz/8 tbsp butter in a large microwaveproof jug and microwave on HIGH for 1½ minutes until melted. Whisk in 45ml/3 tbsp lemon juice, 2 egg yolks, a pinch of mustard powder and salt and pepper to taste.

2 Microwave on MEDIUM for 1 minute, whisk and serve. This sauce is delicious with poached salmon or cooked asparagus. Serves 4–6.

RED LENTILS

1 Place 225g/8oz/1 cup lentils in a large microwaveproof bowl. Add a little chopped onion, celery and lemon juice, if liked. Cover with 900ml/1½ pints/3¾ cups boiling water or stock and add salt and pepper to taste.

2 Cover, leaving a gap for steam to escape, and microwave on HIGH for 15–25 minutes, stirring once halfway through cooking. Time the cooking according to requirements: if you want the lentils to retain some shape, use the shorter time; if you want soft lentils for a soup or dip, use the longer cooking time. Serves 4.

QUICK SOAKING OF DRIED BEANS

1 To shorten the soaking time for dried beans, place them in a microwaveproof bowl and cover with boiling water.

2 Cover and microwave on HIGH for 5 minutes. Leave to stand for 1½ hours, then drain, rinse and cook the beans.

VEGETABLE RICE

1 Place 225g/8oz/generous 1 cup long grain white rice in a microwaveproof bowl with 550ml/18fl oz/scant 2½ cups boiling water, 5ml/1 tsp salt, and a knob of butter, if liked. Cover loosely with a lid or vented clear film and microwave on HIGH for 3 minutes.

2 Reduce the power setting to MEDIUM and microwave for a further 12 minutes, stirring two or three times.

3 Add 175g/6oz/about 1 cup diced and softened vegetables (for example a single vegetable or selection from peas, beans, peppers, onion and sweetcorn). Stir well to mix, cover and microwave on HIGH for 1½ minutes.

4 Leave to stand, tightly covered, for 5 minutes. Fluff the rice with a fork to separate the grains before serving. Serves 4.

PORRIDGE

1 Traditional and quick-cook varieties of porridge can be prepared quickly and easily in the microwave. To make traditional porridge, place 30g/1¼oz/⅓ cup oatmeal in a microwaveproof bowl with 1.5ml/¼ tsp salt.

2 Stir in 175ml/6 fl oz/¾ cup water or milk, making sure that the oatmeal and liquid are thoroughly mixed.

3 Cover with vented clear film and microwave on LOW for 10–12 minutes, stirring twice. Leave to stand, covered, for 2 minutes before serving.

4 Prepare quick-cook oatmeal as above, but microwave on LOW for 5 minutes. Serves 1.

GARLIC OR HERB BREAD

1 Cut a 115g/4oz short, crusty French stick or Vienna loaf into diagonal slices about 4cm/1½in thick, almost to the base of the loaf but not quite through. Spread garlic or herb butter between the slices and re-form the loaf into a neat shape.

2 Wrap loosely in absorbent kitchen paper and microwave on HIGH for 1½ minutes. Serve at once, while still warm. Serves 4.

Making the Most of Your Microwave

Getting used to the speed of microwave cooking does take time, patience and perseverance, so you are unlikely to become a microwave mastercook overnight. The golden rule is to become a constant clock-watcher until you know your microwave really well. Do not be afraid or intimidated by the microwave – open the door, peer in and poke food as much as you like to see if it is defrosting, cooking or reheating adequately. You will soon be able to cook the recipes in this book successfully, adapt some of your own conventional favourites and halve or double quantities with practised ease.

The following are tips that will provide amusing, useful tricks to make you wonder how you ever managed without a microwave!

PEELING TOMATOES

Place up to 6 tomatoes in a ring on absorbent kitchen paper. Microwave on HIGH for 10–15 seconds. Leave to stand for 15 minutes, then peel the tomatoes.

PEELING PEACHES AND APRICOTS

Place up to 4 peaches in a microwaveproof bowl with very little water. Cover and microwave on HIGH for 1–1½ minutes. Leave the peaches to stand for 5 minutes, then drain and peel them.

TO SOFTEN CHILLED HARD CHEESES

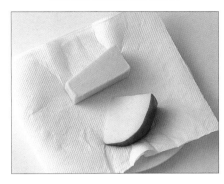

Place about 225g/8oz chilled hard cheese on a microwaveproof serving plate and microwave on LOW for 30–34 seconds, turning over after half the time. Leave to stand for 5 minutes before serving.

TO RIPEN SEMI-SOFT CHEESE

Place about 225g/8oz semi-soft cheese on a microwaveproof serving dish and microwave on LOW for 15–45 seconds depending upon degree of ripeness, checking constantly and turning over after half of the time. Leave to stand for 5 minutes before serving.

SOFTENING BUTTER

Microwave on HIGH for 5–10 seconds, then leave to stand for 5 minutes before using.

BLANCHING ALMONDS

Place 250ml/8fl oz/1 cup water in a jug. Microwave on HIGH for 2½ minutes or until boiling, add the almonds and microwave for 30 seconds. Drain the nuts, then slip off their skins.

TOASTING NUTS

For a golden result, place in a browning dish and microwave on HIGH for 4–5 minutes, stirring each minute. Alternatively, for a lighter result, cook in an ordinary microwaveproof dish.

TOASTING COCONUT

Spread 115g/4oz/1 cup desiccated coconut on a microwaveproof plate. Microwave on HIGH for 5–6 minutes, stirring every 1 minute.

DRYING HERBS AND CITRUS RINDS

Place on a microwaveproof plate and microwave on HIGH until dry. Never leave unattended and check at 1 minute intervals to ensure success.

SQUEEZING CITRUS JUICE

To extract the maximum juice from citrus fruit, prick the skins and microwave on HIGH for 5–10 seconds.

TO DRY BREAD FOR CRUMBS

1 Place a thick slice of bread on a microwaveproof plate and microwave on HIGH for 2½–3½ minutes, until dry.

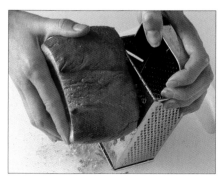

2 Allow the bread to cool completely before crumbling or grating it for use.

TO MAKE CROÛTONS

1 To make dry, oil-free croûtons, dice 175g/6oz bread into cubes. Place on kitchen paper on a large flat microwaveproof plate and microwave on HIGH for 3–4 minutes, stirring once every minute, until dry.

2 To make butter-crisp croûtons, place 25g/1oz/2 tbsp butter in a microwaveproof dish and microwave on HIGH for 30 seconds to melt.

3 Add 175g/6oz bread cubes and toss to coat them in the melted butter. Microwave on HIGH for 3–4 minutes, stirring every minute, until crisp and brown.

COOK'S TIP

Croûtons can be flavoured in a variety of ways to complement the dishes they garnish. A crushed garlic clove or a little dried oregano can be added to the butter for butter-crisp croûtons. Chopped fresh herbs, such as tarragon or parsley, should be tossed with the cooked croûtons. Grated Parmesan cheese or lemon rind can be added to cooked croûtons.

PROVING YEAST DOUGH

1 To rise bread dough quickly, give a 900g/2lb piece of dough short bursts of microwave energy on HIGH for 5–10 second intervals, observing a 10 minute standing time between each heating period.

2 Repeat until the dough has risen to double its size.

DEFROSTING FROZEN SHORTCRUST OR PUFF PASTRY

Place a 400g/14oz packet of pastry on a microwaveproof plate and microwave on DEFROST for 4–4½ minutes, turning over once during the time. Leave to stand for 5 minutes before using.

To Cook Poppadoms

1 Arrange two or three plain or spiced poppadoms on the base of the cooker or on the turntable so that they do not touch or overlap. Microwave on HIGH for 45–60 seconds until puffy and bubbling. Leave to stand on a wire rack for 15 seconds to crisp.

2 To make poppadom cases or cups (ideal for holding salad) position a poppadom over a small microwaveproof bowl and microwave on HIGH for 20–25 seconds. As it cooks, the poppadom will droop in folds over the bowl to make a cup shape. Leave to stand for about 15 seconds to crisp before removing from the bowl.

To Make Biscuit Cups

Ready-made biscuits, like brandy snaps and florentines, can be heated in the microwave over a microwaveproof bowl to form a cup shape that can later hold mousse, ice cream or fruit salad for an almost instant dessert. Position two biscuits over the top of two microwaveproof bowls and microwave on HIGH for 30–45 seconds, until very warm and pliable. While hot, mould the biscuits around the bowls to form cup shapes. Leave until completely cold and firm before removing from the bowls.

Softening Jams and Spreads

Remove any lids and any metal trims or transfer the jam or spread to a microwaveproof dish. Microwave on HIGH for about 5–10 seconds per 450g/1lb.

Dissolving Gelatine

1 Sprinkle the gelatine over cold water, as usual, and leave to stand until spongy.

2 Microwave on HIGH for 30 seconds until clear and completely dissolved.

Clarifying Crystallized Honey

Remove the lid and any metal trims on the jar. Microwave on HIGH for 1–2 minutes. Stir well.

Dissolving Jelly

1 Break up a 135g/4½oz jelly tablet and place in a microwaveproof bowl or jug with 150ml/¼ pint/⅔ cup water.

2 Microwave the jelly on HIGH for 2 minutes.

3 Stir well to dissolve, then make up with cold water according to the packet instructions.

MELTING CHOCOLATE

Break chocolate into pieces and place in a microwaveproof bowl. Microwave on HIGH, for about 1 minute per 25g/1oz.

SOFTENING ICE CREAM FOR SCOOPING

Microwave about 1 litre/ 1¾ pints/4 cups hard (not soft scoop) ice cream on MEDIUM for 45–90 seconds. Leave to stand for 1–2 minutes before scooping.

FLAMBÉING WITH ALCOHOL

Heat the alcohol, such as brandy, in a microwaveproof and flame-proof jug on HIGH for 15 seconds. It will then ignite more easily ready for pouring over Christmas pudding, pancakes or fresh fruit.

TO REHEAT READY-MADE FRESH BLACK COFFEE

Place 600ml/1 pint/2½ cups cold coffee in a microwaveproof jug and microwave on HIGH for 4½–5 minutes.

TO REHEAT A MUG OF TEA OR COFFEE

Make sure the mug is microwave-proof. Heat on HIGH for 30–60 seconds and stir before tasting. Repeat if necessary, always stirring before tasting as hot spots in the liquid can burn the mouth.

WARMING BABY'S BOTTLE

Invert the teat and microwave 250ml/8fl oz/1 cup prepared milk on HIGH for 1 minute to warm. Shake the bottle gently and test the milk to check the temperature before attempting to feed the baby. If in doubt check your baby milk formula instructions for preparing in the microwave.

TO HEAT MILK FOR DRINKS

Frothy hot milk for café au lait, hot chocolate or other beverages can be heated very quickly. Place 300ml/½ pint/1¼ cups cold milk in a microwaveproof jug and microwave on HIGH for 2–2½ minutes. Whisk well until frothy, if liked, and serve at once.

TO MAKE MULLED WINE

Mix 750ml/1¼ pints/3 cups red wine, 12 cloves, 2 small cinnamon sticks, the grated rind and juice of 1 orange and 1 lemon, and 30–45ml/2–3 tbsp brown sugar in a microwaveproof bowl or jug. Microwave on HIGH for 5 minutes, or until almost boiling. Add extra sugar to taste, if liked, and serve the wine warm. This serves about six.

Before You Begin

MICROWAVE POWERS AND SETTINGS

• All the recipes and charts in this book were created and tested using microwave ovens with a maximum power output of 650–700 watts.

• The ovens had variable power and the descriptions used refer to the following power outputs.

HIGH = 650–750 watts or 100%
MEDIUM HIGH = 500–550 watts
or 75%
MEDIUM = 400 watts or 55–60%
LOW = 250 watts or 40%
DEFROST = 200 watts or 30%

• The chart below gives the approximate power input in watts at these levels and relative cooking times.

• The microwave ovens used for testing had turntables - if yours does not and tends to have an irregular heating pattern with hot and cold spots, then follow the rules on turning, rotating and rearranging foods.

• Metric measurements may vary from one recipe to another within the book, and it is essential to follow EITHER metric or Imperial. The recipes have been carefully balanced to get the very best results using only one set of measures and cannot be interchanged.

UNLESS OTHERWISE STATED

• eggs are size 3
• all spoon quantities are measured level

FOODS TO AVOID

The following foods do not cook well in the microwave and they are best avoided.

Eggs in Shells
These are liable to explode due to the build-up of pressure within the shell. Eggs can however be baked, scrambled, poached and "fried" in the microwave with superb results.

Popcorn
This can prove to be too dry to attract microwave energy, although some manufacturers have produced microwave popcorn, sold in a special bag with seasonings and flavourings, and this works superbly. A special microwave popcorn machine can also be purchased to cook ordinary popcorn in the microwave.

Batter-based and Some Air-incorporated Recipes
Items like Yorkshire pudding, soufflé, pancakes, choux pastry, batter-coated fish and whisked sponge mixtures need conventional cooking to become crisp and firm. The microwave will, however, make the basic sauce for a soufflé and will reheat pancakes perfectly.

Conventional Meringues
These should be cooked in the conventional oven since they do not dry sufficiently and become crisp in the microwave.

Deep-fat Frying
This is not recommended since it requires prolonged heating, it is difficult to control the temperature of the fat and the food may burn.

Liquid in Bottles and Pots
Check that bottles do not have necks that are too narrow to allow sufficient escape since steam as built-up pressure may cause them to shatter. Similarly, tall coffee pots, with slim spouts can break or cause coffee to spurt out.

GUIDE TO COMPARITIVE MICROWAVE OVEN CONTROL SETTINGS

Settings used in these recipes	Setting variations on popular microwave ovens			Approximate % power input	Approximate power outputs in watts	Cooking times in minutes – for times greater than 10 minutes simply add together the figures in the appropriate columns									
	1	keep warm	low	2	25%	150W	4	8	12	16	20	24	28	32	36	40
Defrost	2	simmer	simmer	3	30%	200W	3¼	6¼	10	13¼	16¼	20	26¼	26¼	30	33¼
Low	3	stew	medium/low 4		40%	250W	2½	5	7½	10	12½	15	17½	20	22½	25
	4	defrost	medium	5	50%	300W	2	4	6	8	10	12	14	16	18	20
Medium	5	bake	medium	6	60%	400W	1¼	3¼	5	6¼	8¼	10	12	13¼	15	16½
Medium High	6	roast	high	7–8	75%	500–600W	1¼	2¼	4	5¼	6¼	8	9¼	10¼	12	13¼
High	7	full/high	normal	10	100%	700W	1	2	3	4	5	6	7	8	9	10

SOUPS AND STARTERS

Chunky Bean and Vegetable Soup

A substantial soup, not unlike minestrone, using a selection of vegetables, with cannellini beans for extra protein and fibre. Serve with a hunk of wholegrain bread.

INGREDIENTS

Serves 4

30ml/2 tbsp olive oil

2 celery sticks, chopped

2 leeks, sliced

3 carrots, sliced

2 garlic cloves, crushed

400g/14oz can chopped tomatoes
    with basil

1.2 litres/2 pints/5 cups hot
    vegetable stock

425g/15oz can cannellini beans (or mixed
    pulses), drained

15ml/1 tbsp pesto sauce

salt and ground black pepper

shavings of Parmesan cheese, to serve

1 Place the olive oil in a large microwaveproof bowl with the celery, leeks, carrots and garlic. Microwave on HIGH for 4 minutes, stirring halfway through cooking, until softened.

2 Stir in the tomatoes and the stock. Cover and microwave on HIGH for 10 minutes, stirring halfway through cooking.

3 Stir in the beans and pesto, with salt and pepper to taste. Microwave on HIGH for a further 3–5 minutes, stirring halfway through cooking. Serve in heated bowls, sprinkled with shavings of Parmesan cheese.

COOK'S TIP

Canned chick-peas give the soup a delicious nutty flavour. Flageolet beans are more delicate and borlotti beans are slightly more substantial.

Italian Fish Soup

INGREDIENTS

Serves 4

30ml/2 tbsp olive oil

1 onion, thinly sliced

a few saffron threads

5ml/1 tsp dried thyme

large pinch of cayenne pepper

2 garlic cloves, finely chopped

2 x 400g/14oz cans peeled tomatoes,
   drained and chopped

175ml/6fl oz/³⁄₄ cup dry white wine

1.85 litres/3¼ pints/8 cups hot fish stock

350g/12oz white, skinless fish fillets, cut
   into pieces

450g/1lb monkfish, membrane removed,
   cut into pieces

450g/1lb mussels in the shell,
   thoroughly scrubbed

225g/8oz small squid, cleaned and cut
   into rings

30ml/2 tbsp chopped fresh parsley

salt and ground black pepper

thickly sliced bread, to serve

1 Place the oil in a large microwaveproof bowl. Stir in the onion, saffron, thyme, cayenne pepper and salt to taste. Microwave on HIGH for 3 minutes, until soft. Add the garlic and microwave on HIGH for 1 minute.

2 Stir in the tomatoes, white wine and fish stock. Cover and microwave on HIGH for 10 minutes, stirring halfway through the cooking time.

3 Add the fish fillet and monkfish pieces to the bowl. Cover and microwave on HIGH for 2 minutes, stirring once.

4 Mix in the mussels and squid. Cover and microwave on HIGH for 2–3 minutes, stirring once, until the mussels open. Stir in the parsley and season with salt and pepper.

5 Ladle into warmed soup bowls and serve immediately, with warm crusty bread.

Creamy Cod Chowder

Serves 4–6

350g/12oz smoked cod fillet
1 small onion, finely chopped
1 bay leaf
4 black peppercorns
900ml/1½ pints/3¾ cups skimmed milk
10ml/2 tsp cornflour
10ml/2 tsp water
200g/7oz canned sweetcorn kernels
15ml/1 tbsp chopped fresh parsley

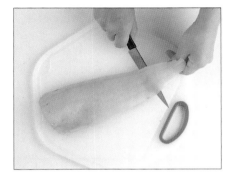

1 Skin the fish fillet. Hold the tail firmly and cut the fish off its skin using a sharp knife. Cut at an acute angle, taking care not to cut the skin and folding back the fish fillet.

2 Place the fish in a large microwaveproof bowl with the onion, bay leaf and peppercorns. Pour in the milk.

3 Cover and microwave on HIGH for 8–10 minutes, stirring twice, or until the fish is just cooked.

4 Using a slotted spoon, lift out the fish and flake it into large chunks. Remove and discard the bay leaf and peppercorns.

5 Blend the cornflour with the water and add to the milk mixture. Microwave on HIGH for 2–3 minutes, stirring twice, until slightly thickened.

6 Drain the sweetcorn kernels and add to the milk mixture with the flaked fish and parsley.

7 To reheat the chowder, microwave on HIGH for 2–3 minutes until piping hot, stirring twice, but do not boil. Ladle the chowder into four or six soup bowls and serve straight away.

Chilli Prawns

*This delightful, spicy combination
makes a tempting light main course
for a casual supper. Serve with rice,
noodles or freshly cooked pasta and
a leafy salad.*

Serves 3–4

45ml/3 tbsp olive oil

2 shallots, chopped

2 garlic cloves, chopped

1 fresh red chilli, chopped

450g/1lb ripe tomatoes, peeled, seeded
   and chopped

15ml/1 tbsp tomato purée

1 bay leaf

1 thyme sprig

90ml/6 tbsp dry white wine

450g/1lb peeled cooked large prawns

salt and ground black pepper

roughly torn basil leaves, to garnish

1 Place the oil, shallots, garlic
and chilli in a microwaveproof
bowl and microwave on HIGH for
2 minutes, stirring once.

2 Add the tomatoes, tomato
purée, bay leaf, thyme, wine
and seasoning. Cover and
microwave on HIGH for 6–7
minutes, stirring twice. Discard
the herbs.

3 Stir the prawns into the sauce
and microwave on HIGH
for 2–3 minutes, stirring once.
Taste and adjust the seasoning.
Garnish with torn basil leaves and
serve at once.

COOK'S TIP

For a milder flavour, scrape and
then rinse out all the seeds from
the chilli before chopping it.

Scallops with Ginger

*Scallops cook very well in the
microwave. Rich and creamy, this
dish is very simple to make and
quite delicious.*

Serves 4

40g/1½oz/3 tbsp butter

8–12 scallops, shelled

2.5cm/1in piece fresh root ginger,
   finely chopped

1 bunch spring onions, diagonally sliced

30ml/2 tbsp white vermouth

250ml/8fl oz/1 cup crème fraîche

salt and ground black pepper

chopped fresh parsley, to garnish

1 Place the butter in a shallow
microwaveproof dish.
Microwave on HIGH for
30 seconds to melt.

2 Remove the tough muscle
opposite the red coral on each
scallop. Separate the coral and cut
the white part of the scallop in half
horizontally. Add the scallops,
including the corals, cover and
microwave on HIGH for
4–6 minutes, rearranging once.

3 Lift out the scallops with a
slotted spoon and transfer
them to a warmed serving dish.
Keep warm.

4 Add the ginger and spring
onions to the juices in the
bowl and microwave on HIGH for
1 minute. Pour in the vermouth
and microwave on HIGH for
30 seconds. Stir in the crème
fraîche and microwave on HIGH
for 1–1½ minutes, stirring twice.
Taste and adjust the seasoning.

5 Pour the sauce over the
scallops, sprinkle with parsley
and serve.

Eggs en Cocotte

A classic starter, these baked eggs are cooked on a flavoursome base of ratatouille, making them ideal for microwave cooking. They are also excellent for lunch or supper, with plenty of warm crusty bread.

Serves 4

4 eggs
20ml/4 tsp freshly grated Parmesan cheese
chopped fresh parsley, to garnish

For the ratatouille
1 small red pepper
15ml/1 tbsp olive oil
1 onion, finely chopped
1 garlic clove, crushed
2 courgettes, diced
400g/14oz can chopped tomatoes
   with basil
salt and ground black pepper

1 First prepare the vegetables: cut the red pepper in half on a board and remove the seeds. Then dice the pepper flesh.

2 Place the oil in a microwave-proof bowl. Add the onion, garlic, courgettes and pepper, and microwave on HIGH for 3–4 minutes, stirring once, until softened. Stir in the tomatoes, with salt and pepper to taste, and microwave on HIGH for 3–4 minutes, stirring once.

3 Divide the ratatouille between four individual microwave-proof dishes or large ramekins, each with a capacity of about 300ml/½ pint/1¼ cups.

4 Make a small hollow in the centre of each portion of ratatouille and break in an egg.

5 Grind some black pepper over the top of each cocotte and sprinkle with the cheese. Gently prick each yolk with a needle or wooden cocktail stick. Microwave on HIGH for 4–6 minutes or until the eggs are just set. Sprinkle with the fresh parsley and serve at once.

Mushroom Pâté

This is a vegetarian alternative to liver-based pâtés. Cooking the onion in butter gives a rich flavour, but you can use oil instead, if preferred.

INGREDIENTS

Serves 4

30ml/2 tbsp olive oil or butter

2 onions, chopped

350g/12oz/4½ cups mushrooms, chopped
  or roughly sliced

225g/8oz/1 cup ground almonds

a handful of parsley, stalks removed

salt and ground black pepper

flat leaf parsley, to garnish

thin slices of toast, cucumber, chicory and
  celery sticks, to serve

1 Place the olive oil or butter in a microwaveproof bowl with the onions. Microwave on HIGH for 5−7 minutes, stirring twice.

2 Add the mushrooms and microwave on HIGH for 3−3½ minutes, stirring halfway through cooking. Season well.

3 Transfer the cooked onion and mushrooms to a blender or food processor with their juices. Add the ground almonds and parsley, and process briefly. The pâté can either be smooth or you can leave it slightly chunky. Taste again for seasoning.

4 Spoon the pâté into individual pots. Garnish with flat leaf parsley and serve with thin slices of toast and sticks of cucumber, chicory and celery.

Stuffed Vine Leaves

Based on the Greek dolmas (or dolmades) but with a wholegrain vegetarian stuffing, this makes an excellent low-fat, high-fibre starter, snack or buffet dish. This is a quick version of the traditional speciality – the leaves and filling are cooked separately, rather than by long, slow cooking together for the authentic dish.

INGREDIENTS

Makes about 40

15ml/1 tbsp sunflower oil
5ml/1 tsp sesame oil
1 onion, finely chopped
225g/8oz/1⅓ cups brown rice
600ml/1 pint/2½ cups hot vegetable stock
1 small yellow pepper, seeded and finely chopped
115g/4oz/⅔ cup ready-to-eat dried apricots, finely chopped
2 lemons
50g/2oz/½ cup pine nuts
45ml/3 tbsp chopped fresh parsley
30ml/2 tbsp chopped fresh mint
2.5ml/½ tsp mixed spice
225g/8oz packet vine leaves preserved in brine, drained
150ml/¼ pint/⅔ cup water
30ml/2 tbsp olive oil
ground black pepper
lemon wedges, to garnish

To serve

300ml/½ pint/1¼ cups low-fat natural yogurt
30ml/2 tbsp chopped fresh mixed herbs
cayenne pepper

1 Place the sunflower and sesame oils together in a large microwaveproof bowl. Microwave on HIGH for 30 seconds. Add the onion and microwave on HIGH for 2 minutes, stirring once.

2 Add the rice and stir to coat the grains in oil. Pour in the stock, cover loosely and microwave on HIGH for 3 minutes. Reduce the power setting to MEDIUM and microwave for a further 25 minutes, stirring two or three times.

3 Stir in the chopped pepper and apricots. Replace the cover and leave to stand for 5 minutes.

4 Grate the rind off 1 lemon, then squeeze both lemons. Drain off any stock that has not been absorbed by the rice. Stir in the pine nuts, herbs, mixed spice, lemon rind and half the juice. Season with pepper and set aside.

5 Place the vine leaves in a bowl with the water, cover and microwave on HIGH for 4 minutes. Drain the leaves well, then lay them shiny side down on a board. Cut out any coarse stalks.

6 Place a heap of the rice mixture in the centre of a vine leaf. Fold over first the stem end, then the sides and finally the pointed end to make a neat parcel. Repeat with the remaining leaves.

7 Pack the parcels closely together in a shallow serving dish. Mix the remaining lemon juice with the olive oil and pour over the vine leaves. Cover and chill before serving.

8 Serve the vine leaves, garnished with lemon wedges. Spoon the yogurt into a bowl, stir in the chopped herbs and sprinkle with a little cayenne. Offer this light sauce with the chilled stuffed vine leaves.

COOK'S TIP

If vine leaves are not available, the leaves of Swiss chard, young spinach or cabbage can be used instead.

FISH AND SEAFOOD

Mediterranean Plaice

Sun-dried tomatoes, toasted pine nuts and anchovies make a flavoursome combination for the stuffing mixture.

INGREDIENTS

Serves 4

4 plaice fillets, about 225g/8oz each, skinned
75g/3oz/6 tbsp butter
1 small onion, chopped
1 celery stick, finely chopped
115g/4oz/2 cups fresh white breadcrumbs
45ml/3 tbsp chopped fresh parsley
30ml/2 tbsp pine nuts, toasted
3–4 pieces sun-dried tomatoes in oil, drained and chopped
50g/2oz can anchovy fillets, drained and chopped
75ml/5 tbsp fish stock
ground black pepper

1 Using a sharp knife, cut the plaice fillets in half lengthways to make eight smaller fillets.

2 Place the butter in a microwaveproof bowl and add the onion and celery. Cover and microwave on HIGH for 2 minutes, stirring halfway through cooking.

3 Mix together the bread-crumbs, parsley, pine nuts, sun-dried tomatoes and anchovies. Stir in the softened vegetables with their buttery juices and season with pepper.

4 Divide the stuffing into eight portions. Taking one portion at a time, form the stuffing into balls, then roll up each one inside a plaice fillet. Secure each roll with a wooden cocktail stick.

5 Place the rolled fillets in a buttered microwaveproof dish. Pour in the stock and cover the dish. Microwave on HIGH for 6–8 minutes, or until the fish flakes easily. Remove the cocktail sticks, then serve with a little of the cooking juices drizzled over.

Fisherman's Casserole

A perfect dish for microwaving as it's cooked in one dish.

INGREDIENTS

Serves 4–6

450g/1lb mixed firm fish fillets, such as
    cod, haddock and monkfish
50g/2oz/4 tbsp butter
1 onion, sliced
1 celery stick, sliced
350g/12oz potatoes, cut into chunks
750ml/1¼ pints/3 cups hot fish stock
bouquet garni
150g/5oz frozen broad beans
300ml/½ pint/1¼ cups milk
115g/4oz peeled cooked prawns
8 mussels, shelled
salt and ground black pepper
chopped parsley, to garnish

1 Skin the fish and cut the flesh into bite-sized chunks using a large sharp knife. Place the butter in a microwaveproof dish and microwave on HIGH for 1 minute, until melted. Add the onion, celery and potatoes, cover and microwave on HIGH for 4 minutes, stirring once during cooking.

2 Stir in the stock, bouquet garni and beans. Cover and microwave on HIGH for 10 minutes, stirring twice.

3 Add the fish and milk, re-cover and microwave on HIGH for 5–7 minutes until the fish flakes. Stir in the prawns, mussels and seasoning and microwave on HIGH for 1–2 minutes to warm through. Sprinkle with parsley and serve.

Potato-topped Fish Pie

Cheese-topped potatoes enclose a creamy mixture of fish, prawns and hard-boiled eggs.

INGREDIENTS

Serves 4

400ml/14fl oz/1⅔ cups hot milk
1 bay leaf
¼ onion, sliced
450g/1lb haddock or cod fillet
225g/8oz smoked haddock fillet
3 hard-boiled eggs, chopped
65g/2½oz/5 tbsp butter
25g/1oz/2 tbsp plain flour
115g/4oz/1 cup frozen peas
75g/3oz peeled cooked prawns
30ml/2 tbsp chopped fresh parsley
lemon juice, to taste
500g/1¼lb cooked potatoes, mashed
60ml/4 tbsp grated Cheddar cheese
salt and ground black pepper

1 Place 120ml/4fl oz/½ cup of the milk, the bay leaf and onion in a microwaveproof dish, then add the white and smoked fish. Cover and microwave on HIGH for 7–8 minutes, rearranging once. Strain and reserve the milk. Flake the fish into a microwaveproof pie dish, discarding the skin and any bones. Add the eggs.

2 Place 25g/1oz/2 tbsp of the butter, the flour and remaining milk in a microwaveproof jug. Whisk in the reserved cooking liquid from the fish. Microwave on HIGH for 5–7 minutes, stirring every 1 minute, until smooth, boiling and thickened. Stir in the peas and cooked prawns.

3 Add the parsley, lemon juice and seasoning to taste. Pour the sauce over the fish and eggs and carefully mix the ingredients.

4 Spoon the mashed potato evenly over the fish and fork up the surface. Dot with the remaining butter.

5 Sprinkle the cheese over the pie, then microwave on HIGH for 5–6 minutes. Brown under a preheated hot grill, if liked. Serve piping hot.

COMBINATION MICROWAVE

This recipe is suitable for cooking in a combination microwave. Follow your oven manufacturer's timing guide for good results.

Tuna and Mixed Vegetable Pasta

Cook this simple and very speedy sauce in the microwave while the pasta cooks conventionally.

INGREDIENTS

Serves 4

30ml/2 tbsp olive oil

175g/6oz/1½ cups button mushrooms, sliced

1 garlic clove, crushed

½ red pepper, seeded and chopped

15ml/1 tbsp tomato purée

300ml/½ pint/1¼ cups tomato juice

115g/4oz frozen peas

15–30ml/1–2 tbsp drained pickled green peppercorns, crushed

275g/10oz/2½ cups wholewheat pasta shapes

200g/7oz can tuna chunks in brine, drained

6 spring onions, diagonally sliced

1 Place the oil in a microwave-proof bowl with the mushrooms, garlic and pepper. Cover and microwave on HIGH for 4 minutes, stirring halfway through cooking. Stir in the tomato purée, then add the tomato juice, peas and some or all of the crushed peppercorns, depending on how spicy you like the sauce.

2 Cover the bowl and microwave on HIGH for a further 4 minutes, stirring halfway through cooking.

3 Bring a large saucepan of lightly salted water to the boil on the hob and cook the pasta for about 12 minutes, or according to the packet instructions, until just tender. When the pasta is almost ready, add the tuna to the sauce and microwave on HIGH for 1 minute to heat though. Stir in the spring onions. Drain the pasta and tip it into a warmed bowl. Pour the sauce over the pasta and toss to mix. Serve at once.

Sweet and Sour Fish

Serve this tasty, nutritious dish with brown rice and stir-fried cabbage or spinach for a delicious, light lunch-time meal.

INGREDIENTS

Serves 4

60ml/4 tbsp cider vinegar

45ml/3 tbsp light soy sauce

50g/2oz/¼ cup granulated sugar

15ml/1 tbsp tomato purée

25ml/1½ tbsp cornflour

250ml/8fl oz/1 cup water

1 green pepper, seeded and sliced

225g/8oz can pineapple pieces in fruit juice

225g/8oz tomatoes, peeled and chopped

225g/8oz/2 cups button mushrooms, sliced

675g/1½lb chunky haddock fillets, skinned

salt and ground black pepper

1 Mix the vinegar, soy sauce, sugar and tomato purée in a microwaveproof bowl. Gradually blend the cornflour to a smooth paste with the water, then add to the bowl, stirring well. Microwave on HIGH for 2–2½ minutes, stirring three times during cooking, until smooth, boiling and thickened.

2 Add the green pepper, canned pineapple pieces (with juice), tomatoes and mushrooms to the sauce and microwave on HIGH for 2 minutes, stirring halfway through cooking. Season to taste with salt and pepper.

3 Place the fish in a single layer in a shallow microwaveproof dish and pour over the sauce. Cover and microwave on HIGH for 8–10 minutes, rotating the dish twice during cooking. Leave to stand for 5 minutes before serving.

Green Fish Curry

INGREDIENTS

Serves 4

1.5ml/¼ tsp ground turmeric

30ml/2 tbsp lime juice

pinch of salt

4 portions cod fillets, skinned and cut into
  5cm/2in chunks

1 onion, chopped

1 green chilli, roughly chopped

1 garlic clove, crushed

25g/1oz/¼ cup cashew nuts

2.5ml/½ tsp fennel seeds

30ml/2 tbsp desiccated coconut

30ml/2 tbsp oil

1.5ml/¼ tsp cumin seeds

1.5ml/¼ tsp ground coriander

1.5ml/¼ tsp ground cumin

1.5ml/¼ tsp salt

150ml/¼ pint/⅔ cup water

175ml/6fl oz/¾ cup single cream

45ml/3 tbsp finely chopped fresh
  coriander

fresh coriander sprig, to garnish

rice with vegetables, to serve

1 Mix the turmeric, lime juice and pinch of salt, then rub the mixture over the fish. Cover and leave to marinate for 15 minutes.

2 Meanwhile, process the onion, chilli, garlic, cashew nuts, fennel seeds and coconut to a paste in a blender or food processor. Spoon the paste into a bowl and set it aside.

3 Place the oil in a large microwaveproof bowl. Add the cumin seeds and microwave on HIGH for 1–1½ minutes or until the seeds begin to splutter. Add the paste, ground coriander, cumin, salt and water and mix well. Cover and microwave on HIGH for 3–5 minutes, stirring twice during cooking.

4 Stir in the cream and fresh coriander. Microwave on HIGH for a further 2–3 minutes, stirring halfway through cooking.

5 Gently mix in the fish. Cover and microwave on HIGH for 7–10 minutes, stirring twice, until cooked. Serve, garnished with coriander, with rice and vegetables or pilau.

COOK'S TIP

Whole and ground spices, lime, garlic, chilli and coconut make a superb sauce. Fresh coriander and single cream balance and enliven the flavours.

Prawn Curry

This rich prawn curry is flavoured with coconut and a delicious blend of aromatic spices.

INGREDIENTS

Serves 4

675g/1½lb uncooked tiger prawns

4 dried red chillies

50g/2oz/1 cup desiccated coconut

5ml/1 tsp black mustard seeds

1 large onion, chopped

45ml/3 tbsp oil

4 bay leaves

2.5cm/1in piece fresh root ginger, finely
    chopped

2 garlic cloves, crushed

15ml/1 tbsp ground coriander

5ml/1 tsp chilli powder

5ml/1 tsp salt

4 tomatoes, finely chopped

175ml/6fl oz/¾ cup water

plain rice, to serve

1 Peel the prawns. Run a sharp knife along the back of each prawn to make a shallow cut and carefully remove the thin black intestinal vein.

2 Put the dried red chillies, coconut, mustard seeds and onion in a large microwaveproof bowl. Microwave on HIGH for 8 minutes, stirring twice. Process the mixture to a coarse paste in a blender or food processor.

3 Place the oil in a microwave-proof bowl with the bay leaves. Add the ginger and garlic, cover and microwave on HIGH for 2 minutes, stirring twice during cooking.

4 Stir in the coriander, chilli powder, salt and the paste. Cover and microwave on HIGH for 2–3 minutes, stirring halfway through cooking.

5 Stir in the tomatoes and water, cover and microwave on HIGH for 4–6 minutes, stirring halfway through cooking, until thickened slightly.

6 Mix in the prawns, cover and microwave on HIGH for 4 minutes or until they turn pink and their edges curl slightly. Serve with plain boiled rice.

Seafood Pilaff

This all-in-one main course makes a satisfying meal for any day of the week. For a special meal, substitute dry white wine for the orange juice.

INGREDIENTS

Serves 4

10ml/2 tsp olive oil

250g/9oz/1¼ cups long grain rice

5ml/1 tsp ground turmeric

1 red pepper, seeded and diced

1 small onion, finely chopped

2 courgettes, sliced

150g/5oz/2 cups button mushrooms, halved

350ml/12fl oz/1½ cups fish or chicken stock

150ml/¼ pint/⅔ cup orange juice

350g/12oz white fish fillets, skinned

12 cooked mussels, shelled

salt and ground black pepper

grated rind of 1 orange, to garnish

1 Mix the oil with the rice and turmeric in a large microwaveproof bowl. Microwave on HIGH for 1 minute.

2 Add the pepper, onion, courgettes and mushrooms. Stir in the stock and orange juice. Cover and microwave on HIGH for 13 minutes, stirring halfway through cooking. Leave to stand, covered.

3 Place the fish on a microwave-proof plate. Cover and microwave on HIGH for 4–5 minutes, until cooked. Flake the fish and stir it into the rice mixture. Stir in the mussels and microwave on HIGH for a further 1 minute. Adjust the seasoning, sprinkle with orange rind and serve hot.

Salmon Pasta with Parsley Sauce

INGREDIENTS

Serves 4

450g/1lb salmon fillet, skinned

225g/8oz/3 cups pasta shapes, such as penne or twists

175g/6oz cherry tomatoes, halved

150ml/¼ pint/⅔ cup low-fat crème fraîche

45ml/3 tbsp chopped fresh parsley

finely grated rind of ½ orange

salt and ground black pepper

COOK'S TIP

If low-fat crème fraîche is not available, use ordinary crème fraîche or double cream instead.

1 Cut the salmon into bite-sized pieces, arrange them on a microwaveproof plate and cover with greaseproof paper. Microwave on HIGH for 2–2½ minutes, rearranging halfway through cooking. Leave to stand for 5 minutes.

2 Cook the pasta in a saucepan of boiling water on the hob, following the packet instructions.

3 Alternatively, cook the pasta in 1.2 litres/2 pints boiling water with 5ml/1 tsp oil in a large microwaveproof bowl. Microwave on HIGH for 10–12 minutes.

4 Drain the pasta and toss it with the tomatoes and salmon. Mix the crème fraîche, parsley, orange rind and pepper to taste, then toss this sauce into the salmon and pasta and serve hot.

Whole Cooked Salmon

Farmed salmon has made this fish more affordable and less of a treat, but a whole salmon still features as a centrepiece at parties. As with all fish, the taste depends first on freshness and second on not overcooking it. Although you need to start early, the cooking time is short. Cooked salmon is, of course, also delicious served hot with a buttery hollandaise sauce. New potatoes and fine green beans are perfect accompaniments.

INGREDIENTS

Serves 6–8 as part of a buffet
1.8kg/4lb whole salmon
1 lemon, sliced
salt and ground black pepper
lemon wedges, cucumber ribbons and
    fresh dill sprigs, to garnish

1 Wash the salmon and dry it well, inside and out. Prick the skin in several places to prevent bursting and place the salmon in a shallow microwaveproof dish.

2 Put a few slices of lemon inside the salmon and arrange some more on the top. Season well and sprinkle a little boiling water over to moisten the fish.

3 Cover with greaseproof paper or vented clear film and microwave on HIGH for 20–22 minutes, rotating the dish three times during cooking. Leave to stand, covered, for 5 minutes, before serving hot. If serving cold, leave to cool completely before uncovering.

4 To serve hot with hollandaise sauce, peel away the skin and transfer the salmon to a heated serving dish. Keep warm while preparing the sauce.

5 To serve cold and on the same day, remove the skin from the cooked fish and arrange it on a large platter. Garnish with lemon wedges, cucumber cut into thin ribbons and sprigs of dill. If you intend serving the salmon the following day, leave the skin on and chill the fish overnight before adding the garnish.

HOLLANDAISE SAUCE

Place 115g/4oz/8 tbsp butter in a large microwaveproof jug and microwave on HIGH for 1½ minutes. Whisk in 45ml/3 tbsp lemon juice, 2 egg yolks, a pinch of mustard powder and salt and pepper to taste. Microwave on MEDIUM for 1 minute, then whisk and serve.

COOK'S TIP

To prevent the head and tail ends of fish from overcooking in the microwave, they can be shielded with small pieces of smooth foil. This may be done at the beginning of the cooking time or after a few minutes if cooking progress is being carefully watched.

MEAT AND
POULTRY

~

Lamb Pie with a Potato Crust

Serves 4

675g/1½lb potatoes, diced

45ml/3 tbsp water

30ml/2 tbsp skimmed milk

15ml/1 tbsp wholegrain or
   French mustard

1 onion, chopped

2 celery sticks, sliced

2 carrots, diced

450g/1lb lean minced lamb

150ml/¼ pint/⅔ cup beef stock

60ml/4 tbsp rolled oats

15ml/1 tbsp Worcestershire sauce

30ml/2 tbsp chopped fresh rosemary

salt and ground black pepper

1 Place the potatoes in a microwaveproof bowl with the water. Cover and microwave on HIGH for 8–10 minutes, until tender, stirring once. Drain and mash until smooth, then stir in the milk and mustard.

2 Place the onion, celery and carrots in a large microwave-proof bowl. Cover and microwave on HIGH for 5 minutes, stirring once. Add the minced lamb, mixing well. Microwave on HIGH for 2 minutes, stirring once.

3 Stir in the stock, rolled oats, Worcestershire sauce and rosemary, and season to taste with salt and pepper. Cover loosely and microwave on HIGH for 20–25 minutes, until cooked, stirring twice.

4 Turn the meat mixture into a 1.75 litre/3 pint/7½ cup microwaveproof dish that is suitable for grilling. Swirl the potato evenly over the top. Microwave, uncovered, on HIGH for 4–5 minutes until hot. Brown under a grill, if liked. Serve with freshly cooked vegetables.

COMBINATION MICROWAVE

This recipe is suitable for cooking in a combination microwave. Follow the oven manufacturer's timing guide for good results.

Beef and Mushroom Burgers

It's worth making your own burgers to cut down on fat – in these, the meat is extended with mushrooms for extra fibre.

INGREDIENTS

Serves 4

1 small onion, chopped

150g/5oz/2 cups small cup mushrooms

450g/1lb lean minced beef

50g/2oz/1 cup fresh wholemeal
   breadcrumbs

5ml/1 tsp dried mixed herbs

15ml/1 tbsp tomato purée

plain flour, for shaping

salt and ground black pepper

relish, lettuce, burger buns or pitta bread,
   to serve

1 Place the onion and mushrooms in a food processor and process until finely chopped. Add the beef, bread-crumbs, herbs, tomato purée and seasoning. Process for a few seconds, until the mixture binds together but still has some texture.

2 Divide the mixture into four, then press into burger shapes using lightly floured hands.

3 To cook, place the burgers on a microwaveproof roasting rack and microwave, uncovered, for 6–7 minutes, turning over once. Leave to stand for 2–3 minutes.

4 Alternatively, for a browner and crisper result, preheat a microwave browning dish according to the manufacturer's instructions. Add the burgers, pressing down well on to the base and microwave on HIGH for 5–5½ minutes, turning over once. Leave to stand for 2–3 minutes. Serve with relish and lettuce, in burger buns or pitta bread.

VARIATION

To make Lamb and Mushroom Burgers, substitute lean minced lamb for the minced beef.

COMBINATION MICROWAVE

This recipe is suitable for cooking in a combination microwave. Follow the oven manufacturer's timing guide for good results.

Stuffed Tomatoes

Ever popular, this simple recipe demonstrates the versatility of mince as a stuffing.

Serves 4

4 beef tomatoes

7.5ml/1½ tsp oil

75g/3oz/¾ cup minced beef

1 small red onion, thinly sliced

25g/1oz/¼ cup bulgur wheat

30ml/2 tbsp freshly grated
   Parmesan cheese

15g/½oz/1 tbsp cashew nuts, chopped

1 small celery stick, chopped

salt and ground black pepper

crisp green salad, to serve

1 Trim the tops from the tomatoes, scoop out the flesh with a teaspoon and reserve.

2 Place the oil in a large microwaveproof bowl, add the minced beef and onion, cover and microwave on HIGH for 5–6 minutes or until the beef is cooked, stirring twice to break up the meat. Stir in the tomato flesh.

3 Place the bulgur wheat in a bowl, cover with boiling water and leave to soak for 10 minutes. Drain if necessary.

4 Mix the mince and bulgur, Parmesan cheese, nuts and celery. Season well.

5 Spoon the filling into the tomatoes and place in a shallow microwaveproof dish. Microwave on HIGH for 3–5 minutes or until the tomatoes and their filling are tender. Serve with a crisp green salad.

Spicy Bolognese

*A spicy version of a popular dish.
Worcestershire sauce and chorizo
sausages add an extra element to
this perfect family standby.*

INGREDIENTS

Serves 4

15ml/1 tbsp oil

1 onion, chopped

225g/8oz/2 cups minced beef

5ml/1 tsp ground chilli powder

15ml/1 tbsp Worcestershire sauce

25g/1oz/2 tbsp plain flour

150ml/¼ pint/⅔ cup beef stock

4 chorizo sausages

200g/7oz can chopped tomatoes

50g/2oz baby sweetcorn

15ml/1 tbsp chopped fresh basil

salt and ground black pepper

1 Place the oil and onion in a
large microwaveproof bowl.
Microwave on HIGH for
2 minutes. Add the minced beef
and chilli powder, mixing well.
Microwave on HIGH for 4–5
minutes, breaking up the mince
twice during cooking.

2 Stir in the Worcestershire
sauce and flour. Microwave on
HIGH for 30 seconds, stirring
once, before pouring in the stock.

3 Slice the chorizo sausages and
halve the corn lengthways.

4 Stir in the sausages, tomatoes,
sweetcorn and chopped basil.
Season well, cover loosely and
microwave on HIGH for 15–20
minutes, stirring twice. Serve
with spaghetti, garnished with
fresh basil.

COOK'S TIP

If you like, cool the Bolognese
sauce and freeze it in conveniently sized portions for up to
2 months.

Hot Chilli Chicken

Not for the faint-hearted, this fiery, hot curry is made with a spicy chilli masala paste.

INGREDIENTS

Serves 4

30ml/2 tbsp tomato purée
2 garlic cloves, roughly chopped
2 green chillies, roughly chopped
5 dried red chillies
2.5ml/½ tsp salt
1.5ml/¼ tsp sugar
5ml/1 tsp chilli powder
2.5ml/½ tsp paprika
15ml/1 tbsp curry paste
30ml/2 tbsp oil
2.5ml/½ tsp cumin seeds
1 onion, finely chopped
2 bay leaves
5ml/1 tsp ground coriander
5ml/1 tsp ground cumin
1.5ml/¼ tsp ground turmeric
400g/14oz can chopped tomatoes
150ml/¼ pint/⅔ cup water
8 chicken thighs, skinned
5ml/1 tsp garam masala
sliced green chillies, to garnish
chappatis and natural yogurt, to serve

1 Process the tomato purée, garlic, green and dried red chillies, salt, sugar, chilli powder, paprika and curry paste to a smooth paste in a food processor or blender.

2 Place the oil in a large microwaveproof bowl and add the cumin seeds. Microwave on HIGH for 1½ minutes. Add the onion and bay leaves, cover and microwave on HIGH for 3 minutes.

3 Stir in the chilli paste. Cover and microwave on HIGH for 1½ minutes, then mix in the remaining ground spices, chopped tomatoes and water. Cover and microwave on HIGH for 3 minutes.

4 Add the chicken and garam masala. Cover and microwave on HIGH for 18–22 minutes, stirring twice, until the chicken is tender. Garnish with sliced green chillies and serve with chappatis and natural yogurt.

Chicken and Fruit Salad

The chicken may be cooked a day before serving and the salad assembled at the last minute. Serve with warm garlic bread.

INGREDIENTS

Serves 8

4 tarragon or rosemary sprigs
2 x 1.5kg/3–3½lb chickens
65g/2½oz/5 tbsp softened butter
150ml/¼ pint/⅔ cup chicken stock
150ml/¼ pint/⅔ cup white wine
1 small cantaloupe melon
115g/4oz/1 cup walnut pieces
lettuce leaves
450g/1lb seedless grapes or
    cherries, stoned
salt and ground black pepper

For the dressing
30ml/2 tbsp tarragon vinegar
120ml/8 tbsp light olive oil
30ml/2 tbsp chopped mixed fresh herbs,
    for example parsley, mint and tarragon

1 Put the sprigs of tarragon or rosemary inside the chickens and season with salt and pepper. Tie the chickens in a neat shape with string and spread with 50g/2oz/4 tbsp of the softened butter. Place breast-side down in a microwaveproof shallow dish and pour round the stock. Cover loosely and microwave on HIGH for 30–35 minutes, turning breast-side up halfway through cooking. Cover with foil and leave to stand for 10–15 minutes. Prick to release excess juices and leave to cool.

2 Add the wine to the cooking juices. Transfer to a microwaveproof jug or bowl and microwave on HIGH for about 5 minutes or until syrupy. Strain and leave the juices to cool. Scoop the melon into balls or into cubes. Joint the chickens.

3 Place the remaining butter in a microwaveproof bowl with the walnuts. Microwave on HIGH for 2–3 minutes to brown, stirring once. Drain and cool.

4 To make the dressing, whisk the vinegar and oil together with some seasoning. Remove the fat from the chicken juices and add the juices to the dressing with the herbs. Adjust the seasoning.

5 Arrange the chicken pieces on a bed of lettuce, scatter over the grapes or stoned cherries, melon balls or cubes and coat with the herb dressing. Sprinkle with toasted walnuts and serve.

COMBINATION MICROWAVE

This recipe is suitable for cooking in a combination microwave. Follow the oven manufacturer's timing guide for good results.

COOK'S TIP

The chickens can be cooked in roasting bags, but do not use metal ties for securing the bags; replace with elastic bands or string.

Chicken Liver Salad

This salad may be served as a first course on individual plates.

Serves 4

mixed salad leaves, such as frisée and
   oakleaf lettuce or radicchio
1 avocado, diced
2 pink grapefruits, segmented
350g/12oz chicken livers
30ml/2 tbsp olive oil
1 garlic clove, crushed
salt and ground black pepper
crusty bread, to serve

For the dressing
30ml/2 tbsp lemon juice
60ml/4 tbsp olive oil
2.5ml/½ tsp wholegrain mustard
2.5ml/½ tsp clear honey
15ml/1 tbsp snipped fresh chives

1 First prepare the dressing: put
all the ingredients into a
screw-topped jar and shake vigor-
ously to emulsify the mixture.
Taste and adjust the seasoning.

2 Wash and dry the salad.
Arrange attractively on a
serving plate with the avocado and
grapefruit.

3 Dry the chicken livers on
paper towels and remove any
sinew or membrane. Cut the larger
livers in half and leave the smaller
ones whole. Prick thoroughly with
a fork.

4 Place the oil in a large
microwaveproof bowl. Add
the livers and garlic, mixing well.
Cover loosely and microwave on
HIGH for 3–4 minutes, stirring
twice until cooked, but still slightly
pink inside.

5 Season with salt and ground
black pepper and drain on
paper towels.

6 Place the liver on the salad and
spoon the dressing over the
top. Serve immediately, with warm
crusty bread.

PULSES, PASTA
AND GRAINS

Borlotti Beans with Mushrooms

A mixture of wild and cultivated mushrooms helps to give this dish a rich and nutty flavour.

INGREDIENTS

Serves 4

30ml/2 tbsp olive oil

50g/2oz/4 tbsp butter

2 shallots, chopped

2-3 garlic cloves, crushed

675g/1½lb mixed mushrooms,
  thickly sliced

4 sun-dried tomatoes in oil, drained
  and chopped

45ml/3 tbsp dry white wine

400g/14oz can borlotti beans

45ml/3 tbsp grated Parmesan cheese

30ml/2 tbsp chopped fresh parsley

salt and ground black pepper

freshly cooked pappardelle pasta, to serve

1 Place the oil and butter in a microwaveproof bowl with the shallots. Microwave on HIGH for 1 minute.

2 Add the garlic and mushrooms and microwave on HIGH for 3–4 minutes, stirring halfway through cooking. Stir in the sun-dried tomatoes, wine and seasoning to taste.

3 Stir in the borlotti beans and microwave on HIGH for 2–3 minutes or until the beans are heated through.

4 Stir in the grated Parmesan and sprinkle with parsley. Serve immediately with hot pappardelle pasta.

COOK'S TIP

When buying wild mushrooms, examine packs carefully and reject any mushrooms that have tiny holes or show signs of being eaten as they may contain tiny maggots.

Pasta Carbonara

Cooking the pasta conventionally on the hob and the sauce in the microwave makes this a very speedy dish to prepare.

INGREDIENTS

Serves 4

350–450g/12oz–1lb fresh tagliatelle
15ml/1 tbsp olive oil
225g/8oz ham, bacon or pancetta, cut into 2.5cm/1in sticks
115g/4oz button mushrooms (about 10), sliced
4 eggs, lightly beaten
75ml/5 tbsp single cream
30ml/2 tbsp finely grated Parmesan cheese
salt and ground black pepper
fresh basil sprigs, to garnish

1 While preparing the sauce in the microwave, cook the pasta conventionally in a large saucepan of boiling salted water on the hob according to the packet instructions.

2 Meanwhile, place the oil and ham in a microwaveproof bowl. Microwave on HIGH for 3 minutes, then add the mushrooms. Microwave on HIGH for a further 3 minutes, stirring once during cooking. Meanwhile, lightly beat the eggs and cream together and season well.

3 Drain the cooked pasta well and add to the ham and mushroom mixture, mixing well.

4 Pour in the eggs and cream and add half the Parmesan cheese. Stir well and, as you do this, the eggs will cook in the heat of the pasta. If you like your sauce slightly thicker, then microwave on HIGH for 30 seconds, stirring once during cooking. Pile on to warmed serving plates, sprinkle with the remaining Parmesan and garnish with basil.

Baked Macaroni Cheese

A delicious supper-time dish – replace the Cheddar with your family's favourite cheese.

INGREDIENTS

Serves 4

275g/10oz/2⅓ cups macaroni
1.2 litres/2 pints/5 cups boiling water
15ml/1 tbsp olive oil
2 leeks, chopped
50g/2oz/4 tbsp butter
50g/2oz/½ cup plain flour
900ml/1½ pints/3¾ cups milk
225g/8oz/2 cups mature Cheddar cheese, grated
30ml/2 tbsp fromage frais
5ml/1 tsp wholegrain mustard
50g/2oz/1 cup fresh white breadcrumbs
25g/1oz/½ cup Double Gloucester cheese, grated
salt and ground black pepper
15ml/1 tbsp chopped fresh parsley, to garnish

1 Place the macaroni in a large microwaveproof bowl with the boiling water and the olive oil. Add the leeks and microwave on HIGH for 10 minutes, stirring once. Leave to stand, covered, while cooking the sauce.

2 Stir the butter with the flour and milk in a large microwaveproof jug. Microwave on HIGH for 6–8 minutes, whisking every minute, until smooth, boiling and thickened.

3 Whisk in the Cheddar cheese, fromage frais and mustard, adding salt and pepper to taste.

4 Drain the macaroni and leeks and rinse under cold water. Stir the drained macaroni and leeks into the cheese sauce and turn into a dish that is suitable for grilling. Level the top with the back of a spoon and sprinkle over the breadcrumbs and Double Gloucester cheese.

5 Cook under a preheated hot grill until golden and bubbly. Serve hot, garnished with chopped fresh parsley.

Rigatoni with Spicy Sausage and Tomato

This is really a cheat's Bolognese sauce using the wonderful fresh spicy sausages sold in every Italian delicatessen.

Serves 4

450g/1lb fresh spicy Italian sausage

30ml/2 tbsp olive oil

1 onion, chopped

475ml/16fl oz/2 cups passata (smooth, thick, sieved tomatoes)

150ml/¼ pint/⅔ cup dry red wine

6 sun-dried tomatoes in oil, drained

450g/1lb/4 cups rigatoni or similar pasta

salt and ground black pepper

freshly grated Parmesan cheese, to serve

1 Squeeze the sausagemeat out of the skins into a bowl and break it up.

2 While preparing the sauce, cook the pasta conventionally in a saucepan of boiling salted water on the hob according to the packet instructions.

3 Place the oil in a microwave-proof bowl and add the onion. Microwave on HIGH for 3 minutes. Stir in the sausagemeat and microwave on HIGH for 5 minutes, stirring every minute to break up the meat. Stir in the passata and wine. Cover and microwave on HIGH for 4 minutes, stirring once.

4 Slice the sun-dried tomatoes and add them to the sauce. Microwave, uncovered, for 2 minutes, stirring once, then season to taste.

5 Drain the pasta well and top with the sauce. Serve with grated Parmesan cheese.

COOK'S TIP

If you cannot find fresh Italian sausage, season pork sausage-meat with a crushed garlic clove, a little dried oregano, grated nutmeg and a pinch of paprika. Mix well.

Golden Vegetable Paella

Serves 4

pinch of saffron strands or 5ml/1 tsp
    ground turmeric
750ml/1¼ pints/3 cups boiling vegetable
    or spicy stock
90ml/6 tbsp olive oil
2 large onions, sliced
3 garlic cloves, chopped
275g/10oz/1⅓ cups long grain rice
50g/2oz/⅓ cup wild rice
175g/6oz pumpkin or butternut
    squash, chopped
175g/6oz carrots, cut into
    matchstick strips
1 yellow pepper, seeded and sliced
4 tomatoes, peeled and chopped
115g/4oz oyster mushrooms, quartered
salt and ground black pepper
strips of red, yellow and green pepper,
    to garnish

1 If using saffron, place it in a small bowl with 45–60ml/3–4 tbsp of the stock. Leave to stand for 5 minutes. Meanwhile, place the oil in a large microwave-proof bowl with the onions and garlic, then microwave on HIGH for 4–4½ minutes, stirring once.

2 Stir both types of rice into the onion mixture and toss until coated in oil. Add the remaining stock, with the pumpkin or squash, and the saffron strands and liquid or turmeric.

3 Cover and microwave on HIGH for 3 minutes. Add the carrots, pepper, tomatoes, salt and black pepper. Cover again and microwave on HIGH for 2 minutes. Reduce the power setting to MEDIUM and microwave for a further 12 minutes, stirring twice, or until the rice is almost tender.

4 Finally, add the oyster mushrooms, check the seasoning, cover and microwave on HIGH for 1 minute. Leave to stand for 10 minutes, fluff up the rice with a fork, top with the peppers and serve.

Ravioli with Four Cheese Sauce

This is a smooth cheese sauce that coats the pasta very evenly.

INGREDIENTS

Serves 4

350g/12oz ravioli

1.75 litres/3 pints/7½ cups boiling water

50g/2oz/¼ cup butter

50g/2oz/¼ cup plain flour

475ml/16fl oz/2 cups milk

50g/2oz Parmesan cheese

50g/2oz Edam cheese

50g/2oz Gruyère cheese

50g/2oz fontina cheese

salt and ground black pepper

chopped fresh parsley, to garnish

1 Place the ravioli in a large microwaveproof bowl and pour in the boiling water. Microwave on HIGH for 10 minutes, stirring halfway through cooking. Leave to stand for 3 minutes.

2 Whisk the butter, flour and milk together in a microwaveproof jug. Microwave on HIGH for 5–7 minutes, whisking every minute, until smooth, boiling and thickened.

3 Grate the cheeses and stir them into the sauce until they are just beginning to melt. Add seasoning to taste.

4 Drain the pasta thoroughly and turn it into a large serving bowl. Pour over the sauce and toss to coat. Serve immediately, garnished with chopped parsley.

COOK'S TIP

If you cannot find all of the recommended cheeses, simply substitute your favourite types. Strong-flavoured hard cheeses are best for this type of sauce.

Mushroom, Leek and Cashew Nut Risotto

INGREDIENTS

Serves 4

225g/8oz/1⅓ cups brown rice

900ml/1½ pints/3 cups boiling vegetable
   stock or a mixture of boiling stock and
   dry white wine in the ratio 5:1

15ml/1 tbsp walnut or hazelnut oil

2 leeks, sliced

225g/8oz/2 cups mixed wild or cultivated
   mushrooms, trimmed and sliced

50g/2oz/½ cup cashew nuts

grated rind of 1 lemon

30ml/2 tbsp chopped fresh thyme

25g/1oz/scant ¼ cup pumpkin seeds

salt and ground black pepper

fresh thyme sprigs and lemon wedges,
   to garnish

1 Place the rice in a large microwaveproof bowl with the boiling stock (or stock and wine). Cover loosely and microwave on HIGH for 3 minutes. Reduce the power setting to MEDIUM and microwave for a further 25 minutes, stirring twice. Leave to stand, covered, while cooking the vegetable and nut mixture.

2 Place the oil in a large microwaveproof bowl with the leeks and mushrooms. Cover and microwave on HIGH for 3–4 minutes, stirring once.

3 Add the cashew nuts, grated lemon rind and chopped fresh thyme to the leeks and mushrooms and microwave on HIGH for 1 minute. Season to taste with salt and freshly ground black pepper.

4 Drain off any excess stock from the cooked rice and stir in the vegetable mixture. Turn the risotto into a serving dish. Scatter the pumpkin seeds over the top and garnish with the fresh thyme sprigs and lemon wedges. Serve the risotto at once.

Spiced Lentils and Rice

Lentils are cooked with whole and ground spices, potatoes, rice and onions to produce an authentic Indian-style risotto.

Serves 4

150g/5oz/¾ cup toovar dhal or split red lentils

115g/4oz basmati rice

1 large potato

1 large onion

30ml/2 tbsp sunflower oil

4 whole cloves

1.5ml/¼ tsp cumin seeds

1.5ml/¼ tsp ground turmeric

10ml/2 tsp salt

300ml/½ pint/1¼ cups boiling water

1 Wash the toovar dhal or lentils and rice in several changes of cold water. Then leave to soak in plenty of cold water for 15 minutes. Drain well.

2 Peel the potato and cut it into 2.5cm/1in chunks.

3 Thinly slice the onion and set it aside until the whole spices are lightly cooked.

4 Place the sunflower oil in a large microwaveproof bowl with the cloves and cumin seeds. Microwave on HIGH for 2 minutes.

5 Add the onion and potatoes, cover and microwave on HIGH for 4 minutes, stirring once. Stir in the lentils and rice, turmeric, salt and water.

6 Cover and microwave on HIGH for 3 minutes. Reduce the power setting to MEDIUM and microwave for a further 12 minutes, stirring twice. Leave to stand, covered, for about 10 minutes before serving.

Sweet Vegetable Couscous

A wonderful combination of sweet vegetables and spices, this makes a substantial winter dish.

Serves 4-6

1 generous pinch of saffron threads

45ml/3 tbsp boiling water

15ml/1 tbsp olive oil

1 red onion, sliced

2 garlic cloves, crushed

1-2 fresh red chillies, seeded and finely chopped

2.5ml/½ tsp ground ginger

2.5ml/½ tsp ground cinnamon

400g/14oz can chopped tomatoes

300ml/½ pint/1¼ cups hot vegetable stock or water

4 carrots, peeled and cut into 5mm/¼in slices

2 turnips, peeled and cut into 2cm/¾in cubes

450g/1lb sweet potatoes, peeled and cut into 2cm/¾in cubes

75g/3oz/⅓ cup raisins

2 courgettes, cut into 5mm/¼in slices

400g/14oz can chick-peas, drained and rinsed

45ml/3 tbsp chopped fresh parsley

45ml/3 tbsp chopped fresh coriander leaves

450g/1lb quick-cook couscous

1 Sprinkle the saffron into the boiling water and set this aside to infuse.

2 Place the oil in a large microwaveproof bowl. Add the onion, garlic and chillies. Microwave on HIGH for 2 minutes, stirring halfway through cooking.

3 Add the ground ginger and cinnamon and microwave on HIGH for 1 minute.

4 Stir in the tomatoes, stock or water, infused saffron and liquid, carrots, turnips, sweet potatoes and raisins. Cover and microwave on HIGH for 15 minutes, stirring twice during cooking.

5 Add the courgettes, chick-peas, parsley and coriander, cover and microwave on HIGH for 5–8 minutes, stirring once, until the vegetables are tender.

6 Meanwhile, prepare the couscous following the packet instructions and serve it with the vegetables.

VEGETABLES
AND SALADS

Mixed Mushroom Ragout

*These mushrooms are delicious
served hot or cold and can be made
up to two days in advance.*

INGREDIENTS

Serves 4

1 small onion, finely chopped
1 garlic clove, crushed
5ml/1 tsp coriander seeds, crushed
30ml/2 tbsp red wine vinegar
15ml/1 tbsp soy sauce
15ml/1 tbsp dry sherry
10ml/2 tsp tomato purée
10ml/2 tsp soft light brown sugar
75ml/5 tbsp hot vegetable stock
115g/4oz baby button mushrooms
115g/4oz chestnut mushrooms, quartered
115g/4oz oyster mushrooms, sliced
salt and ground black pepper
sprig of fresh coriander, to garnish

1 Mix the onion, garlic, coriander
 seeds, red wine vinegar, soy
sauce, sherry, tomato purée, sugar
and stock in a large microwaveproof
bowl. Cover and microwave on
HIGH for 3 minutes, stirring once.
Uncover and microwave on HIGH
for a further 2–3 minutes, or until
the liquid has reduced by half.

2 Add the mushrooms, mixing
 well. Cover and microwave on
HIGH for 3–4 minutes, stirring
once, until tender.

3 Remove the mushrooms with
 a slotted spoon and transfer
them to a warmed serving dish.

4 Microwave the juices on
 HIGH for about 3–5 minutes,
or until reduced to about
75ml/5 tbsp. Season to taste with
salt and ground black pepper.

COOK'S TIP

If coriander is a favourite spice
of yours, then it is worth buying
a pepper mill and filling it with
coriander seeds. This way, you
can grind a little coriander into
all sorts of savoury dishes to add
a hint of exotic seasoning.

5 Allow to cool for 2–3 minutes,
 then pour over the
mushrooms. Serve hot or well
chilled, garnished with a sprig of
fresh coriander.

Spring Vegetable Medley

*A colourful, dazzling medley of fresh
and sweet young vegetables.*

INGREDIENTS

Serves 4

15ml/1 tbsp peanut oil

1 garlic clove, sliced

2.5cm/1in piece fresh ginger root,
   finely chopped

115g/4oz baby carrots

115g/4oz patty pan squash

115g/4oz baby sweetcorn

115g/4oz French beans, topped and tailed

115g/4oz sugar snap peas, topped
   and tailed

115g/4oz young asparagus, cut into
   7.5cm/3in pieces

8 spring onions, trimmed and cut into
   5cm/2in pieces

115g/4oz cherry tomatoes

For the dressing

juice of 2 limes

15ml/1 tbsp runny honey

15ml/1 tbsp soy sauce

5ml/1 tsp sesame oil

1 Place the peanut oil in a large
microwaveproof bowl.

2 Add the garlic and ginger, and
microwave on HIGH for
30 seconds.

3 Stir in the carrots, patty pan
squash, sweetcorn and beans.
Cover and microwave on HIGH
for 5 minutes, stirring halfway
through cooking.

4 Add the sugar snap peas,
asparagus, spring onions and
cherry tomatoes. Cover and
microwave on HIGH for 3–4
minutes, stirring halfway through
cooking.

5 Mix the dressing ingredients
together and add to the bowl.

6 Stir well, then cover again and
microwave on HIGH for 1–2
minutes, or until the vegetables are
just tender but still crisp.

Middle-Eastern Vegetable Stew

A spiced dish of mixed vegetables makes a delicious and filling vegetarian main course. Children may prefer less chilli.

INGREDIENTS

Serves 4-6

45ml/3 tbsp vegetable stock
1 green pepper, seeded and sliced
2 courgettes, sliced
2 carrots, sliced
2 celery sticks, sliced
2 potatoes, diced
400g/14oz can chopped tomatoes
5ml/1 tsp chilli powder
30ml/2 tbsp chopped fresh mint
15ml/1 tbsp ground cumin
400g/14oz can chick-peas, drained
salt and ground black pepper
mint sprigs, to garnish

1 Place the vegetable stock in a large microwaveproof casserole with the sliced pepper, courgettes, carrots and celery. Cover and microwave on HIGH for 2 minutes.

COOK'S TIP

Chick-peas are traditional in this type of Middle-Eastern dish, but if you prefer, red kidney or haricot beans can be used instead.

2 Add the potatoes, tomatoes, chilli powder, fresh mint, ground cumin and chick-peas to the vegetable dish and stir well. Cover the dish and microwave on HIGH for 15–20 minutes, remembering to stir twice during the cooking time.

3 Leave to stand, covered, for 5 minutes, until all the vegetables are tender. Season to taste with salt and pepper and serve hot, garnished with mint leaves.

VARIATION

Other vegetables can be substituted for those in the recipe, just use whatever you have to hand – try swede, sweet potato or parsnips.

Potato, Leek and Tomato Bake

This simple dish is delicious for lunch or supper – a real winner with all the family. Select the best tomatoes you can for a good flavour; if this means using small fruit, then add one or two extra.

Serves 4

675g/1½lb potatoes

2 leeks, trimmed and sliced

3 large tomatoes, sliced

a few fresh rosemary sprigs, crushed

1 garlic clove, crushed

300ml/½ pint/1¼ cups hot vegetable stock

15ml/1 tbsp olive oil

salt and ground black pepper

1 Scrub and thinly slice the potatoes. Then layer them with the leeks and tomatoes in a 1.2 litre/2 pint/5 cup microwave-proof dish that is suitable for grilling, scattering some rosemary between the layers and ending with a layer of potatoes.

2 Add the garlic to the stock, stir in salt and pepper to taste and pour over the vegetables. Brush the top layer of potatoes with the olive oil.

3 Cover and microwave on HIGH for 15–18 minutes or until the potatoes are tender. Leave to stand for 5 minutes, then remove the cover. Brown under a preheated hot grill, if liked, and serve hot.

COMBINATION MICROWAVE

This recipe is suitable for cooking in a combination microwave. Follow the oven manufacturer's timing guide for good results.

Summer Vegetable Braise

Tender, young vegetables are ideal for speedy cooking methods and the microwave ensures they stay tender-crisp.

INGREDIENTS

Serves 4

175g/6oz/2½ cups baby carrots

175g/6oz/2 cups sugar snap peas or mangetouts

115g/4oz/1¼ cups baby corn

90ml/6 tbsp vegetable stock

10ml/2 tsp lime juice

salt and black pepper

chopped fresh parsley and snipped fresh chives, to garnish

1 Place the carrots, peas and baby corn in a large microwaveproof bowl with the vegetable stock and lime juice.

2 Cover and microwave on HIGH for 7–9 minutes, stirring halfway through cooking, until the vegetables are just tender.

3 Season the vegetables to taste with salt and pepper, then stir in the chopped fresh parsley and snipped chives. Microwave on HIGH for 1 minute, until the vegetables are well flavoured with the herbs. Then serve at once.

VARIATION

To make a more substantial dish, tip the cooked vegetables into a gratin dish and top with a mixture of grated cheese and breadcrumbs, then grill until golden and bubbling.

COOK'S TIP

You can make this dish in the winter too, but cut larger, tougher vegetables into chunks and cook them for slightly longer.

Broccoli and Chestnut Terrine

Served hot or cold, this versatile terrine is equally suitable for a dinner party as for a picnic.

INGREDIENTS

Serves 4–6

450g/1lb broccoli, cut into small florets
60ml/4 tbsp water
225g/8oz cooked chestnuts,
    roughly chopped
50g/2oz/1 cup fresh wholemeal
    breadcrumbs
60ml/4 tbsp low-fat natural yogurt
30ml/2 tbsp freshly grated
    Parmesan cheese
salt and ground black pepper
grated nutmeg
2 eggs, beaten

1 Line a 900g/2lb glass loaf dish with clear film.

2 Place the broccoli in a microwaveproof bowl with the water. Cover and microwave on HIGH for 6 minutes, stirring once. Drain well. Reserve a quarter of the smallest florets and chop the rest finely.

3 Mix together the chestnuts, breadcrumbs, yogurt and Parmesan, adding seasoning and grated nutmeg to taste.

4 Fold in the chopped broccoli, reserved small florets and the beaten eggs.

5 Spoon the broccoli mixture into the prepared dish. Cover and microwave on HIGH for 3 minutes. Reduce the power setting to MEDIUM and microwave for a further 5–8 minutes, or until just firm and set. Leave to stand for 5 minutes.

6 Turn out the terrine on to a flat plate or tray. Serve cut into thick slices. New potatoes and salad are suitable accompaniments.

Salade Niçoise

INGREDIENTS

Serves 4

90ml/6 tbsp olive oil

30ml/2 tbsp tarragon vinegar

5ml/1 tsp tarragon or Dijon mustard

1 small garlic clove, crushed

12 small new or salad potatoes

115g/4oz/1 cup French beans

3–4 Little Gem lettuces, roughly chopped

200g/7oz can tuna in oil, drained

6 anchovy fillets, halved lengthways

12 black olives, stoned

4 tomatoes, chopped

4 spring onions, finely chopped

10ml/2 tsp capers

30ml/2 tbsp pine nuts

2 hard-boiled eggs, chopped

salt and ground black pepper

1 Mix the oil, vinegar, mustard, garlic and seasoning in a large salad bowl.

2 Place the potatoes in a microwaveproof bowl with 30ml/2 tbsp water. Cover and microwave on HIGH for 6–8 minutes, stirring halfway through cooking. Leave to stand, covered, for 3 minutes, then drain thoroughly.

3 Place the beans in a microwaveproof bowl with 15ml/1 tbsp water. Cover and microwave on HIGH for 3 minutes, stirring once. Leave to stand, covered, for 2 minutes, then drain.

4 Mix the potatoes and beans with the lettuce, tuna, anchovies, olives, tomatoes, spring onions and capers.

5 Just before serving, place the pine nuts on a small microwaveproof plate and microwave on HIGH for 3–4 minutes, stirring once every minute, until brown.

6 Sprinkle the pine nuts over the salad while still hot, add the eggs and toss all the ingredients together well. Serve with chunks of hot crusty bread.

DESSERTS

Plum and Walnut Crumble

Walnuts add a lovely crunch to the fruit layer in this crumble – almonds would be equally good.

INGREDIENTS

Serves 4–6

1kg/2¼lb plums, halved and stoned

75g/3oz/¾ cup walnut pieces, toasted

175g/6oz/scant 1 cup demerara sugar

75g/3oz/6 tbsp butter or hard
   margarine, diced

175g/6oz/1½ cups plain flour

1 Butter a 1.2 litre/2 pint/5 cup microwaveproof dish that is suitable for grilling. Put the plums in the dish, then stir in the nuts and half the demerara sugar.

2 Rub the butter or margarine into the flour until the mixture resembles coarse crumbs. Stir in the remaining sugar and continue to rub in the fat until fine crumbs are formed.

3 Cover the fruit with the crumb mixture and press it down lightly. Microwave the crumble on HIGH for 14–16 minutes, rotating the dish three times during cooking. Brown the top under a preheated hot grill until golden and crisp, if liked, before serving.

VARIATION

To make Oat and Cinnamon Crumble, substitute rolled oats for half the flour in the crumble mixture and add 2.5–5ml/½–1 tsp ground cinnamon.

COMBINATION MICROWAVE

This recipe is suitable for cooking in a combination microwave. Follow your oven manufacturer's timing guide for good results.

Gingerbread Upside-down Pudding

A proper pudding goes down well on a cold winter's day.

Serves 4–6

sunflower oil, for brushing

15ml/1 tbsp soft brown sugar

8 walnut halves

4 medium peaches, halved and stoned, or canned peach halves

For the base

130g/4½oz/½ cup wholemeal flour

2.5ml/½ tsp bicarbonate of soda

7.5ml/1½ tsp ground ginger

5ml/1 tsp ground cinnamon

115g/4oz/½ cup molasses sugar

1 egg

120ml/4fl oz/½ cup skimmed milk

50ml/2fl oz/¼ cup sunflower oil

1 For the topping, brush the base and sides of a 23cm/9in round deep microwaveproof dish with oil. Line the base with grease-proof paper, oil the paper then sprinkle the base with sugar.

2 Place a walnut half in each peach half, then arrange the peaches cut-side down in the dish.

3 For the base, sift together the flour, bicarbonate of soda, ginger and cinnamon, then stir in the sugar. Beat together the egg, milk and oil, then mix into the dry ingredients until smooth.

4 Pour the mixture evenly over the peaches and microwave on MEDIUM for 6–8 minutes, or until the mixture has shrunk away from the sides of the dish, but the surface still looks wet. Leave to stand for 5 minutes. Turn out into a serving plate. Serve hot with yogurt or custard.

Spiced Pears in Cider

INGREDIENTS

Serves 4

250ml/8fl oz/1 cup dry cider

thinly pared strip of lemon rind

1 cinnamon stick

30ml/2 tbsp soft brown sugar

4 firm pears

5ml/1 tsp arrowroot

15ml/1 tbsp water

ground cinnamon, to sprinkle

low-fat fromage frais, to serve

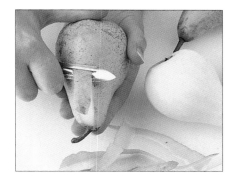

1 Place the cider, lemon rind, cinnamon stick and sugar in a microwaveproof bowl. Microwave on HIGH for 3–5 minutes until boiling, stirring frequently to dissolve the sugar. Meanwhile, peel the pears thinly, leaving them whole with the stems on.

2 Add the pears to the cider syrup. Spoon the syrup over the pears. Three-quarters cover the dish with clear film or with a lid. Microwave on HIGH for 5–6 minutes until the pears are just tender, turning and repositioning them in the bowl two or three times.

3 Carefully transfer the pears to another bowl using a slotted spoon. Microwave the cider syrup, uncovered, on HIGH for 15–17 minutes until it is reduced by half.

4 Mix the arrowroot with the water in a small bowl until smooth, then stir it into the syrup. Microwave on HIGH for 1 minute, stirring twice, until clear and thickened.

5 Pour the sauce over the pears and sprinkle with ground cinnamon. Leave to cool slightly, then serve warm with low-fat fromage frais.

VARIATIONS

Other fruits can be poached in this spicy liquid; try apples, peaches or nectarines. Cook the fruit whole or cut in half or quarters. The apples are best peeled before poaching, but you can cook the peaches and nectarines with their skins on.

C O O K ' S   T I P

Any variety of pear can be used, but it is best to choose firm pears, or they will break up easily – Conference are a good choice.

Honey Fruit Yogurt Ice

INGREDIENTS

Serves 4–6

2 dessert apples, peeled, cored and finely
    chopped
4 ripe bananas, roughly chopped
15ml/1 tbsp lemon juice
30ml/2 tbsp clear honey
250g/9oz/1 cup Greek-style yogurt
2.5ml/½ tsp ground cinnamon
crisp biscuits, flaked hazelnuts and
    banana slices, to serve

1 Place the apples in a small microwaveproof bowl, cover and microwave on HIGH for 2 minutes, stirring once. Allow to cool.

2 Place the bananas in a food processor or blender with the lemon juice, honey, yogurt and cinnamon. Process until smooth and creamy. Add the cooked apples and process briefly to mix.

3 Pour the mixture into a freezer container and freeze until almost solid. Spoon back into the food processor and process again until smooth.

4 Return to the freezer until firm. Allow to soften at room temperature for 15 minutes, then serve in scoops, with crisp biscuits, flaked hazelnuts and banana slices.

Autumn Pudding

INGREDIENTS

Serves 6

10 slices bread, at least one day old
1 Bramley cooking apple, peeled, cored
    and sliced
225g/8oz ripe red plums, halved
    and stoned
225g/8oz blackberries
60ml/4 tbsp water
75g/3oz/6 tbsp caster sugar

1 Remove the crusts from the bread and stamp out a 7.5cm/ 3in round from one slice. Cut the remaining bread in half.

2 Place the bread round in the base of a 1.2 litre/2 pint/5 cup pudding basin, then overlap the fingers around the sides, saving some for the top.

3 Mix the apple, plums, black-berries, water and caster sugar in a microwaveproof bowl. Cover and microwave on HIGH for 7–8 minutes or until the sugar dissolves, the juices begin to flow and the fruit softens. Stir twice during cooking.

4 Reserve the juice and spoon the fruit into the bread-lined basin. Top with the reserved bread, then spoon over the reserved fruit juices.

5 Cover the basin with a saucer and place weights on top. Chill the pudding overnight. Turn out on to a serving plate and serve with low-fat yogurt or fromage frais.

Tangerine Trifle

An unusual variation on a traditional trifle – of course, you can add a little alcohol if you wish.

Serves 4

5 trifle sponges, halved lengthways

30ml/2 tbsp apricot conserve

15-20 ratafia biscuits

142g/4¾oz packet tangerine jelly

300g/11oz can mandarin oranges, drained, juice reserved

600ml/1 pint/2½ cups prepared custard

whipped cream and shreds of orange rind, to decorate

caster sugar, for sprinkling

1 Spread the halved sponge cakes with apricot conserve and arrange them in the base of a deep serving bowl or glass dish. Sprinkle over the ratafia biscuits.

2 Break up the jelly into a microwaveproof jug, add the juice from the canned mandarins and microwave on HIGH for 2 minutes, then stir to dissolve the jelly.

3 Make up the jelly to 600ml/1 pint/2½ cups with ice-cold water, stir well and leave to cool for up to 30 minutes. Scatter the mandarin oranges over the cakes and ratafias.

4 Pour the jelly over the mandarin oranges, cake and ratafias and chill for 1 hour, or until the jelly has set.

5 Pour the custard over the trifle and chill again. When ready to serve, pipe the whipped cream over the custard. Place the orange rind shreds in a sieve and rinse under cold water, then sprinkle them with caster sugar and use to decorate the trifle.

Baked Apples with Apricots

INGREDIENTS

Serves 6

75g/3oz/½ cup ready-to-eat dried
   apricots, chopped
50g/2oz/½ cup walnuts, chopped
5ml/1 tsp grated lemon rind
2.5ml/½ tsp ground cinnamon
80g/3½oz/½ cup soft light brown sugar
15g/1oz/2 tbsp butter, at
   room temperature
6 large eating apples
15ml/1 tbsp melted butter
120ml/4fl oz/½ cup water or fruit juice

1 Place the apricots, walnuts, lemon rind and cinnamon in a bowl. Add the sugar and butter and stir until thoroughly mixed.

2 Core the apples, without cutting all the way through to the base. Peel the top of each apple and slightly widen the top of each opening to make plenty of room for the filling.

3 Spoon the filling into the apples, packing it down lightly into their middles.

4 Place the stuffed apples in a microwaveproof dish large enough to hold them neatly side by side.

5 Brush the apples with the melted butter and pour the water or fruit juice around them. Microwave on HIGH for 9–10 minutes, rearranging halfway through cooking, until the apples are tender. Serve hot.

BAKING

Sage Soda Bread

This wonderful loaf, quite unlike bread made with yeast, has a velvety texture and a powerful sage aroma.

INGREDIENTS

Makes 1 loaf

350g/12oz/3 cups wholemeal flour

115g/4oz/1 cup strong white flour

5ml/1 tsp salt

10ml/2 tsp bicarbonate of soda

30ml/2 tbsp shredded fresh sage

300–450ml/½–¾ pint/1¼–1¾ cups buttermilk

1 Sift the dry ingredients into a large mixing bowl.

2 Stir in the sage and add enough buttermilk to make a soft dough.

COOK'S TIP

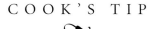

As an alternative to the sage, try using finely chopped rosemary.

3 Shape the dough into a round loaf and place on a lightly oiled plate and cut a deep cross in the top.

4 Microwave on MEDIUM for 5 minutes, give the plate a half turn and microwave on HIGH for a further 3 minutes. Brown the top under a preheated hot grill, if liked. Allow to stand for 10 minutes, then transfer to a wire rack to cool. Best eaten on the day of making.

COMBINATION MICROWAVE

This recipe is suitable for cooking in a combination microwave. Follow the oven manufacturer's timing guide for good results.

Cheese and Marjoram Scones

INGREDIENTS

Makes 18

115g/4oz/1 cup wholemeal flour

115g/4oz/1 cup self-raising flour

pinch of salt

40g/1½oz/3 tbsp butter

1.5ml/¼ tsp dry mustard

10ml/2 tsp dried marjoram

50–75g/2–3oz/½–⅔ cup Cheddar cheese,
   finely grated

about 125ml/4fl oz/½ cup milk

50g/2oz/⅓ cup pecans or walnuts,
   chopped

1 Sift the two types of flour into a bowl and add the salt. Cut the butter into small pieces, and rub it into the flour until the mixture resembles fine bread-crumbs.

2 Add the mustard, marjoram and grated cheese, then mix in sufficient milk to make a soft dough. Knead the dough lightly.

3 Roll out the dough on a floured surface to about a 2cm/¾in thickness and cut out about 18 scones using a 5cm/2in square cutter.

4 Brush the scones with a little milk and sprinkle the chopped pecans or walnuts over the top. Place the scones on a piece of non-stick parchment in the microwave, spacing them well apart. Microwave on HIGH for 3–3½ minutes, repositioning the scones twice during cooking.

5 Insert a skewer into the centre of each scone: if it comes out clean, the scone is cooked. Return any uncooked scones to the microwave and microwave on HIGH for a further 30 seconds. Brown under a preheated hot grill until golden, if liked. Serve warm, split and buttered.

VARIATION

For Herb and Mustard Scones, use 30ml/2 tbsp chopped fresh parsley or chives instead of the dried marjoram and 5ml/1 tsp Dijon mustard instead of the dry mustard. Substitute 50g/2oz chopped pistachio nuts for the pecans or walnuts.

Oat Florentines

These irresistible "bakes" make the best of familiar flapjacks and old-fashioned, chocolate-coated florentine biscuits.

INGREDIENTS

Makes 16

75g/3oz/6 tbsp butter

45ml/3 tbsp/¼ cup golden syrup

115g/4oz/1¼ cups rolled oats

25g/1oz/2 tbsp soft brown sugar

25g/1oz/2 tbsp chopped mixed
candied peel

25g/1oz/2 tbsp glacé cherries,
coarsely chopped

25g/1oz/¼ cup hazelnuts,
coarsely chopped

115g/4oz/⅔ cup plain chocolate

1 Lightly grease a 20cm/8in square microwaveproof shallow dish and line the base with a sheet of rice paper.

2 Place the butter and golden syrup in a microwaveproof bowl and microwave on HIGH for 1½ minutes to melt. Stir well.

3 Add the oats, sugar, peel, cherries and hazelnuts, mixing well to blend.

COOK'S TIP

Rice paper is used for cooking in traditional recipes as well as in microwave methods. It prevents mixtures, such as this sweet oat base, from sticking by cooking on to them. When cooked, the rice paper can be eaten with the biscuits or other items.

4 Spoon the mixture into the dish and level the surface with the back of a spoon. Microwave on MEDIUM HIGH for 6 minutes, giving the dish a half turn every 2 minutes. Allow to cool slightly then cut into 16 fingers and place on a wire rack to cool.

5 Break the chocolate into pieces and place in a microwaveproof bowl. Microwave on HIGH for 2–3 minutes, stirring twice, until melted and smooth. Spread over the tops of the florentines and mark in a zig-zag pattern with the prongs of a fork. Leave to set.

Blueberry Crumble Tea Bread

Makes 8 pieces

50g/2oz/4 tbsp butter or margarine, at
   room temperature

175g/6oz/²⁄₃ cup caster sugar

1 egg, at room temperature

120ml/4fl oz/¹⁄₂ cup milk

225g/8oz/2 cups plain flour

10ml/2 tsp baking powder

2.5ml/¹⁄₂ tsp salt

275g/10oz fresh blueberries or bilberries

For the topping

115g/4oz sugar

40g/1¹⁄₂oz/6 tbsp plain flour

2.5ml/¹⁄₂ tsp ground cinnamon

50g/2oz/4 tbsp butter, cut in pieces

1   Grease a 23 x 18cm/9 x 7in microwaveproof dish.

2   Cream the butter or margarine with the caster sugar until light and fluffy. Beat in the egg, then mix in the milk.

3   Sift over the flour, baking powder and salt and stir just enough to blend the ingredients.

4   Add the berries and stir them in lightly. Spoon the mixture into the prepared dish.

5   For the topping, place the sugar, flour, ground cinnamon and butter in a mixing bowl. Rub in the butter until the mixture resembles coarse breadcrumbs; alternatively, cut in the butter with a pastry blender.

6   Sprinkle the topping over the mixture in the baking dish. Microwave on MEDIUM for 12 minutes, rotating the dish twice during cooking. Brown under a preheated hot grill, if liked. Leave to stand for 5 minutes. Serve warm or cold.

Maple and Banana Tea Bread

Serves 8–10

115g/4oz/1 cup wholemeal flour

5ml/1 tsp bicarbonate of soda

2 bananas, mashed

60ml/4 tbsp natural yogurt

50g/2oz/4 tbsp soft light brown sugar

65g/2½oz/5 tbsp unsalted butter

1 egg, beaten

30ml/2 tbsp maple syrup

75g/3oz/½ cup dried dates,
    coarsely chopped

icing sugar, to dust

1 Lightly grease a 23 x 13cm/ 9 x 5in microwaveproof loaf dish and line the base with grease-proof paper.

2 Sift the wholemeal flour with the bicarbonate of soda, adding the bran left in the sieve.

3 Mix the bananas with the yogurt, brown sugar, butter, egg and syrup, blending well. Add the flour mixture and dates and mix into a smooth batter. Spoon the mixture evenly into the loaf dish and spread it out slightly.

4 To prevent the ends of the cake from over-cooking, wrap a 5cm/2in wide strip of smooth foil over each end of the dish. Place the dish on an inverted plate in the oven and microwave on MEDIUM for 10 minutes, giving the dish a quarter turn every 2½ minutes.

5 Increase the power setting to HIGH and microwave for a further 2 minutes. Remove the foil, give the dish a quarter turn and microwave for 1–3 minutes more, until the tea bread shrinks from the sides of the dish. Leave to stand for 10 minutes before turning out to cool on a wire rack.

6 Sift a light coating of icing sugar over the top of the cake before serving. Serve warm or cold.

Hot Chocolate Cake

This is wonderfully wicked, either hot as a pudding, to serve with a white chocolate sauce, or cold as a cake. The basic cake freezes well – thaw, then warm it in the microwave before serving.

Makes 10–12 slices
200g/7oz/1¾ cups self-raising
   wholemeal flour
25g/1oz/¼ cup cocoa powder
pinch of salt
175g/6oz/¾ cup soft margarine
175g/6oz/¾ cup soft light brown sugar
few drops vanilla essence
4 eggs
75g/3oz white chocolate, roughly chopped
chocolate leaves and curls, to decorate

For the white chocolate sauce
75g/3oz white chocolate
150ml/¼ pint/⅔ cup single cream
30–40ml/2–3 tbsp milk

1 Sift the flour, cocoa powder and salt into a bowl, adding the bran from the sieve.

2 Cream the margarine, sugar and vanilla essence together until light and fluffy, then gently beat in one egg.

3 Gradually stir in the remaining eggs, one at a time, alternately folding in some of the flour, until all the flour mixture is well blended in.

4 Stir in the white chocolate and spoon the mixture into a 675–900g/1½–2lb greased microwaveproof loaf dish. Shield each end of the dish with a small piece of smooth foil, shiny side in. Cover with clear film and microwave on HIGH for 8–9 minutes, giving the dish a quarter turn three or four times during cooking. Remove the clear film and foil for the last 1½ minutes of the cooking time. The cake is cooked when a skewer inserted in the centre comes out clean. Leave to stand while making the sauce.

5 Place the chocolate and cream for the sauce in a microwave-proof bowl and microwave on MEDIUM for 2–3 minutes, until the chocolate has melted. Add the milk and stir until cool.

6 Serve the cake sliced, in a pool of sauce, decorated with chocolate leaves and curls.

COMBINATION MICROWAVE

This recipe is suitable for cooking in a combination microwave. Follow your oven manufacturer's timing guide for good results.

Coconut Pyramids

Without the danger of using a conventional cooker, making a batch of these all-time favourites is an ideal wet-afternoon occupation for young children.

INGREDIENTS

Makes about 15

225g/8oz/1 cup unsweetened
   desiccated coconut
115g/4oz/½ cup caster sugar
2 egg whites
oil, for greasing

1 Mix together the desiccated coconut and sugar. Lightly whisk the egg whites. Fold enough egg white into the coconut to make a fairly firm mixture. You may not need quite all the egg whites.

2 Form the mixture into pyramid shapes by taking a teaspoonful and rolling it first into a ball. Flatten the base and press the top into a point. Arrange the pyramids on greaseproof paper, leaving space between them.

3 Microwave on HIGH for 2–3 minutes or until the pyramids are just firm, but still soft inside. Transfer to a baking sheet and place under a preheated hot grill to tinge the tops golden, if liked.

COOK'S TIP
~

To freeze biscuits, arrange in a single layer on a tray. When hard, pack in bags or boxes. Thaw for 1 hour before use.

4 Slide a palette knife under the pyramids to loosen them, and leave to cool before removing from the baking sheet.

COOKING AND
DEFROSTING
CHARTS

~

Cooking Fish and Shellfish

COD
steamed steaks and fillets

450g/1lb fillets
2 x 225g/8oz steaks
4 x 225g/8oz steaks

HIGH

Arrange fish fillets in a microwaveproof dish so that the thinner tail ends are to the centre. Fold in any flaps of skin on steaks and secure with wooden cocktail sticks. Dot with a little butter, sprinkle with seasoning and add a dash of lemon juice. Cover and microwave for 5–7 minutes for 450g/1lb fillets; 5 minutes for 2 x 225g/8oz steaks; and 8–9 minutes for 4 x 225g/8oz steaks, rearranging once halfway through cooking. Leave to stand, covered, for 3 minutes before serving.

FISH CAKES

4 x 75g/3oz

HIGH

Place in a shallow microwaveproof dish and brush with a little melted butter if liked. Microwave for 5 minutes, turning over once, halfway through cooking. Times refer to chilled or fresh fish cakes (thaw frozen fish cakes before cooking). Leave to stand for 2–3 minutes before serving. If liked, the fish cakes can be cooked in a preheated browning dish.

FISH FINGERS

2
4
6
8
12

HIGH

For best results cook in a preheated browning dish. Microwave for 1½ minutes for 2; 2 minutes for 4; 3 minutes for 6; 4 minutes for 8; and 5 minutes for 12 fish fingers, turning over once, halfway through cooking. Times refer to frozen fish fingers. Leave to stand for 1–2 minutes before serving.

FISH ROES

115g/4oz
225g/8oz

LOW

Rinse the fish roes and place in a microwaveproof dish with a large knob of butter and seasoning to taste. Cover and microwave for 4–4½ minutes for 115g/4oz; and 6–8 minutes for 225g/8oz fish roes, stirring once halfway through cooking. Leave to stand, covered, for 2 minutes before serving.

HADDOCK
steamed steaks and fillets

450g/1lb fillets
2 x 225g/8oz steaks
4 x 225g/8oz steaks

HIGH

Arrange the fish fillets in a microwaveproof dish so that the thinner tail ends are to the centre. Fold in any flaps of skin on steaks and secure with wooden cocktail sticks. Dot with a little butter, sprinkle with seasoning and add a dash of lemon juice. Cover and microwave for 5–7 minutes for 450g/1lb fillets; 5 minutes for 2 x 225g/8oz steaks; and 8–9 minutes for 4 x 225g/8oz steaks, rearranging once halfway through cooking. Leave to stand, covered, for 3 minutes before serving.

HALIBUT
steaks

2 x 225g/8oz steaks

HIGH

Fold in any flaps of skin and secure with wooden cocktail sticks. Place in a shallow microwaveproof dish and dot with a little butter. Season with salt, pepper and lemon juice. Cover and microwave for 4–5 minutes. Leave to stand, covered, for 2–3 minutes before serving.

HERRING
fresh whole

per 450g/1lb

HIGH

Remove heads and clean and gut before cooking. Slash the skin in several places to prevent bursting during cooking. Place in a shallow microwave-proof dish and season to taste. Shield the tail ends of the fish if liked. Cover with greaseproof paper and microwave for 3–4 minutes per 450g/1lb, turning over once halfway through cooking. Leave to stand, covered, for 2–3 minutes before serving.

KIPPERS
fillets

2
4
8

HIGH

If buying whole fish then remove heads and tails. Place skin-side down in a shallow microwaveproof cooking dish. Cover loosely and microwave for 1–2 minutes for 2 fillets; 3–4 minutes for 4 fillets; and 6–7 minutes for 8 fillets, rearranging once halfway through cooking. Leave to stand, covered, for 2–3 minutes before serving.

LOBSTER
to reheat cooked whole lobster and tails

450g/1lb whole
450g/1lb tails

HIGH

Place in a shallow microwaveproof dish and cover loosely. Microwave for 6–8 minutes for 450g/1lb whole; and 5–6 minutes for 450g/1lb tails, turning over once halfway through cooking. Leave to stand, covered, for 5 minutes before serving.

MACKEREL fresh whole	per 450g/1lb	HIGH	Remove heads and clean and gut before cooking. Slash the skin in several places to prevent bursting during cooking. Place in a shallow microwave-proof dish and season to taste. Shield the tail ends of the fish if liked. Cover with greaseproof paper and microwave for 3–4 minutes per 450g/1lb, turning over once halfway through cooking. Leave to stand, covered, for 2–3 minutes before serving.
MUSSELS fresh steamed	675g/1½lb	HIGH	Sort the mussels and scrub thoroughly with cold running water. Place in a microwaveproof dish with 75ml/5 tbsp water, fish stock or dry white wine. Cover loosely and microwave for 5 minutes, stirring once halfway through cooking. Remove with a slotted spoon, discarding any mussels that do not open. Thicken the cooking juices with a little beurre manié, (butter and flour paste), if liked, to serve with the mussels.
PLAICE steamed fillets	450g/1lb fillets	HIGH	Arrange fish fillets in a microwaveproof dish so that the thinner tail ends are to the centre of the dish. Dot with a little butter, sprinkle with seasoning and add a dash of lemon juice. Cover and microwave for 4–6 minutes, rearranging once halfway through cooking. Leave to stand, covered, for 3 minutes before serving.
RED OR GREY MULLET fresh whole	2 x 250g/9oz 4 x 250g/9oz	HIGH	Clean and gut before cooking. Place in a shallow microwaveproof dish and slash the skin in several places to prevent bursting during cooking. Cover and microwave for 4–5 minutes for 2 x 250g/9oz mullet; and 8–9 minutes for 4 x 250g/9oz mullet, turning over once halfway through cooking. Leave to stand, covered, for 5 minutes before serving.
SALMON steamed steaks	2 x 225g/8oz 4 x 225g/8oz	HIGH	Place in a shallow microwaveproof dish so that the narrow ends are to the centre of the dish. Dot with butter and sprinkle with lemon juice and salt and pepper. Cover with greaseproof paper and microwave for 2½–3 minutes for 2 x 225g/8oz steaks; and 4½–5¾ minutes for 4 x 225g/8oz steaks, turning over once halfway through cooking. Leave to stand, covered, for 5 minutes before serving.
	4 x 175g/6oz steaks	MEDIUM	Prepare and cook as above but use MEDIUM power and allow 10½–11½ minutes.
whole salmon and salmon trout	450g/1lb 900g/2lb 1.5kg/3–3½lb 1.75kg/4–4½lb	HIGH	Remove the head if liked. Slash or prick the skin in several places to prevent bursting during cooking. Place in a microwaveproof dish with 150ml/¼ pint/⅔ cup boiling water and a dash of lemon juice. Cover and microwave for 4½–5 minutes for a 450g/1lb fish, 8½–10½ minutes for a 900g/2lb fish; 11–14½ minutes for a 1.5kg/3–3½lb fish; and 14½–18½ minutes for a 1.75kg/4–4½lb fish, rotating 3 times during cooking. Leave to stand, covered, for 5 minutes before serving.
SCALLOPS steamed fresh	450g/1lb	MEDIUM	Remove from their shells. Place in a shallow microwaveproof dish and cover with absorbent kitchen paper. Microwave for 8–12 minutes, rearranging once, halfway through cooking. Leave to stand, covered, for 3 minutes before serving.
SHRIMPS AND PRAWNS to boil	450g/1lb 900g/2lb	HIGH	Rinse and place in a microwaveproof dish with 600ml/1 pint/2½ cups water, a dash of vinegar or lemon juice and a bay leaf if liked. Cover and microwave for 6–8 minutes for 450g/1lb; 8–10 minutes for 900g/2lb, stirring once halfway through cooking. Leave to stand, covered, for 3 minutes before draining and shelling.

SOLE steamed fillets	450g/1lb	HIGH	Arrange fish fillets in a microwaveproof dish so that the thinner tail ends are to the centre of the dish. Dot with a little butter, season and add a dash of lemon juice. Cover and microwave for 4–6 minutes, rearranging once half-way through cooking. Leave to stand, covered, for 3 minutes before serving.
SMOKED **HADDOCK** steamed fillets	450g/1lb	HIGH	Arrange fish fillets in a microwaveproof dish so that the thinner tail ends are to the centre of the dish. Dot with butter, sprinkle with seasoning and add a dash of lemon juice. Cover and microwave for 5–6 minutes, rearranging once halfway through cooking. Leave the fish to stand, covered, for 3 minutes before serving.
poached fillets	450g/1lb	HIGH	Place the fillets in a shallow microwaveproof dish with the thinner tail ends to the centre. Pour over 120ml/4fl oz/½ cup milk, dot with a little butter and season to taste. Cover and microwave for 5–6 minutes, rearranging once halfway through cooking. Leave to stand, covered, for 3 minutes before serving.
TROUT whole	2 x 250g/9oz 4 x 250g/9oz	HIGH	Clean and gut before cooking. Place in a shallow microwaveproof dish. Slash the skin in several places to prevent bursting during cooking. Dot with butter if liked and season to taste. Cover and microwave for 4–5 minutes for 2 x 250g/9oz trout; and 8–9 minutes for 4 x 250g/9oz trout, turning over once halfway through cooking. Leave the fish to stand, covered, for 5 minutes before serving.
WHITING steamed fillets	450g/1lb	HIGH	Arrange fish fillets in a microwaveproof dish so that the thinner tail ends are to the centre of the dish. Dot with a little butter, sprinkle with seasoning and add a dash or two of lemon juice. Cover and microwave for 4–6 minutes, rearranging once halfway through cooking. Leave to stand, covered, for 3 minutes before serving.

Cooking Poultry and Game

CHICKEN			
whole roast fresh chicken	1kg/2¼lb 1.5kg/3–3½lb 1.75kg/4–4½lb	HIGH	Rinse, dry and truss the chicken into a neat shape. Season and calculate the cooking time after weighing (and stuffing). Cook breast-side down for half of the cooking time and breast-side up for the remaining cooking time. Brush with a browning agent if liked and shield the wing tips with foil if necessary. Microwave for 12–16 minutes for a 1kg/2¼lb chicken; 18–24 minutes for a 1.5kg/3–3½lb chicken; 25–36 minutes for a 1.75kg/4–4½lb chicken. Cover with foil and leave to stand for 10–15 minutes before carving.
portions	1 x 225g/8oz portion 2 x 225g/8oz portions 4 x 225g/8oz portions	HIGH	Prick with a fork and brush with a browning agent if liked. Alternatively, crisp and brown under a preheated hot grill after cooking. Cover with buttered greaseproof paper to cook. Microwave for 5–7 minutes for 225g/8oz portion; 10–12 minutes for 2 x 225g/8oz portions; 18–24 minutes for 4 x 225g/8oz portions. Leave to stand, covered, for 5–10 minutes before serving.
drumsticks	2 4 8	HIGH	Prick with a fork and brush with a browning agent if liked. Alternatively, crisp and brown under a preheated hot grill after cooking. Cover with buttered greaseproof paper to cook. Microwave for 3–5 minutes for 2 drumsticks; 8–9 minutes for 4 drumsticks; 16–19 minutes for 8 drumsticks. Leave to stand, covered, for 5–10 minutes before serving.
thighs	8	HIGH	Prick with a fork and brush with a browning agent if liked. Alternatively, crisp and brown under a preheated hot grill after cooking. Cover with buttered greaseproof paper to cook. Microwave 8 thighs for 17–20 minutes. Leave to stand, covered, for 5–10 minutes before serving.
breasts	2 4	HIGH	Prick with a fork and brush with a browning agent if liked. Alternatively, crisp and brown under a preheated hot grill after cooking. Cover with buttered greaseproof paper to cook. Microwave for 2–3 minutes for 2 breasts; 3½–4 minutes for 4 breasts. Leave to stand, covered, for 5–10 minutes before serving.
livers, fresh or thawed frozen	225g/8oz 450g/1lb	HIGH	Rinse well and prick to prevent bursting during cooking. Place in a microwaveproof dish with a knob of butter. Cover loosely and microwave for 2–3 minutes for 225g/8oz; and 5–6 minutes for 450g/1lb, stirring twice during cooking. Leave to stand for 2 minutes before serving or using.
DUCK			
whole roast fresh duck	1.75kg/4–4½lb 2.25kg/5–5¼lb per 450g/1lb	HIGH	Rinse, dry and truss the duck into a neat shape, securing any tail-end flaps of skin to the main body. Prick thoroughly and place on a rack or upturned saucer in a microwaveproof dish for cooking. Cook breast-side down for half of the cooking time, and breast-side up for the remaining cooking time. Microwave for 28–32 minutes for a 1.75kg/4–4½lb duck; 35–40 minutes for a 2.25kg/5–5¼lb duck; or calculate times at 7–8 minutes per 450g/1lb. Drain away excess fat 3 times during cooking and shield tips, tail end and legs with foil if necessary. Cover with foil and leave to stand for 10–15 minutes before serving. Crisp the skin under a preheated hot grill if liked.
GAME BIRDS			
whole roast	1 x 450g/1lb 2 x 450g/1lb 1 x 900g/2lb 2 x 900g/2lb	HIGH	Rinse, dry and truss the birds into a neat shape. Brush with a browning agent if liked. Cover with greaseproof paper to cook. Microwave for 9–10 minutes for 450g/1lb bird; 18–22 minutes for 2 x 450g/1lb birds; 20–22 minutes for 900g/2lb bird; and 35–40 minutes for 2 x 900g/2lb birds, turning over twice during cooking. Leave to stand, covered, for 5 minutes before serving.

TURKEY

whole roast fresh	2.75kg/6lb 4kg/9lb 5.5kg/12lb larger birds over 5.5kg/12lb *per* *450g/1lb*	HIGH	Rinse, dry and stuff the turkey if liked. Truss into a neat shape and weigh to calculate the cooking time. Brush with melted butter or browning agent if liked. Divide the cooking time into quarters and cook breast-side down for the first quarter, on one side for the second quarter, on the remaining side for the third quarter and breast-side up for the final quarter. Shield any parts that start to cook faster than others with small strips of foil. Microwave for 42 minutes for a 2.75kg/6lb bird; 63 minutes for a 4kg/9lb bird; 84 minutes for a 5.5kg/12lb bird; or allow 7 minutes per 450g/1lb for larger birds. When cooked, cover with foil and leave to stand for 10–25 minutes (depending upon size of bird) before carving.
drumsticks	2 x 350g/12oz	HIGH *then* MEDIUM	Place on a roasting rack, meaty sections downwards. Baste with a browning agent if liked. Cover and microwave on HIGH for 5 minutes, then on MEDIUM for 13–15 minutes, turning once. Leave to stand, covered, for 5 minutes before serving.
breasts	2 x 225g/8oz breasts 4 x 225g/8oz breasts	MEDIUM	Beat out flat if preferred and place in a shallow dish. Baste with browning agent if liked. Microwave for 8–10 minutes for 2 x 225g/8oz breasts; and 16–18 minutes for 4 x 225g/8oz breasts, turning over once. Leave to stand for 2–3 minutes before serving.

Cooking Meat

BACON back and streaky rashers	4 rashers 450g/1lb	HIGH	Place small quantities between sheets of kitchen paper, larger quantities on a plate or microwaveproof bacon rack covered with kitchen paper. Microwave for 3½–4 minutes for 4 rashers; and 12–14 minutes for 450g/1lb, turning over once. Leave to stand for 1–2 minutes before serving.
joint	900g/2lb joint	HIGH	Remove any skin and score the fat into a diamond pattern. Sprinkle with a little brown sugar and stud with cloves if liked. Place on a microwaveproof roasting rack or upturned saucer in a dish. Microwave for 20–24 minutes, rotating the dish twice. Leave to stand, covered with foil, for 10–15 minutes before serving.
BEEF roast joint	per 450g/1lb	HIGH *then* MEDIUM	Ideally place the joint on a microwaveproof roasting rack or upturned saucer inside a roasting bag. Calculate the cooking time according to weight and microwave on HIGH for the first 5 minutes then on MEDIUM for the remaining time. Turn the joint over halfway through the cooking time.

per 450g/1lb

topside or sirloin (boned and rolled)

rare	8–9 minutes
medium	11–12 minutes
well done	15–16 minutes

forerib or back rib (on the bone)

rare	7–8 minutes
medium	13–14 minutes
well done	15 minutes

forerib or back rib (boned and rolled)

rare	11–12 minutes
medium	13–14 minutes
well done	15–16 minutes

Cover with foil after cooking and leave to stand for 10–15 minutes before carving.

minced beef	450g/1lb	HIGH	Place in a microwaveproof dish, cover and microwave for 10–12 minutes, breaking up and stirring twice.
hamburgers	1 x 115g/4oz 2 x 115g/4oz 3 x 115g/4oz 4 x 115g/4oz	HIGH	Ideally cook in a preheated browning dish. If this isn't possible then cook on a roasting rack and increase the times slightly. Microwave for 2½–3 minutes for 1; 3½–4 minutes for 2; 4½–5 minutes for 3; and 5–5½ minutes for 4, turning over once halfway through the cooking time. Leave to stand for 2–3 minutes before serving.
meatloaf	450g/1lb loaf	HIGH	Place your favourite 450g/1lb seasoned beef mixture in a microwaveproof loaf dish, packing in firmly and levelling the surface. Microwave for 7 minutes, allow to stand for 5 minutes, then microwave for a further 5 minutes. Leave to stand, covered with foil, for 3 minutes before serving.
steaks	2 x 225g/8oz rump, sirloin or fillet steaks 4 x 225g/8oz rump, sirloin or fillet steaks	HIGH	Cook with or without the use of a browning dish. If cooking without, then brush with a browning agent if liked prior to cooking. Place in a lightly oiled microwaveproof dish and turn over halfway through the cooking time. Microwave for 5–5½ minutes for 2 x 225g/8oz steaks; and 7½–8½ minutes for 4 x 225g/8oz steaks. If using a browning dish then preheat first, add a little oil and brush to coat the base. Add the steaks, pressing down well. Turn the steaks over halfway through the cooking time. Microwave for 2¼–2½ minutes for 2 x 225g/8oz steaks; and 3½–4 minutes for 4 x 225g/8oz steaks. Leave to stand for 1–2 minutes before serving.

GAMMON			
braised steaks	4 x 115g/4oz steaks	HIGH	Remove the rind and scissor-snip the fat off the gammon steaks. Place in a large shallow microwaveproof dish. Add 150ml/¼ pint/⅔ cup wine, cider or fruit juice (and marinate for 1 hour if liked). Microwave for 4 minutes, rearranging once. Leave to stand, covered, for 5 minutes before serving.
raw joint	per 450g/1lb	HIGH	Place in a pierced roasting bag in a microwaveproof dish. Microwave for 12–14 minutes per 450g/1lb, turning over halfway through the cooking time. Cover with foil and leave to stand for 10 minutes before carving.

KIDNEYS			
fresh lamb's, pig's or ox	115g/4oz 225g/8oz 450g/1lb	HIGH	Halve and core the kidneys. Preheat a browning dish. Add 5ml/1 tsp oil and the kidneys. Microwave for 4 minutes for 115g/4oz; 6–8 minutes for 225g/8oz; and 12–15 minutes for 450g/1lb, turning and rearranging twice. Leave to stand, covered, for 3 minutes before serving.

LAMB			
roast joint	per 450g/1lb	HIGH *then* MEDIUM	Place the joint on a microwaveproof roasting rack or upturned saucer inside a dish and shield any thin or vulnerable areas with a little foil. Calculate the cooking time according to weight and microwave on HIGH for the first 5 minutes, then on MEDIUM for the remaining time. Turn the joint over halfway through the cooking time.

per 450g/1lb

leg joint with bone	
rare	8–10 minutes
medium	10–12 minutes
well done	12–14 minutes
boned leg joints	
rare	10–12 minutes
medium	13–15 minutes
well done	16–18 minutes
shoulder joints	
rare	7–9 minutes
medium	9–11 minutes
well done	11–13 minutes

chops and steaks	2 loin chops 4 loin chops 2 chump chops 4 chump chops	HIGH	Brush with a browning agent if liked, or cook in a browning dish. Microwave for 6–7 minutes for 2 loin chops; 8–9 minutes for 4 loin chops; 6–8 minutes for 2 chump chops; and 8–10 minutes for 4 chump chops, turning over halfway through the cooking time. Leave to stand for 2–3 minutes before serving.
rack	1.2kg/2–2½lb rack with 7 ribs	HIGH	Chop rack in half and place both pieces together, bones interleaved guard-of-honour style, then tie in place. Place on a microwaveproof roasting rack. Microwave for 12 minutes for rare; 13 minutes for medium; and 14½–15 minutes for well-done lamb, rotating the dish every 3 minutes. Cover with foil and leave to stand for 10 minutes before carving.

LIVER			
fresh lamb's liver	450g/1lb	HIGH	Preheat a browning dish. Add 15ml/1 tbsp oil and 15g/½oz/1 tbsp butter. Add sliced, washed and dried liver, pressing down well. Microwave for 1 minute, turn over and microwave for a further 4–5 minutes, rearranging once. Leave to stand for 2 minutes before serving.

PORK

roast joint	per 450g/1lb	HIGH *or* MEDIUM	Place the joint in a microwaveproof dish on a rack if possible. Times are given for roasting on HIGH or MEDIUM. Both methods work well but the latter tends to give a crisper crackling. Turn the joint over halfway through cooking. Brown and crisp under a preheated hot grill after cooking if liked and before the standing time. Calculate the cooking time according to weight and microwave for: *per 450g/1lb* loin, leg and hand joints on bone HIGH 8–9 minutes *or* MEDIUM 12–14 minutes loin and leg joints (boned) HIGH 8–10 minutes *or* MEDIUM 13–15 minutes Cover with foil after cooking and leave to stand for 10–20 minutes before carving.
chops	2 loin chops 4 loin chops 2 chump chops 4 chump chops	HIGH	Brush with a browning agent if liked, or cook in a browning dish. Microwave for 4–5 minutes for 2 loin chops; 6–8 minutes for 4 loin chops; 8–10 minutes for 2 chump chops; and 11–13 minutes for 4 chump chops, turning over once halfway through cooking. Leave to stand for 5 minutes before serving.
pork fillet or tenderloin	350g/12oz	HIGH *then* MEDIUM	Shield the narrow, thin ends of the fillet with a little foil. Place on a microwaveproof roasting rack or upturned saucer in a dish. Microwave on HIGH for 3 minutes, then on MEDIUM for 10–15 minutes, turning over once. Leave to stand, covered with foil, for 5–10 minutes before serving.
sausages standard 50g/2oz size	2 4 8	HIGH	Prick and place on a microwaveproof roasting rack in a dish if possible. Brush with a browning agent if liked or cook in a preheated browning dish. Microwave for 2½ minutes for 2; 4 minutes for 4; and 5 minutes for 8 sausages, turning over once halfway through the cooking time. Leave to stand for 2 minutes before serving.

VEAL

roast joint	per 450g/1lb	HIGH *or* MEDIUM	Place the joint on a microwaveproof rack or upturned saucer in a dish. Times are given for cooking on HIGH or MEDIUM. Both methods work well, but the latter is ideal for less-tender cuts or large joints. Calculate the cooking time according to weight and microwave for: *per 450g/1lb* HIGH 8½–9 minutes *or* MEDIUM 11–12 minutes Turn the joint over halfway through the cooking time. Cover with foil after cooking and leave to stand for 15–20 minutes before carving.

Beef and Mushroom Burgers.

Cooking Vegetables

ARTICHOKES globe	1 2 4	HIGH	Discard the tough, outer leaves. Snip the tops off the remaining leaves and trim the stems to the base. Wash and stand upright in a microwaveproof bowl. Pour over the water and lemon juice for 90ml/6 tbsp water and 7.5ml/1½ tsp lemon juice for 1; 120ml/4fl oz/½ cup water and 15ml/1 tbsp lemon juice for 2; and 150ml/¼ pint/⅔ cup water and 30ml/2 tbsp lemon juice for 4. Cover and microwave for 5–6 minutes for 1; 10–11 minutes for 2; and 15–18 minutes for 4, basting and rearranging twice. Leave to stand for 5 minutes before serving.
Jerusalem	450g/1lb	HIGH	Peel and cut into even-size pieces. Place in a microwaveproof bowl with 60ml/4 tbsp water or 25g/1oz/2 tbsp butter. Cover and microwave for 8–10 minutes, stirring once. Leave to stand, covered, for 3–5 minutes before serving.
ASPARAGUS fresh whole spears	450g/1lb	HIGH	Prepare and arrange in a shallow microwaveproof dish with pointed tops to the centre. Add 120ml/4fl oz/½ cup water. Cover and microwave for 12–14 minutes, rearranging the spears half way through the time but still keeping the tips to the centre of the dish.
fresh cut spears	450g/1lb	HIGH	Prepare and place in a large shallow microwaveproof dish. Add 120ml/4fl oz/½ cup water. Cover and microwave for 9–11 minutes, rearranging once. Leave to stand, covered, for 5 minutes before serving.
AUBERGINES fresh cubes	450g/1lb	HIGH	Cut unpeeled aubergine into 2cm/¾in cubes. Place in a microwaveproof bowl with 25g/1oz/2 tbsp butter. Cover and microwave for 7–10 minutes, stirring every 3 minutes. Leave to stand, covered, for 4 minutes. Season *after* cooking.
fresh whole	225g/8oz 2 x 225g/8oz	HIGH	Peel off stalks, rinse and dry. Brush with a little oil and prick. Place on kitchen paper and microwave for 3–4 minutes for 1 aubergine; 4–6 minutes for 2, turning over once. Leave to stand for 4 minutes. Scoop out flesh and use as required.
BEANS fresh green	225g/8oz whole 450g/1lb whole 225g/8oz cut 450g/1lb cut	HIGH	Place whole or cut beans in a microwaveproof bowl and add 30ml/2 tbsp water. Cover and microwave for 8–10 minutes for 225g/8oz whole beans; 15–18 minutes for 450g/1lb whole beans; 7–9 minutes for 225g/8oz cut beans; and 12–15 minutes for 450g/1lb cut beans, stirring once. Leave to stand, covered, for 2–3 minutes before serving.
fresh baby green whole or French whole	225g/8oz 450g/1lb	HIGH	Place in a microwaveproof bowl with 30ml/2 tbsp water. Cover and microwave for 7–9 minutes for 225g/8oz; 12–15 minutes for 450g/1lb, stirring 3 times. Leave to stand, covered, for 2–3 minutes, before serving.
fresh sliced runner beans	225g/8oz 450g/1lb	HIGH	Place in a microwaveproof bowl with 30ml/2 tbsp water. Cover and microwave for 7–9 minutes for 225g/8oz; 12–15 minutes for 450g/1lb, stirring 3–4 times. Leave to stand, covered, for 2–3 minutes before serving.
fresh shelled broad beans	225g/8oz 450g/1lb	HIGH	Place in a microwaveproof bowl and add the water: 75ml/5 tbsp for 225g/8oz beans; and 120ml/4fl oz/½ cup for 450g/1lb beans. Cover and microwave for 5–7 minutes for 225g/8oz; 6–10 minutes for 450g/1lb, stirring once. Leave to stand, covered, for 2–3 minutes before serving.
BEETROOT fresh	4 medium	HIGH	Wash the beetroot and pierce the skin with a fork but do not peel. Place in a shallow microwaveproof dish with 60ml/4 tbsp water. Cover loosely and microwave for 14–16 minutes, rearranging twice. Leave to stand, covered, for 5 minutes before removing skins to serve or use.

BROCCOLI

fresh spears	225g/8oz 450g/1lb	HIGH	Place spears in a large shallow microwaveproof dish with tender heads to centre of dish. Add 60ml/4 tbsp water. Cover and microwave for 4–5 minutes for 225g/8oz; 8–9 minutes for 450g/1lb, rotating the dish once. Leave to stand, covered, for 2–4 minutes before serving.
fresh pieces	225g/8oz 450g/1lb	HIGH	Cut into 2.5cm/1in pieces. Place in a microwaveproof bowl with 60ml/4 tbsp water. Cover and microwave for 4½–5 minutes for 225g/8oz; 8½–9½ minutes for 450g/1lb, stirring once. Leave to stand, covered, for 3–5 minutes before serving.

BRUSSELS SPROUTS

fresh	450g/1lb 900g/2lb	HIGH	Remove outer leaves, trim and cross-cut base. Place in a microwaveproof dish and add water: 60ml/4 tbsp for 450g/1lb; 120ml/4/fl oz/½ cup for 900g/2lb. Cover and microwave for 6–7 minutes for 450g/1lb; 12–14 minute for 900g/2lb, stirring once. Leave to stand, covered, for 3–5 minutes before serving.

CABBAGE

fresh	225g/8oz 450g/1lb	HIGH	Core and shred, and place in a large microwaveproof dish. Add water: 60ml/4 tbsp for 225g/8oz; 120ml/4/fl oz/½ cup for 450g/1lb. Cover and microwave for 7–9 minutes for 225g/8oz; 9–11 minutes for 450g/1lb, stirring once. Leave to stand, covered, for 2 minutes before serving.

CARROTS

fresh baby whole and sliced	450g/1lb whole 450g/1lb sliced	HIGH	Place in a microwaveproof dish with 60ml/4 tbsp water. Cover and microwave for 12–14 minutes for whole; 10–12 minutes for sliced. Leave to stand, covered, for 3–5 minutes before serving.

CAULIFLOWER

fresh whole	675g/1½lb	MEDIUM	Trim but leave whole, and place floret-side down in a microwaveproof dish with 250ml/8fl oz/1 cup water. Cover and microwave for 16–17 minutes, turning over once. Leave to stand for 3–5 minutes before serving.
fresh florets	225g/8oz 450g/1lb	HIGH	Place in a microwaveproof dish with water: 45ml/3 tbsp for 225g/8oz; 60ml/4 tbsp for 450g/1lb. Cover and microwave for 7–8 minutes for 225g/8oz; 10–12 minutes for 450g/1lb, stirring once. Leave to stand for 3 minutes before serving.

CELERY

fresh sliced	1 head (about 9 stalks)	HIGH	Slice into 5mm/¼in pieces and place in a shallow microwaveproof dish with 30ml/2 tbsp water and 25g/1oz/2 tbsp butter. Cover and microwave for 5–6 minutes, stirring once. Leave to stand, covered, for 3 minutes before serving.
fresh celery hearts	4 hearts	HIGH	Halve each celery heart lengthways and place in a shallow microwaveproof dish. Add 30ml/2 tbsp water and a knob of butter if liked. Cover and microwave for 4½–5 minutes, turning once. Leave to stand, covered, for 3 minutes before serving.

CHINESE CABBAGE

fresh	450g/1lb	HIGH	Slice and place in a large microwaveproof dish. Add 30–45ml/2–3 tbsp water. Cover and microwave for 6–8 minutes, stirring once. Leave to stand, covered, for 3–5 minutes. Season after cooking.

COURGETTES

fresh	225g/8oz 450g/1lb	HIGH	Top and tail, and slice thinly. Place in a microwaveproof dish with butter: 25g/1oz/2 tbsp for 225g/8oz; 40g/1½oz/3 tbsp for 450g/1lb. Cover loosely and microwave for 4–6½ minutes for 225g/8oz; 6–8 minutes for 450g/1lb, stirring once. Leave to stand, covered, for 2–3 minutes before serving.

CURLY KALE fresh	450g/1lb	HIGH	Remove the thick stalk and stems, then shred. Place in a microwaveproof bowl with 150ml/¼ pint/⅔ cup water. Cover and microwave for 15–17 minutes, stirring every 5 minutes. Leave to stand for 2 minutes before serving.
FENNEL fresh sliced	450g/1lb	HIGH	Place in a microwaveproof bowl with 45ml/3 tbsp water. Cover and microwave for 9–10 minutes, stirring once. Leave to stand, covered, for 2–3 minutes before serving.
KOHLRABI fresh sliced	450g/1lb 900g/2lb	HIGH	Trim away the root ends and stems, scrub and peel the bulb and cut into 5mm/¼in slices. Place in a microwaveproof bowl with water: 45ml/3 tbsp for 450g/1lb; and 75ml/5 tbsp for 900g/2lb. Cover and microwave for 5–6 minutes for 450g/1lb; 9–11 minutes for 900g/2lb, stirring twice. Leave to stand, covered, for 3–4 minutes. Drain to serve.
LEEKS fresh whole	450g/1lb 900g/2lb	HIGH	Trim and slice from the top of the white to the green leaves in 2–3 places. Wash thoroughly and place in a microwaveproof dish with water: 45ml/3 tbsp for 450g/1lb; and 75ml/5 tbsp for 900g/2lb. Cover and microwave for 3–5 minutes for 450g/1lb; 6–8 minutes for 900g/2lb, rearranging twice. Leave to stand, covered, for 3–5 minutes before serving.
fresh sliced	450g/1lb	HIGH	Place in a microwaveproof dish with 45ml/3 tbsp water. Cover and microwave for 8–10 minutes, stirring once. Leave to stand, covered, for 2–3 minutes before serving.
MANGETOUTS fresh	115g/4oz 225g/8oz	HIGH	Trim and place in a microwaveproof bowl with water: 15ml/1 tbsp for 115g/4oz; 30ml/2 tbsp for 225g/8oz. Cover and microwave for 3–4 minutes for 115g/4oz; and 4–5 minutes for 225g/8oz, stirring once. Leave to stand, covered, for 2 minutes before serving.
MARROW fresh	450g/1lb	HIGH	Peel, remove seeds and cut into small neat dice. Place in a microwaveproof dish without water. Cover loosely and microwave for 7–10 minutes, stirring once. Leave to stand, covered, for 2–3 minutes before serving.
MUSHROOMS fresh whole	225g/8oz 450g/1lb	HIGH	Trim and wipe mushrooms. Place in a microwaveproof dish with water or butter: 25g/1oz/2 tbsp butter or 30ml/2 tbsp water for 225g/8oz mushrooms; and 40g/1½oz/3 tbsp butter or 45ml/3 tbsp water for 450g/1lb mushrooms. Cover and microwave for 3–4 minutes for 225g/8oz; and 4–5 minutes for 450g/1lb, stirring twice. Leave to stand for 1–2 minutes before serving. Season after cooking.
fresh sliced	225g/8oz 450g/1lb	HIGH	As above but microwave for 2–3 minutes for 225g/8oz mushrooms; and 3–4 minutes for 450g/1lb mushrooms.
OKRA fresh	450g/1lb	HIGH	Top and tail, and sprinkle lightly with salt. Leave to drain for 30 minutes. Rinse and place in a microwaveproof dish with 30ml/2 tbsp water or 25g/1oz/2 tbsp butter. Cover and microwave for 8–10 minutes, stirring once. Leave to stand, covered, for 3 minutes before serving.
ONIONS fresh whole	450g/1lb or 4 medium	HIGH	Peel and place in a microwaveproof dish. Cover and microwave for 10–12 minutes, rearranging and rotating once. Leave to stand, covered, for 2 minutes before serving.
fresh sliced	450g/1lb	HIGH	Peel and cut into thin wedges or slices. Place in a microwaveproof dish with 25g/1oz/2 tbsp butter and 30ml/2 tbsp water. Cover loosely and microwave for 7–10 minutes, stirring once. Leave to stand, covered, for 5 minutes before serving.

PAK CHOI (or bok choy cabbage)	450g/1lb	HIGH	Slice stalks and leaves and place in a large microwaveproof dish. Add 30ml/ 2 tbsp water and microwave for 6–8 minutes, stirring once. Leave to stand for 3–5 minutes before serving.
PARSNIPS fresh whole	450g/1lb	HIGH	Peel and prick with a fork. Arrange in a microwaveproof dish with tapered ends to the centre. Dot with 15g/½oz/1 tbsp butter and add 45ml/3 tbsp water and 15ml/1 tbsp lemon juice. Cover and microwave for 9–12 minutes, rearranging once. Leave to stand, covered, for 3 minutes before serving.
fresh slices	450g/1lb	HIGH	Peel and slice. Place in a microwaveproof dish with 15g/½oz/1 tbsp butter, 45ml/3 tbsp water and 15ml/1 tbsp lemon juice. Cover and microwave for 9–12 minutes, stirring twice. Leave to stand, covered, for 3 minutes before serving.
PEAS fresh	115g/4oz 225g/8oz 450g/1lb	HIGH	Place shelled peas in a microwaveproof bowl with butter and water: 15g/½oz/ 1 tbsp butter and 10ml/2 tsp water for 115g/4oz peas; 25g/1oz/2 tbsp butter and 15ml/1 tbsp water for 225g/8oz peas; and 50g/2oz/4 tbsp butter and 30ml/2 tbsp water for 450g/1lb peas. Cover and microwave for 3 minutes for 115g/4oz; 4–5 minutes for 225g/8oz; and 6–8 minutes for 450g/1lb, stirring once. Leave to stand, covered, for 3–5 minutes before serving.
POTATOES mashed or creamed	900g/2lb	HIGH	Peel and cut into 1.5cm/½in cubes. Place in a microwaveproof bowl with 75ml/ 5 tbsp water. Cover and microwave for 11–13 minutes, stirring once. Leave to stand, covered, for 5 minutes. Drain and mash with butter and seasoning to taste.
new potatoes or old, peeled and quartered	450g/1lb	HIGH	Scrub and scrape new potatoes if liked. Peel and quarter old potatoes. Place in a microwaveproof dish with 60ml/4 tbsp water. Cover and microwave for 7–10 minutes for new; and 6–8 minutes for old, stirring once. Leave to stand, covered, for 5 minutes before serving.
jacket baked	175g/6oz 2 x 175g/6oz 3 x 175g/6oz 4 x 175g/6oz	HIGH	Scrub and prick the skin. Place on a double sheet of absorbent kitchen paper. Microwave for 4–6 minutes for 1; 6–8 minutes for 2; 8–12 minutes for 3; 12–15 minutes for 4, turning over once. If cooking more than 2 potatoes, arrange in a ring pattern. Leave to stand for 5 minutes, before serving.
PUMPKIN fresh	450g/1lb	HIGH	Remove the skin, seeds and membrane and cut into 2.5cm/1in cubes. Place in a microwaveproof dish with 15g/½oz/1 tbsp butter. Cover and microwave for 4–6 minutes, stirring twice. Leave to stand for 3 minutes, then season to serve plain, or mash with cream and herbs.
SPINACH fresh	450g/1lb	HIGH	Chop or shred and rinse. Place in a microwaveproof bowl without any extra water. Cover and microwave for 6–8 minutes, stirring once. Leave to stand for 2 minutes before serving. Season after cooking.
SQUASH fresh	450g/1lb	HIGH	Pierce whole squash with a knife several times. Microwave for 3–5 minutes per 450g/1lb until the flesh pierces easily with a skewer. Leave to stand for 5 minutes. Halve, scoop out the seeds and fibres and discard. Serve fresh in chunks or mash with butter.
SWEDES fresh	450g/1lb	HIGH	Peel and cut into 1cm/½in cubes. Place in a microwaveproof bowl with 15g/½oz/1 tbsp butter and 30ml/2 tbsp water. Cover and microwave for 10–12 minutes, stirring twice. Leave to stand, covered, for 4 minutes. Drain to serve.

SWEETCORN

corn on the cob, fresh husked	1 x 175g/6oz 2 x 175g/6oz 3 x 175g/6oz 4 x 175g/6oz	HIGH	Wrap individually in clear film or place in a microwaveproof dish with 60ml/4 tbsp water and cover. Place or arrange evenly in the oven and microwave for 3–4 minutes for 1; 5–6 minutes for 2; 7–8 minutes for 3; and 9–10 minutes for 4, rotating and rearranging once. Leave to stand, covered, for 3–5 minutes before serving.

SWEET POTATOES

fresh	450g/1lb, whole 450g/1lb, cubed	HIGH	If cooking whole, prick the skins and place on absorbent kitchen paper. Microwave for 7–9 minutes, turning twice. Allow to cool for handling and peel away the skins to serve. To cook cubes, place in a microwaveproof bowl with 45ml/3 tbsp water. Cover and microwave for 6–8 minutes, stirring twice. Drain and toss with butter and seasoning. Leave to stand for 2 minutes before serving.

SWISS CHARD

fresh	450g/1lb	HIGH	Remove and discard the thick stalk and shred the leaves. Place in a microwaveproof dish with 150ml/¼ pint/⅔ cup water. Cover and microwave for 5½–6½ minutes, stirring every 3 minutes. Leave to stand for 2 minutes before serving. Season after cooking.

TOMATOES

whole and halves	1 medium 4 medium 4 large (beef)	HIGH	Prick whole and/or halved tomatoes, arrange in a circle on a plate, cut-sides up. Dot with butter and season to taste. Microwave for ½ minute for 1 medium; 2–2½ minutes for 4 medium; and 3½–4 minutes for 4 large (beef) tomatoes, according to size and ripeness. Leave to stand for 1–2 minutes before serving.

TURNIPS

whole	450g/1lb	HIGH	Choose only small to medium turnips. Peel and prick with a fork. Arrange in a ring pattern in a shallow microwaveproof dish. Dot with 15g/½oz/1 tbsp butter and add 45ml/3 tbsp water. Cover and microwave for 14–16 minutes, rearranging once. Leave to stand, covered, for 3 minutes before serving.
sliced or cubed	450g/1lb	HIGH	Place slices or cubes in a microwaveproof dish with 15g/½oz/1 tbsp butter and 45ml/3 tbsp water. Cover and microwave for 11–12 minutes for slices; and 12–14 minutes for cubes. Leave to stand, covered, for 3 minutes before serving.

Broccoli and Chestnut Terrine.

Middle-Eastern Vegetable Stew.

Cooking Frozen Vegetables

ASPARAGUS frozen whole spears	450g/1lb	HIGH	Place in a microwaveproof dish with 120ml/4fl oz/½ cup water. Cover and microwave for 9–12 minutes, rearranging once. Leave to stand for 5 minutes before serving.
BEANS frozen green beans	225g/8oz whole 450g/1lb whole 225g/8oz cut 450g/1lb cut	HIGH	Place in a microwaveproof bowl with water, cover and microwave with 30ml/2tbsp water for 9–10 minutes for 225g/8oz whole beans; 60ml/4 tbsp water and 14–15 minutes for 450g/1lb whole beans; 30ml/2 tbsp water and 6–7 minutes for 225g/8oz cut beans; and 60ml/4 tbsp water and 10–12 minutes for 450g/1lb cut beans, stirring once. Leave to stand, covered, for 2–3 minutes before serving.
frozen baby green or French whole beans	225g/8oz 450g/1lb	HIGH	Place in a microwaveproof bowl with water, cover and microwave with 30ml/2 tbsp water for 8–9 minutes for 225g/8oz beans; and 60ml/4 tbsp water and 13–15 minutes for 450g/1lb beans, stirring 3 times. Leave to stand, covered, for 2–3 minutes before serving.
frozen sliced runner beans	225g/8oz 450g/1lb	HIGH	Place in a microwaveproof bowl with water, cover and microwave with 30ml/2 tbsp water for 6–7 minutes for 225g/8oz beans; and 60ml/4 tbsp water and 10–12 minutes for 450g/1lb beans, stirring twice. Leave to stand, covered, for 2–3 minutes before serving.
frozen shelled broad beans	225g/8oz 450g/1lb	HIGH	Place in a microwaveproof bowl with water, cover and microwave with 60ml/4 tbsp water for 6–7 minutes for 225g/8oz beans; and 120ml/4½fl oz/½ cup and 10–11 minutes for 450g/1lb beans, stirring twice. Leave to stand, covered, for 2–3 minutes before serving.
BROCCOLI frozen spears	450g/1lb	HIGH	Place in a microwaveproof dish with 60ml/4 tbsp water. Cover and microwave for 13–14 minutes, stirring once. Leave to stand, covered, for 2–3 minutes before serving.
BRUSSELS SPROUTS frozen	450g/1lb	HIGH	Place in a microwaveproof dish with 30ml/2 tbsp water. Cover and microwave for 10–11 minutes, stirring once. Leave to stand, covered, for 3–5 minutes before serving.
CABBAGE frozen	225g/8oz 450g/1lb	HIGH	Place in a large microwaveproof dish with water, cover and microwave with 60ml/4 tbsp water for 6–8 minutes for 225g/8oz; and 120ml/4½fl oz/½ cup water and 8–10 minutes for 450g/1lb, stirring once. Leave to stand, covered, for 2 minutes before serving.
CARROTS frozen whole and sliced	450g/1lb whole 450g/1lb sliced	HIGH	Place in a microwaveproof dish with water. Cover and microwave with 30ml/2 tbsp water for 10–12 minutes for whole carrots; and 30ml/2 tbsp water and 8–10 minutes for sliced carrots, stirring once. Leave to stand, covered, for 2–3 minutes before serving.
CAULIFLOWER frozen florets	450g/1lb	HIGH	Place in a microwaveproof dish with 60ml/4 tbsp water. Cover and microwave for 8–9 minutes, stirring once. Leave to stand, covered, for 2–3 minutes before serving.
COURGETTES frozen sliced	450g/1lb	HIGH	Place in a shallow microwaveproof dish with 40g/1½oz/3 tbsp butter if liked. Cover loosely and microwave for 7–8 minutes, stirring once. Leave to stand, covered, for 2–3 minutes before serving.

LEEKS frozen sliced	450g/1lb	HIGH	Place in a microwaveproof dish with 45ml/3 tbsp water. Cover and microwave for 11–12 minutes, stirring once. Leave to stand, covered, for 2–3 minutes before serving.
MANGETOUTS frozen	225g/8oz	HIGH	Place in a microwaveproof dish with 30ml/2 tbsp water. Cover and microwave for 3–4 minutes, stirring once. Leave to stand, covered, for 2–3 minutes before serving.
MIXED VEGETABLES frozen	225g/8oz 450g/1lb	HIGH	Place in a microwaveproof dish with water. Cover and microwave with 30ml/2 tbsp water for 4–5 minutes for 225g/8oz; and 30ml/2 tbsp water and 7–8 minutes for 450g/1lb, stirring once. Leave to stand, covered, for 2 minutes before serving.
MUSHROOMS frozen whole button	115g/4oz 225g/8oz	HIGH	Place in a shallow microwaveproof dish with a knob of butter. Cover and microwave for 3–4 minutes for 115g/4oz; and 5–6 minutes for 225g/8oz, stirring twice. Leave to stand, covered, for 1–2 minutes. Season to taste to serve.
PARSNIPS frozen whole	450g/1lb	HIGH	Arrange in a shallow microwaveproof dish with tapered ends to centre. Cover and microwave for 9–10 minutes, rearranging once. Toss in butter and seasonings to serve. Leave to stand, covered, for 2–3 minutes before serving.
PEAS frozen	225g/8oz 450g/1lb	HIGH	Place in a microwaveproof dish with water. Cover and microwave with 30ml/2 tbsp water for 4–6 minutes for 225g/8oz; and 60ml/4 tbsp water and 6–8 minutes for 450g/1lb, stirring once. Leave to stand, covered, for 3 minutes.
SPINACH frozen	275g/10oz packet	HIGH	Place in a microwaveproof dish. Cover and microwave for 7–9 minutes, stirring twice to break up during cooking. Season *after* cooking.
SWEDES frozen cubed swede	450g/1lb	HIGH	Place in a microwaveproof dish, cover and microwave for 8–10 minutes, stirring twice. Leave to stand, covered, for 2–3 minutes. Toss in butter and seasonings or mash with same to a purée.
SWEETCORN frozen sweetcorn kernels	450g/1lb	HIGH	Place in a microwaveproof dish with 60ml/4 tbsp water. Cover and microwave for 7–8 minutes, stirring once. Leave to stand, covered, for 2–3 minutes before serving.

Summer Vegetable Braise.

Mixed Mushroom Ragout.

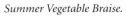

Cooking Pasta, Pulses and Grains

BARLEY pot barley	175g/6oz	HIGH *then* MEDIUM	Toast if liked before cooking. Place in a microwaveproof dish with 1 litre/ 1¾ pints/4 cups boiling water and a pinch of salt if liked. Cover loosely and microwave on HIGH for 3 minutes, then on MEDIUM for 40 minutes. Leave to stand for 5–10 minutes before fluffing with a fork to serve.
BULGUR grains	225g/8oz	HIGH *then* MEDIUM	Place in a microwaveproof dish with 550ml/18fl oz/2¼ cups boiling water and a pinch of salt if liked. Cover loosely and microwave on HIGH for 3 minutes, then on MEDIUM for 9–12 minutes. Leave to stand for 5–10 minutes before fluffing with a fork to serve.
COUSCOUS pre-cooked	350g/12oz	MEDIUM	Place in a microwaveproof dish with 250ml/8fl oz/1 cup boiling water and 50g/2oz/4 tbsp butter. Cover loosely and microwave for 15 minutes. Leave to stand for 5–10 minutes before fluffing with a fork to serve.
DRIED BEANS aduki black black-eyed borlotti broad butter cannellini flageolet haricot mung pinto red kidney soya	225g/8oz	HIGH *then* MEDIUM	Soak dried beans overnight in cold water or hasten soaking by par-cooking in the microwave. Place the dried beans in a microwaveproof bowl with boiling water to cover. Cover and microwave on HIGH for 5 minutes. Leave to stand, covered, for 1½ hours before draining to cook. Place soaked or par-cooked beans in a microwaveproof dish and cover with boiling water. Cover and microwave all beans on HIGH for 10 minutes. Reduce the power to MEDIUM and microwave aduki, black-eyed, mung and pinto beans for 10–15 minutes; and black, borlotti, broad, butter, cannellini, flageolet, haricot, red kidney and soya beans for 20–25 minutes, adding extra boiling water to cover if needed. Drain to use.
DRIED CHICK- PEAS	225g/8oz	HIGH *then* MEDIUM	Soak dried peas overnight or according to packet instructions. Place soaked peas in a microwaveproof dish and cover with boiling water. Cover and microwave on HIGH for 10 minutes, then on MEDIUM for 20–25 minutes, adding extra boiling water to cover if needed. Drain to use.
DRIED WHOLE GREEN PEAS	225g/8oz	HIGH *then* MEDIUM	Soak dried peas overnight or according to packet instructions. Place soaked peas in a microwaveproof dish and cover with boiling water. Cover and microwave on HIGH for 10 minutes, then on MEDIUM for 10–15 minutes, adding extra boiling water to cover if needed. Drain to use.
DRIED SPLIT PEAS	225g/8oz	HIGH	Soak dried peas overnight or according to packet instructions. Place soaked peas in a microwaveproof dish and cover with boiling water. Cover and microwave on HIGH for 10 minutes. Drain to use.
DRIED LENTILS	225g/8oz	HIGH	Place the lentils in a microwaveproof dish with a few seasoning vegetables such as chopped onion, celery, carrot or bouquet garni and a squeeze of lemon juice. Add 900ml/1½ pints/3¾ cups boiling water or stock. Cover and microwave for 15–25 minutes, stirring once halfway through cooking. Cook for the shorter length of time if the lentils are to be served in a salad mixture or as a meal accompaniment, the longer time if the lentils are to be puréed for use.
MILLET	225g/8oz	HIGH *then* MEDIUM	Toast if liked before cooking. Place in a microwaveproof dish with 650ml/ 22fl oz/2¾ cups boiling water and a pinch of salt if liked. Cover loosely and microwave on HIGH for 3 minutes, then on MEDIUM for 12 minutes. Leave to stand for 5–10 minutes before fluffing with a fork to serve.

OATS grains	175g/6oz	HIGH *then* MEDIUM	Toast if liked before cooking. Place in a microwaveproof dish with 750ml/ 1¼ pints/3 cups boiling water and a pinch of salt if liked. Cover loosely and microwave on HIGH for 3 minutes, then on MEDIUM for 20–22 minutes. Leave to stand for 5–10 minutes before fluffing with a fork to serve.
PASTA fresh: egg noodles spaghetti tagliatelle ravioli	225g/8oz	HIGH	Place the pasta in a large microwaveproof dish. Cover with 750ml/ 1¼ pints/3 cups boiling water and add 5ml/1 tsp oil. Cover loosely and microwave for 2–2½ minutes for egg noodles; 4–6 minutes for spaghetti; 2–3 minutes for tagliatelle; and 6–8 minutes for ravioli, stirring once halfway through the cooking time. Leave to stand for 2 minutes before draining to serve.
dried: egg noodles spaghetti tagliatelle short-cut macaroni pasta shapes ravioli	225g/8oz	HIGH	Place the pasta in a large microwaveproof dish. Add a generous 1.2 litres/ 2 pints/5 cups of boiling water and 5ml/1 tsp oil. Cover loosely and microwave: 6 minutes for egg noodles; 10–12 minutes for spaghetti; 6 minutes for tagliatelle; 10 minutes for short-cut macaroni; 10-12 minutes for pasta shapes; and 10 minutes for ravioli, stirring once halfway through the cooking time. Leave to stand for 3–5 minutes before draining to use.
RICE long grain white	115g/4oz 225g/8oz	HIGH *then* MEDIUM	Place the rice in a large microwaveproof dish. Add boiling water: 300ml/ ½ pint/1¼ cups for 115g/4oz rice; and 550ml/18fl oz/2¼ cups for 225g/8oz rice with a pinch of salt and knob of butter if liked. Cover loosely and microwave on HIGH for 3 minutes. Stir well then re-cover and microwave on MEDIUM for 12 minutes. Leave to stand, covered, for 5 minutes before fluffing with a fork to serve.
long grain brown	115g/4oz 225g/8oz	HIGH *then* MEDIUM	Place the rice in a large microwaveproof dish. Add boiling water: 300ml/ ½ pint/1¼ cups for 115g/4oz; 550ml/18fl oz/2¼ cups for 225g/8oz rice with a pinch of salt and knob of butter if liked. Cover loosely and microwave on HIGH for 3 minutes. Stir well then re-cover and microwave on MEDIUM for 25 minutes. Leave to stand, covered, for 5 minutes before fluffing with a fork to serve.
long grain and wild rice mix	400g/14oz packet	HIGH *then* MEDIUM	Place the rice mix in a microwaveproof dish with 650ml/22fl oz/2¾ cups boiling water, a pinch of salt and knob of butter if liked. Cover loosely and microwave on HIGH for 3 minutes. Stir well, re-cover and microwave on MEDIUM for 12 minutes, stirring once. Leave to stand, covered, for 5 minutes before fluffing with a fork to serve.
RYE grains	175g/6oz	HIGH *then* MEDIUM	Soak the rye grains for 6–8 hours in cold water then drain. Place in a microwaveproof dish with 750ml/1¼ pints/3 cups boiling water. Cover loosely and microwave on HIGH for 3 minutes, then on MEDIUM for 40 minutes. Leave to stand 5–10 minutes before fluffing with a fork to serve.
WHEAT grains	175g/6oz	HIGH *then* MEDIUM	Soak wheat grains for 6–8 hours in cold water then drain. Place in a microwaveproof dish with 1 litre/1¾ pints/4 cups boiling water. Cover loosely and microwave on HIGH for 3 minutes, then on MEDIUM for 40 minutes. Leave to stand 5–10 minutes before fluffing with a fork to serve.

Cooking Fruit

APPLES poached in light syrup	450g/1lb	HIGH	Peel, core and slice apples and place in a microwaveproof bowl with 300ml/½ pint/1¼ cups hot sugar syrup. Cover loosely and microwave for 3 minutes, stirring once. Leave to stand, covered, for 5 minutes.
	900g/2lb	HIGH	As above, but microwave for 5–6 minutes.
stewed	450g/1lb	HIGH	Peel, core and slice apples and place in a microwaveproof bowl with 115g/4oz/½ cup sugar. Cover loosely and microwave for 6–8 minutes, stirring once. Leave to stand, covered, for 2–3 minutes.
baked	4 large	HIGH	Wash and remove cores from the apples and score around the middle to prevent bursting. Place in a microwaveproof dish, stuff with a little dried fruit if liked. Pour 120ml/4fl oz/½ cup water around fruit and microwave for 9–10 minutes, rearranging once. Leave to stand, covered, for 3–4 minutes before serving.
APRICOTS poached in light syrup	6–8	HIGH	Skin, halve and stone, slicing if preferred. Place in a microwaveproof bowl with 300ml/½ pint/1¼ cups hot sugar syrup. Cover loosely and microwave for 3–4 minutes, stirring once. Leave to stand, covered, for 5 minutes.
stewed	6–8	HIGH	Stone and wash. Place in a microwaveproof bowl, sprinkle with 115g/4oz/½ cup sugar. Cover and microwave for 6–8 minutes, stirring once. Leave to stand, covered, for 5 minutes before serving.
BANANAS baked	2 large	HIGH	Peel and halve the bananas lengthways. Place in a microwaveproof dish with a little sugar and fruit juice. Microwave for 3–4 minutes, stirring or rearranging twice.
BLACKBERRIES poached in light syrup	450g/1lb	HIGH	Hull and rinse. Place in a microwaveproof bowl with 300ml/½ pint/1¼ cups hot sugar syrup. Cover loosely and microwave for 2 minutes, stirring once. Leave to stand, covered, for 5 minutes.
BLACKCURRANTS fresh	450g/1lb	HIGH	Top and tail and place in a microwaveproof dish with 115g/4oz/½ cup sugar and 30ml/2 tbsp water. Cover loosely and microwave for 5 minutes, stirring once. Leave to stand, covered, for 5 minutes.
CHERRIES poached in light syrup	450g/1lb	HIGH	Prick and stone if preferred. Place in a microwaveproof bowl with 300ml/½ pint/1¼ cups of hot sugar syrup. Cover loosely and microwave for 2–3 minutes, stirring once. Leave to stand, covered, for 5 minutes.
stewed	450g/1lb	HIGH	Stone, wash and place in a microwaveproof bowl with 115g/4oz/½ cup sugar and a little grated lemon rind if liked. Cover and microwave for 4–5 minutes, stirring once. Leave to stand, covered, for 3–5 minutes.
CRANBERRIES cranberry sauce	450g/1lb	HIGH	Place the cranberries, 90ml/6 tbsp water and 350g/12oz/1¾ cups sugar in a large microwaveproof bowl. Cover with vented cling film and microwave for 18–20 minutes, stirring every 6 minutes, until pulpy.
DAMSONS poached in light syrup	450g/1lb, whole or halved	HIGH	Prick whole damsons or halve and stone if preferred. Place in a microwaveproof bowl with 300ml/½ pint/1¼ cups hot sugar syrup. Cover loosely and microwave for 3 minutes for whole damsons; 2 minutes for halves, stirring once. Leave to stand, covered, for 5 minutes.

stewed	450g/1lb	HIGH	Stone and wash. Place in a microwaveproof bowl with 115g/4oz/½ cup sugar and a little grated lemon rind if liked. Cover and microwave for 4–5 minutes, stirring once. Leave to stand, covered, for 3–5 minutes.
GOOSEBERRIES fresh	450g/1lb	HIGH	Top and tail and place in a microwaveproof bowl with 30ml/2 tbsp water. Cover and microwave for 4–6 minutes. Stir in 115g/4oz/½ cup sugar and leave to stand, covered, for 5 minutes.
GREENGAGES poached in light syrup	450g/1lb whole or halved	HIGH	Prick whole greengages or halve and stone if preferred. Place in a microwave-proof bowl with 300ml/½ pint/1¼ cups hot sugar syrup. Cover loosely and microwave for 3 minutes for whole greengages; 2 minutes for halves, stirring once. Leave to stand, covered, for 5 minutes.
stewed	450g/1lb	HIGH	Stone and wash. Place in a microwaveproof bowl with 115g/4oz/½ cup sugar and a little grated lemon rind if liked. Cover and microwave for 4–5 minutes, stirring once. Leave to stand, covered, for 3–5 minutes.
NECTARINES poached in light syrup	8	HIGH	Skin and prick thoroughly. Place in a microwaveproof bowl with 300ml/½ pint/1¼ cups hot sugar syrup and a dash of lemon juice. Cover loosely and microwave for 6 minutes, stirring once. Leave to stand, covered, for 5 minutes.
stewed	4 medium	HIGH	Stone, wash and slice. Place in a microwaveproof bowl with 115g/4oz/½ cup sugar. Cover and microwave for 4–5 minutes, stirring once. Leave to stand, covered, for 5 minutes.
ORANGES poached in light syrup	4	HIGH	Peel if preferred, or scrub the skin, then finely slice. Place in a microwaveproof bowl with 300ml/½ pint/1¼ cups hot sugar syrup. Cover loosely and microwave for 3 minutes, stirring once. Leave to stand, covered, for 5 minutes.
PEACHES poached in light syrup	4 whole or sliced	HIGH	Skin and prick thoroughly or skin, stone and slice. Place in a microwaveproof bowl with 300ml/½ pint/1¼ cups hot sugar syrup. Cover loosely and microwave for 4 minutes for whole peaches; 3 minutes for slices, stirring once. Leave to stand, covered, for 5 minutes.
stewed	4 medium	HIGH	Stone, wash and slice. Place in a microwaveproof bowl with 115g/4oz/½ cup sugar. Cover and microwave for 4–5 minutes, stirring once. Leave to stand, covered, for 5 minutes.
PEARS poached in light syrup	900g/2lb whole dessert 900g/2lb whole cooking 900g/2lb halved dessert	HIGH	Peel and prick if kept whole, or halve and core. Place in a microwaveproof bowl with 300ml/½ pint/1¼ cups hot sugar syrup. Cover loosely and microwave for 5 minutes for whole dessert pears; 10 minutes for whole cooking pears: and 3 minutes for halved dessert pears, stirring once. Leave to stand, covered, for 5 minutes.
stewed	6 medium	HIGH	Peel, halve and core. Dissolve 75g/3oz/⅓ cup sugar in a little water and pour over the pears. Cover loosely and microwave for 8–10 minutes, stirring once. Leave to stand, covered, for 5 minutes.
PINEAPPLE poached in light syrup	900g/2lb	HIGH	Peel, core and cut into bite-size pieces. Place in a microwaveproof bowl with 300ml/½ pint/1¼ cups hot sugar syrup. Cover loosely and microwave for 5 minutes, stirring once. Leave to stand, covered, for 5 minutes.

PLUMS poached in light syrup	450g/1lb whole or halved	HIGH	Prick if kept whole or halve and stone. Place in a microwaveproof bowl with 300ml/½ pint/1¼ cups hot sugar syrup. Cover loosely and microwave for 3 minutes for whole plums; 2 minutes for halved, stirring once. Leave to stand, covered, for 5 minutes.
stewed	450g/1lb	HIGH	Stone and wash. Place in a microwaveproof bowl with 115g/4oz/½ cup sugar and a little grated lemon rind if liked. Cover and microwave for 4–5 minutes, stirring once. Leave to stand, covered, for 3–5 minutes.
RASPBERRIES poached in light syrup	450g/1lb	HIGH	Hull and rinse. Place in a microwaveproof bowl with 300ml/½ pint/1¼ cups hot sugar syrup. Cover loosely and microwave for 2 minutes, stirring once. Leave to stand, covered, for 5 minutes.
REDCURRANTS fresh	450g/1lb	HIGH	Top and tail and place in a microwaveproof bowl with 115g/4oz/½ cup sugar and 30ml/2 tbsp water. Cover loosely and microwave for 5 minutes, stirring once. Leave to stand for 5 minutes.
RHUBARB fresh	350g/12oz	HIGH	Cut into 2.5cm/1in lengths. Place in a microwaveproof bowl with 30ml/2 tbsp water. Cover loosely and microwave for 6–7 minutes, stirring once. Stir in 115g/4oz/½ cup sugar and 5ml/1 tsp lemon juice. Leave to stand, covered, for 2–3 minutes.
poached in light syrup	450g/1lb	HIGH	Cut into 2.5cm/1in lengths. Place in a microwaveproof bowl with 300ml/½ pint/1¼ cups hot sugar syrup. Cover loosely and microwave for 4 minutes, stirring once. Leave to stand, covered, for 5 minutes.
STRAWBERRIES poached in light syrup	450g/1lb	HIGH	Hull and rinse. Place in a microwaveproof bowl with 300ml/½ pint/1¼ cups hot sugar syrup. Cover loosely and microwave for 2 minutes, stirring once. Leave to stand, covered, for 5 minutes.

SUGAR SYRUP

To make sugar syrup for poaching fruits: place 115g/4oz/½ cup sugar and 300ml/½ pint/1¼ cups water in a microwaveproof jug. Microwave on HIGH for 4–5 minutes, stirring 3 times. Use as required. Makes 300ml/½ pint/1¼ cups.

Plum and Walnut Crumble.

Baked Apples with Apricots.

Defrosting Fish and Shellfish

COD

frozen steaks	1 x 225g/8oz 2 x 225g/8oz 4 x 225g/8oz	DEFROST	To defrost, place in a microwaveproof dish, cover and microwave for 2–2 ½ minutes for 1 steak; 3–4 minutes for 2 steaks; and 6–7 minutes for 4 steaks, turning over or rearranging once. Leave to stand, covered, for 10 minutes before using.
frozen fillets	450g/1lb	DEFROST	To defrost, place in a microwaveproof dish with the thicker portions to the outer edge. Cover and microwave for 7–8 minutes, rearranging once. Leave to stand for 5 minutes before using.

CRABMEAT

frozen	225g/8oz	DEFROST	Leave in wrappings. Microwave for 4 minutes, turning over once. Leave to stand for 2 minutes, then flake to use.

FISHCAKES

frozen	4 x 75g/3oz	DEFROST	To defrost, unwrap and place in a shallow microwaveproof dish. Cover and microwave for 5–6½ minutes, rearranging once. Leave to stand for 2 minutes before cooking.

HADDOCK

frozen steaks	1 x 225g/8oz 2 x 225g/8oz 4 x 225g/8oz	DEFROST	To defrost, place in a microwaveproof dish, cover and microwave for 2–2½ minutes for 1 steak; 3–4 minutes for 2 steaks; and 6–7 minutes for 4 steaks, turning over or rearranging once. Leave to stand for 10 minutes before using.
frozen fillets	450g/1lb	DEFROST	To defrost, place in a microwaveproof dish with the thicker portions to the outer edge. Cover and microwave for 7–8 minutes, rearranging once. Leave to stand for 5 minutes before using.

HALIBUT

frozen steaks	1 x 225g/8oz 2 x 225g/8oz 4 x 225g/8oz	DEFROST	To defrost, place in a microwaveproof dish, cover and microwave for 2–2½ minutes for 1 steak; 3–4 minutes for 2 steaks; and 6–7 minutes for 4 steaks, turning over or rearranging once. Leave to stand for 10 minutes before using.

HERRING

frozen whole	per 450g/1lb	DEFROST	To defrost, place in a shallow microwaveproof dish and microwave for 5–7 minutes per 450g/1lb, turning over once. Leave to stand for 10 minutes before using.

KIPPERS

frozen fillets	175g/6oz boil-in-the-bag	HIGH	To defrost *and* cook, place the frozen boil-in-the-bag on a plate and snip a couple of vents in the bag. Microwave for 5–6 minutes, turning over once. Leave to stand for 2–3 minutes before serving.

LOBSTER

frozen whole cooked	per 450g/1lb	DEFROST	To defrost, place in a microwaveproof dish, cover and microwave for 12–15 minutes per 450g/1lb, giving the dish a quarter turn every 2 minutes and turning over after 6 minutes. Leave to stand for 5 minutes before serving.

MACKEREL

frozen whole	per 450g/1lb	DEFROST	To defrost, place in a shallow microwaveproof dish and microwave for 5–7 minutes per 450g/1lb, turning over once. Leave to stand for 10 minutes before using.

MUSSELS

frozen cooked shelled	225g/8oz	DEFROST	To defrost, spread the mussels out on a plate in a single layer. Microwave for 3½–4 minutes, stirring to rearrange once. Leave to stand for 2 minutes before using.

PLAICE

frozen fillets	450g/1lb	DEFROST	To defrost, place in a microwaveproof dish with the thicker portions to the outer edge. Cover and microwave for 7–8 minutes, rearranging once. Leave to stand for 5 minutes before using.

frozen whole	1 x 275g/10oz 2 x 275g/10oz	DEFROST	To defrost, place on a plate, cover and microwave for 4–6 minutes for 1 plaice; and 10–12 minutes for 2 plaice, shielding the tail end with a little foil halfway through cooking if necessary. Leave to stand for 5 minutes before using.
PRAWNS AND SHRIMPS frozen cooked	450g/1lb	DEFROST	To defrost, place in a microwaveproof dish and microwave for 7–8 minutes, stirring twice. Leave to stand for 2–3 minutes before using.
RED OR GREY MULLET frozen whole	2 x 200–250g/7–9oz 4 x 200–250g/7–9oz	DEFROST	To defrost, place in a shallow microwaveproof dish and microwave for 9–11 minutes for 2 whole fish; and 19–21 minutes for 4 whole fish, turning or rearranging twice. Leave to stand for 5 minutes before using.
RED SNAPPER frozen whole	450–550g/1–1¼lb	MEDIUM	To defrost individually (for best results), place in a shallow microwaveproof dish, cover and microwave for 2½–3½ minutes, turning over once. Rinse in cold water then pat dry. Leave to stand for 2–3 minutes before using.
SALMON AND SALMON TROUT frozen steaks	2 x 225g/8oz 4 x 225g/8oz 4 x 175g/6oz	DEFROST	To defrost, place in a shallow microwaveproof dish, cover and microwave for 4–5 minutes for 2 x 225g/8oz steaks; 10–12 minutes for 4 x 225g/8oz steaks; and 10 minutes for 4 x 175g/6oz steaks, turning over and rearranging once. Leave to stand, covered, for 5–10 minutes before using.
frozen whole salmon or salmon trout	450g/1lb 900g/2lb 1.5kg/3–3½lb 1.75kg/4–4½lb	DEFROST	To defrost, place in a shallow microwaveproof dish, cover and microwave for 6–8 minutes for a 450g/1lb fish; 12–16 minutes for a 900g/2lb fish; 18–20 minutes for a 1.5kg/3–3½lb fish; and 22–24 minutes for a 1.75kg/4–4½lb fish, turning over and rotating the dish twice. Shield the head and tail with a little foil as necessary. Leave to stand, covered, for 5–10 minutes before using.
SCALLOPS frozen	350g/12oz packet 450g/1lb	DEFROST	To defrost, place in a microwaveproof bowl, cover and microwave for 6–8 minutes for 350g/12oz; and 7½–10 minutes for 450g/1lb, stirring and breaking apart twice. Leave to stand, covered, for 5 minutes before using.
SCAMPI frozen cooked	450g/1lb	DEFROST	To defrost, place in a shallow microwaveproof dish and microwave for 7–8 minutes, stirring twice. Leave to stand, covered, for 5 minutes before using.
SMOKED HADDOCK frozen fillets	175g/6oz boil-in-the-bag	HIGH	To defrost *and* cook, place bag on a plate and snip a couple of vent holes. Microwave for 5–6 minutes, turning over once. Leave to stand for 2–3 minutes before using.
SMOKED SALMON frozen sliced	90–115g/3–4oz packet	DEFROST	To defrost, unwrap the salmon and separate the slices. Arrange evenly on a plate and microwave for 1½–2 minutes, turning once.
SOLE frozen fillets	450g/1lb	DEFROST	To defrost, place in a microwaveproof dish with thicker portions to the outer edge. Cover and microwave for 7–8 minutes, rearranging once. Leave to stand for 5 minutes before using.
TROUT frozen whole	2 x 225–275g/8–10oz 4 x 225–275g/8–10oz	DEFROST	To defrost, place in a shallow microwaveproof dish and microwave for 9–11 minutes for 2 whole fish; and 19–21 minutes for 4 whole fish, turning or rearranging twice. Leave to stand for 5 minutes before using.
WHITING frozen fillets	450g/1lb	DEFROST	To defrost, place in a microwaveproof dish with thicker portions to the outer edge. Cover and microwave for 7–8 minutes, rearranging once. Leave to stand for 5 minutes before using.

Defrosting Poultry and Game

CHICKEN frozen quarters	2 x 225g/8oz 4 x 225g/8oz	LOW	To defrost, remove any wrappings and place in a microwaveproof dish so that the meatiest parts are to the outer edge. Microwave for 7–9 minutes for 2 x 225g/8oz quarters; and 15 minutes for 4 x 225g/8oz quarters, turning over and rearranging once. Leave to stand for 10 minutes before using.
frozen drumsticks, about 115g/4oz each	2 4 6	LOW	To defrost, remove any wrappings and place in a shallow microwaveproof dish so that the meatiest parts are to the outer edge. Microwave for 4–5 minutes for 2; 7–8 minutes for 4; and 12 minutes for 6 drumsticks, turning over and rearranging once. Leave to stand for 10 minutes before using.
frozen thighs, about 115g/4oz each	4 8	LOW	To defrost, remove any wrappings and place in a shallow microwaveproof dish so that the meatiest parts are to the outer edge. Microwave for 8 minutes for 4 thighs; and 15 minutes for 8 thighs, turning over and rearranging once. Leave to stand for 10 minutes before using.
frozen wings	450g/1lb 900g/2lb	LOW	To defrost, remove any wrappings and place in a shallow microwaveproof dish. Microwave for 8 minutes for 450g/1lb; and 15 minutes for 900g/2lb wings, turning over and rearranging twice. Leave to stand for 10 minutes before using.
frozen boneless breasts	2 x 225g/8oz 4 x 225g/8oz	LOW	To defrost, remove any wrappings and place in a shallow microwaveproof dish. Microwave for 8 minutes for 2 x 225g/8oz breasts; and 15 minutes for 4 x 225g/8oz breasts, turning over and rearranging once. Leave to stand for 10 minutes before using.
frozen whole chicken	1kg/2¼lb 1.5kg/3–3½lb 1.75kg/4–4½lb	DEFROST	To defrost, remove wrappings and place, breast-side down, on a microwaveproof rack or upturned saucer in a shallow dish. Microwave for 12–14 minutes for a 1kg/2¼lb bird; 18–22 minutes for a 1.5kg/3–3½lb bird; and 24–30 minutes for a 1.75kg/4–4½lb bird, turning over halfway through the time and shielding legs, wing tips or hot spots with foil if necessary. Leave to stand for 15 minutes before using. Remove any giblets at the end of the defrosting time.
frozen chicken livers	225g/8oz carton	DEFROST	To defrost, remove from carton and place in a microwaveproof dish. Cover and microwave for 6–8 minutes, separating livers as they soften. Leave to stand, covered, for 5 minutes before using.
DUCK frozen whole	2.25kg/5–5½lb per 450g/1lb	DEFROST	To defrost, shield the wing tips, tail end and legs with foil as necessary for half of the time. Place breast-side down in a shallow microwaveproof dish and microwave for 10 minutes; turn breast-side up and microwave for a further 15–20 minutes, rotating twice. Stand, covered, for 15 minutes before using. Alternatively, defrost for 5–6 minutes per 450g/1lb.
frozen duck portions	4 x 350–400g/ 12–14oz portions	HIGH *then* DEFROST	To defrost, place in a microwaveproof dish and microwave on HIGH for 7 minutes. Turn over, rearrange and microwave on DEFROST for 10–14 minutes. Leave to stand, covered, for 15 minutes before using.
GAME BIRDS frozen grouse, guinea fowl, partridge, pheasant, pigeon, quail and woodcock	1 x 450g/1lb 2 x 450g/1lb 1 x 900g/2lb 4 x 450g/1lb	DEFROST	To defrost, place on a plate or in a shallow microwaveproof dish, breast-side down. Cover loosely and microwave for half the recommended times: 6–7 minutes for 450g/1lb bird; 12–14 minutes for 2 x 450g/1lb birds; 12–14 minutes for 900g/2lb bird; and 24–28 minutes for 4 x 450g/1lb birds, turning breast-side up after half the time and rearranging if more than 1 bird. Allow to stand, covered, for 5–10 minutes before using.
GIBLETS frozen	1 bag from poultry bird	DEFROST	To defrost, place in a microwaveproof bowl, cover and microwave for 2–3 minutes. Use as required.

TURKEY

frozen whole	2.75kg/6lb 4kg/9lb 5.5kg/12lb 6.8kg/15lb	MEDIUM	To defrost, place the bird breast-side down in a shallow microwaveproof dish and microwave for a quarter of the time. Turn breast-side up and cook for a further quarter of the time. Shield wing tips and legs with small pieces of foil and turn turkey over, cook for the remaining time. Microwave for 21–33 minutes for a 2.75kg/6lb bird; 32–50 minutes for a 4kg/9lb bird; 42–66 minutes for a 5.5kg/12lb bird; and 53–83 minutes for a 6.8kg/15lb bird, checking for hot spots frequently. Leave to stand, covered, for 30–45 minutes, before using.
frozen drumsticks, about 350–400g/ 12–14oz each	2 4	LOW	To defrost, place in a microwaveproof dish with the meatiest parts to the outer edge. Microwave for 12–16 minutes for 2 drumsticks; and 24–26 minutes for 4 drumsticks, turning over and rearranging once. Leave to stand, covered, for 10 minutes before using.
frozen breasts, about 225g/8oz each	2 4	LOW	To defrost, place in a microwaveproof dish. Microwave for 5–7 minutes for 2 breasts; 10–12 minutes for 4 breasts, turning over and rearranging once. Leave to stand, covered, for 10 minutes before using.

Chicken and Fruit Salad.

Defrosting Meat

BACON frozen rashers	225g/8oz vacuum pack	DEFROST	To defrost, place on a plate. Microwave for 2–3 minutes, turning over once.
frozen joint	450g/1lb 900g/2lb	DEFROST	To defrost, if in vacuum pack, then pierce and place on a plate. Microwave for 8 minutes for 450g/1lb joint; 15–17 minutes for 900g/2lb joint, turning over twice. Leave to stand, covered, for 20–30 minutes before using.
BEEF frozen uncooked joint	per 450g/1lb joints on bone per 450g/1lb boneless joints	DEFROST	To defrost, place joint on a microwaveproof roasting rack or upturned saucer in a dish. Microwave for 5–6 minutes per 450g/1lb for joints on bone; and 10 minutes per 450g/1lb for boneless joints, turning over once. Leave to stand, covered, for 30–45 minutes before using.
frozen mince	225g/8oz 450g/1lb 900g/2lb	DEFROST	To defrost, place in a microwaveproof bowl and microwave for 5 minutes for 225g/8oz; 9–10 minutes for 450g/1lb; and 17–18 minutes for 900g/2lb, breaking up twice during the cooking time. Leave to stand for 5–10 minutes before using.
frozen stewing or braising steak cubes	225g/8oz 450g/1lb	DEFROST	To defrost, place in a shallow microwaveproof dish and microwave for 5–7 minutes for 225g/8oz; 8–10 minutes for 450g/1lb, stirring twice. Leave to stand 5–10 minutes before using.
frozen hamburgers	4 x 115g/4oz	DEFROST	To defrost, place on absorbent kitchen paper and microwave for 10–12 minutes, turning over and rearranging twice. Leave to stand 2–3 minutes before using.
frozen steaks	1 x 175–225g/6–8oz 4 x 115–175g/4–6oz 2 x 225g/8oz	DEFROST	Place on a plate. Cover and microwave for 4 minutes for 1 x 175–225g/6–8oz steak, 4–6 minutes for 4 x 115–175g/4–6oz steaks; and 6–8 minutes for 2 x 225g/8oz steaks; turning over once. Leave to stand, covered, for 5–10 minutes before using.
GAMMON frozen uncooked joint	450g/1lb 900g/2lb	DEFROST	To defrost, place joint on a plate and microwave for 4–5 minutes for a 450g/1lb joint; and 8–10 minutes for a 900g/2lb joint. Leave to stand, covered, for 10–15 minutes before using.
frozen steaks	2 x 115g/4oz 4 x 115g/4oz	DEFROST	To defrost, place on a plate and microwave for 3–5 minutes for 2 x 115g/4oz steaks; and 7–9 minutes for 4 x 115g/4oz steaks, turning over once. Leave to stand for 5 minutes before using.
HAM frozen uncooked joint	450g/1lb 900g/2lb	DEFROST	To defrost, place the joint on a plate and microwave for 4–5 minutes for a 450g/1lb joint; and 8–10 minutes for a 900g/2lb joint, turning over once. Leave to stand, covered, for 10–15 minutes before using.
frozen sliced cooked	115g/4oz packet	DEFROST	To defrost, place on a plate and microwave for 3–4 minutes, turning over once. Leave to stand for 5 minutes before using.
KIDNEYS frozen lamb's, pig's or ox	2 lamb's 4 lamb's 2 pig's 4 pig's 225g/8oz ox 450g/1lb ox	DEFROST	To defrost, place in a microwaveproof bowl, cover and microwave for 1½–2 minutes for 2 lamb's; 4 minutes for 4 lamb's; 4 minutes for 2 pig's; 7–8 minutes for 4 pig's; 6 minutes for 225g/8oz ox; and 9–10 minutes for 450g/1lb ox kidney, rearranging 3 times. Leave to stand, covered, for 5 minutes before using.

LAMB

frozen chops	2 x 115–175g/4–6oz loin chops 4 x 115–175g/4–6oz loin chops 2 x 115–175g/4–6oz chump chops 4 x 115–175g/4–6oz chump chops	DEFROST	To defrost, place on a microwaveproof roasting rack and microwave for 3–4 minutes for 2 x 115–175g/4–6oz loin chops; 6–8 minutes for 4 x 115–175g/4–6oz loin chops; 3–4 minutes for 2 x 115–175g/4–6oz chump chops; and 6–8 minutes for 4 x 115–175g/4–6oz chump chops, turning over and rearranging once. Leave to stand, covered, for 10 minutes before using.
frozen uncooked joint	per 450g/1lb boned and rolled joint per 450g/1lb joints on bone	DEFROST	To defrost, place joint on a microwaveproof roasting rack or upturned saucer in a dish. Microwave both types of joint for 5–6 minutes per 450g/1lb, turning over once. Leave to stand, covered, for 30–45 minutes, before using.

LIVER

frozen slices	225g/8oz 450g/1lb	DEFROST	To defrost, spread slices on a plate. Cover and microwave for 4–5 minutes for 225g/8oz; and 8–9 minutes for 450g/1lb, turning twice. Leave to stand, covered, for 5 minutes before using.

PORK

frozen chops	2 x 115–175g/4–6oz loin 4 x 115–175g/4–6oz loin 2 x 225g/8oz chump 2 x 225g/8oz chump	DEFROST	To defrost, place on a microwaveproof roasting rack and microwave for 3–4 minutes for 2 x 115–175g/4–6oz loin chops; 6–8 minutes for 4 x 115–175g/4–6oz loin chops; 7–9 minutes for 2 x 225g/8oz chump chops; and 14–16 minutes for 4 x 225g/8oz chump chops, turning and rearranging once. Leave to stand for 10 minutes before using.
frozen fillet or tenderloin	350g/12oz per 450g/1lb	DEFROST	To defrost, place on a microwaveproof roasting rack and microwave for 3–4 minutes for a 350g/12oz fillet or tenderloin; and 5–6 minutes per 450g/1lb, turning over once. Leave to stand for 10 minutes before using.
frozen uncooked joint	per 450g/1lb joint on bone per 450g/1lb boneless joints	DEFROST	To defrost, place joint on a microwaveproof roasting rack or upturned saucer in a dish. Microwave both types of joint for 7–8 minutes per 450g/1lb, turning over once. Leave to stand, covered, for 20–45 minutes before using.

SAUSAGEMEAT

frozen	450g/1lb	DEFROST	To defrost, remove any wrappings and place in a shallow microwaveproof dish. Cover and microwave for 6–8 minutes, breaking up twice. Leave to stand, covered, for 4–5 minutes before using.

SAUSAGES

frozen	4 standard 8 standard 8 chipolatas 16 chipolatas	DEFROST	To defrost separated or linked sausages, place on a plate, cover and microwave for 3–4 minutes for 4 standard; 5–6 minutes for 8 standard; 3 minutes for 8 chipolatas; and 5 minutes for 16 chipolatas, separating, turning over and rearranging twice. Leave to stand, covered, for 2–5 minutes before using.

VEAL

frozen chops	2 4 6	DEFROST	To defrost, arrange in a microwaveproof dish so that the thicker portions are to the outer edge. Cover and microwave for 5–6 minutes for 2 chops; 8–10 minutes for 4 chops; and 12–15 minutes for 6 chops, turning and rearranging twice. Leave to stand, covered, for 5–10 minutes before using.
frozen roast	900g/2lb 1.5kg/3–3½lb 1.75kg/4–4½lb 2.25kg/5–5¼lb	DEFROST	To defrost, place in a microwaveproof dish and microwave for 16–18 minutes for a 900g/2lb joint; 24–27 minutes for a 1.5kg/3–3½lb joint; 32–36 minutes for a 1.75kg/4–4½lb joint; and 40–45 minutes for a 2.25kg/5–5¼lb joint, turning twice. Shield any thinner areas with foil as they defrost. Leave to stand, covered, for 10–20 minutes before using.

General Defrosting Chart

BISCUITS frozen	225g/8oz	DEFROST	Arrange in a circle around the edge of a plate. Microwave for 1–1½ minutes, turning over once halfway through cooking. Leave to stand for 5 minutes before serving.
BREAD frozen large white or brown sliced or uncut loaf	800g/1¾lb	DEFROST	Loosen wrapper but do not remove. Microwave for 4 minutes. Leave to stand for 5 minutes before slicing or removing ready-cut slices. Leave a further 10 minutes before serving.
frozen individual bread slices and rolls	1 slice/1 roll 2 slices/2 rolls 4 slices/4 rolls	DEFROST	Wrap loosely in kitchen paper and microwave for ¼–½ minute for 1 slice/1 roll; ½–1 minute for 2 slices/2 rolls; and 1½–2 minutes for 4 slices/4 rolls. Leave to stand for 2 minutes before serving.
frozen pitta bread	2 4	DEFROST	Place on a double thickness piece of kitchen paper and microwave for 1½–2 minutes for 2 pittas; and 2–3 minutes for 4 pittas, turning once halfway through the cooking time.
frozen crumpets	2 4	HIGH	To defrost *and* reheat. Place on a double thickness piece of kitchen paper and microwave for ½–¾ minute for 2 crumpets; 1–1½ minutes for 4 crumpets, turning once.
CAKES frozen small light fruit cake	small light fruit cake 1 slice	DEFROST	To defrost, place on a microwaveproof rack and microwave, uncovered, for 5 minutes for a whole small cake; ½–¾ minute for 1 slice, rotating twice. Leave to stand for 10 minutes before serving.
frozen Black Forest gâteau	15cm/6in gâteau	DEFROST	To defrost, place on a serving plate and microwave, uncovered, for 4–6 minutes, checking constantly. Leave to stand for 30 minutes before serving.
frozen cream sponge	15cm/6in sponge	HIGH	To defrost, place on a double thickness piece of kitchen paper and microwave for 45 seconds. Leave to stand for 10–15 minutes before serving.
frozen jam sponge	15–18cm/6–7in sponge	DEFROST	To defrost, place on a double thickness piece of kitchen paper and microwave for 3 minutes. Leave to stand for 5 minutes before serving.
frozen small sponge buns	2 4	DEFROST	To defrost, place on a rack and microwave for 1–1½ minutes for 2 buns; and 1½–2 minutes for 4 buns, checking frequently. Leave to stand for 5 minutes before serving.
frozen chocolate éclairs	2	DEFROST	To defrost, place on a double thickness sheet of kitchen paper and microwave for ¾–1 minute. Leave to stand 5–10 minutes before serving.
frozen doughnuts	2 x cream filled 2 x jam filled	DEFROST	To defrost, place on a double thickness sheet of kitchen paper and microwave for 1–1½ minutes for 2 cream-filled doughnuts; and 1½–2 minutes for 2 jam-filled doughnuts. Leave to stand 3–5 minutes before serving.
CASSEROLES frozen	2 servings 4 servings	HIGH	To defrost *and* reheat. Place in a microwaveproof dish, cover and microwave for 8–10 minutes for 2 servings; 14–16 minutes for 4 servings, breaking up and stirring twice as the casserole thaws. Leave to stand, covered, for 3–5 minutes before serving.
CHEESECAKE frozen	individual fruit-topped individual cream-topped family-size fruit-topped family-size cream-topped	DEFROST	To defrost, remove from container and place on a microwaveproof serving plate. Microwave for 1–1½ minutes for individual fruit-topped; 1–1¼ minutes for individual cream-topped; 5–6 minutes for family-size fruit-topped; and 1½–2 minutes for family-size cream-topped, rotating once and checking frequently. Leave to stand for 5–15 minutes before serving.

CREPES OR PANCAKES frozen	8	MEDIUM	To defrost, place a stack of 8 crêpes or pancakes on a plate and microwave for 1½–2 minutes, rotating once. Leave to stand for 5 minutes, then peel apart to use.
CROISSANTS frozen	2 4	DEFROST	To defrost, place on a double thickness piece of kitchen paper and microwave for ½–1 minute for 2 croissants; and 1½–2 minutes for 4 croissants.
FISH IN SAUCE frozen boil-in-the bag	1 x 170g/6oz 2 x 170g/6oz	DEFROST or MEDIUM	To defrost *and* cook, pierce the bag and place on a plate. Microwave for 11–12 minutes on DEFROST for 1 x 170g/6oz bag; and 10–12 minutes on MEDIUM for 2 x 170g/6oz bags. Shake gently to mix, leave to stand for 2 minutes then snip open to serve.
FLANS & QUICHES frozen unfilled cooked flans	15–18cm/6–7in	DEFROST	To defrost, place on a plate and microwave for 1–1½ minutes. Leave to stand for 5 minutes before using.
frozen filled cooked flans	10cm/4in 20cm/8in	HIGH	To defrost *and* cook, place on a plate and microwave for 1–1½ minutes for a 10cm/4in flan; and 2½–3½ minutes for a 20cm/8in flan. Leave to stand for 5 minutes before serving or using.
FRUIT CRUMBLE frozen cooked frozen uncooked	made with 900g/2lb prepared fruit and 175g/6oz crumble topping (to serve 4)	DEFROST *then* HIGH	To defrost *and* cook, microwave frozen cooked crumble for 15 minutes on DEFROST, then 5 minutes on HIGH; and frozen uncooked crumble for 15 minutes on DEFROST, then 10–14 minutes on HIGH, until cooked or reheated.
LASAGNE frozen prepared	450g/1lb	DEFROST *then* HIGH	To defrost *and* cook, remove any foil packaging and place in a microwave-proof dish. Cover and microwave on DEFROST for 8 minutes. Allow to stand for 5 minutes, then microwave on HIGH for 8–9 minutes. Brown under a preheated hot grill if liked.
ORANGE JUICE frozen concentrated	175ml/6fl oz carton	HIGH	To defrost, remove lid and place in a microwaveproof jug. Microwave for 1–1½ minutes, stirring once. Add water to dilute and serve.
PASTA frozen cooked	275g/10oz	DEFROST	To defrost *and* reheat, place in a microwaveproof dish, cover and microwave for 10 minutes, stirring twice. Leave to stand, covered, for 2–3 minutes before serving.
PASTRY frozen shortcrust and puff	200g/7oz packet 400g/14oz packet	DEFROST	Do not remove from wrappings unless unsuitable for microwave. Microwave for 2½–3 minutes for a 200g/7oz packet; and 4 minutes for a 400g/14oz packet. Leave to stand for 3 minutes before using.
PATE frozen	115g/4oz pack 200g/7oz pack 275g/10oz slice	DEFROST	Unwrap and place on a plate or leave in dish if suitable for microwave. Cover and microwave for 1 minute for 115g/4oz pack; 3–4 minutes for 200g/7oz pack; and 3–4 minutes for 275g/10oz slice, rotating 2–3 times. Leave to stand for 15–20 minutes before serving.
PIZZA frozen	30cm/12in 13cm/5in	HIGH	To defrost *and* cook. Place on a plate and microwave for 3–5 minutes for a 30cm/12in pizza; and 1½–2 minutes for a 13cm/5in pizza, rotating the dish twice.
RICE frozen cooked	225g/8oz 450g/1lb	HIGH	To defrost *and* reheat. Place in a microwaveproof dish, cover and microwave for 5–6 minutes for 225g/8oz; and 7–8 minutes for 450g/1lb, stirring twice. Leave to stand, covered, for 2 minutes before using.

SCONES
frozen | 2 4 | | DEFROST | To defrost, place on a double thickness piece of kitchen paper. Microwave for 1¼–1½ minutes for 2 scones; 3 minutes for 4 scones, rearranging once.

SOUPS
frozen | 300ml/½ pint/1¼ cups 600ml/1 pint/2½ cups | HIGH | To defrost *and* reheat. Place in a bowl, cover and microwave for 4–4½ minutes for 300ml/½ pint/1¼ cups; and 7–7½ minutes for 600ml/ 1 pint/2½ cups, breaking up and stirring 2–3 times.

STOCKS
frozen | 300ml/½ pint/1¼ cups 600ml/1 pint/2½ cups | HIGH | Place in a jug or bowl, microwave uncovered: 2½–3 minutes for 300ml/ ½ pint/1¼ cups; and 5–6 minutes for 600ml/1 pint/2½ cups, stirring and breaking up 2–3 times.

WHITE SAUCE
frozen and variations (such as cheese, parsley or mustard) | 300ml/½ pint/1¼ cups | HIGH | To defrost *and* reheat. Place in a microwaveproof dish and microwave for 4–5 minutes, stirring twice. Whisk to serve.

YOGURT
frozen | 150g/5oz carton | HIGH | To defrost, remove lid and microwave for 1 minute. Stir well and leave to stand for 1–2 minutes before serving.

Maple and Banana Teabread.

Index

A

alcohol, flambéing with, 30
almonds: blanching, 27
apples, cooking, 115
    baked apples with
        apricots, 87
    honey fruit yogurt ice, 84
apricots, cooking, 115
    baked apples with
        apricots, 87
arranging food, 17
artichokes *see* globe
        artichokes; Jerusalem
        artichokes
asparagus, cooking,
        106, 111
aubergines, 106

B

baby food, freezing and
        defrosting, 23
baby's bottles,
        warming, 30
bacon, 8, 103, 122
bananas, cooking, 115
    maple and banana tea
        bread, 93
barley, cooking, 113
batters, 31
beans, dried, 113
    borlotti beans with
        mushrooms, 63
    chunky bean and vegetable
        soup, 33
beef, 103, 122
    beef and mushroom
        burgers, 56
    spicy Bolognese, 58
    stuffed tomatoes, 57
beetroot, 106
biscuits, 124
    biscuit cups, 29
blackberries, 115
blackcurrants, 115
blueberry crumble
        tea bread, 92
bread: croûtons, 28
    garlic or herb bread, 26
    proving yeast
        dough, 28
    sage soda bread, 89
breadcrumbs, 28
broccoli, 107, 111
    broccoli and chestnut
        terrine, 78
browning, 20
browning dishes, 14–15
Brussels sprouts, 107, 111
bulgur wheat, 113
burgers: beef and
        mushroom burgers, 56
butter, softening, 27

C

cabbage, 107, 111
cakes, 124
    coconut pyramids, 95
    hot chocolate
        cake, 94
caper sauce, 24
carbonara, pasta, 64
carrots, 107, 111
casseroles, defrosting, 124
    fisherman's casserole, 44

cauliflower, cooking,
        107, 111
celery, 107
cheese: baked macaroni
        cheese, 64
    cheese and marjoram
        scones, 90
    cheese sauce, 24
    ravioli with four cheese
        sauce, 68
    softening and
        ripening, 27
cheesecake, 124
cherries, 115
chestnuts: broccoli and
        chestnut terrine, 78
chick-peas, 113
chicken, 101, 120
    chicken and fruit
        salad, 60
    hot chilli chicken, 59
chillies: chilli
        prawns, 36
    hot chilli chicken, 59
Chinese cabbage, 107

chocolate: hot chocolate
        cake, 94
    melting, 30
chowder, creamy cod, 35
cider, spiced pears in, 83
citrus juice, squeezing, 28
citrus rinds, drying, 27
cleaning microwave
        cookers, 12
coconut: coconut
        pyramids, 95

toasting, 27
cod, 98, 118
    green fish curry, 48
    see also smoked cod
coffee, reheating, 30
combination cookers, 11
containers, 13–15
corn-on-the-cob, 25
    cooking, 110
courgettes, 107, 111
couscous, sweet
        vegetable, 71
covering food, 18–19
crabmeat, 118
cranberries, 115
crêpes, 125
croissants, 125
croûtons, 28
crumble, plum and
        walnut, 81
curly kale, 108

D

damsons, 115
deep-fat frying, 31

defrosting, 21, 124–6
    fish and shellfish, 118–19
    meat, 122–23
    poultry and game, 120–21
desserts, 80–87
dishes, 13–15
duck, 101, 120

E

eggs, 31
    eggs en cocotte, 38

pasta carbonara, 64
scrambled eggs, 24
equipment, 13–15

F

fennel, 108
fish and seafood, 42–53,
        98–100
fish and shellfish, 7
    defrosting, 118–19
    fishcakes, defrosting, 118
    fisherman's casserole, 44
    Italian fish soup, 34
    see also cod; haddock etc
flambéing with alcohol, 30
florentines, oat, 91
freezers, 21–3
frozen vegetables, 111–12
fruit, 9, 115–17
    autumn pudding, 84
    see also apples; pears etc

G

game, 8, 101–2
    defrosting, 120–21

gammon, 104, 122
garlic bread, 26
gelatine, dissolving, 29
giblets, 120
    giblet stock, 24
ginger: gingerbread upside-
        down pudding, 82
globe artichokes, 106
golden vegetable paella, 67
gooseberries, 116
grains, 9, 113–14
green beans, 106, 111
green fish curry, 48
greengages, 116
grey mullet, 99, 119

H

haddock, 98, 118
    potato-topped fish
        pie, 44
    sweet and sour fish, 46
    see also smoked haddock
halibut, 98, 118
ham, defrosting, 122
    pasta carbonara, 64
herbs: drying, 27
    herb bread, 26
herring, 98, 118
hollandaise sauce, 25
honey: clarifying, 29
    honey fruit yogurt ice, 84
hot chilli chicken, 59

I

ice cream: honey fruit
        yogurt ice, 84
    softening, 30
Italian fish soup, 34

J

jacket potatoes, 25
jams, softening, 29
jelly, dissolving, 29
Jerusalem artichokes, 106

K

kebabs, 8
kidneys, defrosting, 122
kippers, 98, 118
kohlrabi, 108

L

lamb, 104, 123
    lamb pie with a potato
        crust, 55
lasagne, defrosting, 125
leeks, 108, 112
    potato, leek and tomato
        bake, 76
lentils, 26
    cooking, 113
    spiced lentils and rice, 70

liver, 104, 123
  chicken liver salad, 61
lobster, 98, 118

M
macaroni cheese, baked, 64
mackerel, 99, 118
mangetouts, 108, 112
maple and banana
  tea bread, 93
marrow, 108
meat and poultry, 8, 54–61
meat, cooking, 103–5
  defrosting, 122–3
Mediterranean plaice, 43
meringues, 31
microwave cooking, 10–12
Middle-Eastern vegetable
  stew, 75
milk, heating, 30
millet, cooking, 113
mulled wine, 30
mushrooms, 108, 112
  beef and mushroom
    burgers, 56
  borlotti beans with
    mushrooms, 63
  mixed mushroom
    ragout, 73
  mushroom, leek and
    cashew nut risotto, 69
  mushroom pâté, 39
mussels, 99, 118

N
nectarines, cooking, 116
nuts: toasting, 27
  see also almonds;
    walnuts etc

O
oats, cooking, 114
  oat florentines, 91
  porridge, 26
okra, cooking, 108
one-stage sauce, 24
onions, 108
oranges, 116, 125

P
pak choi, cooking, 109
parsley sauce, 24
parsnips, 109, 112
pasta, 9, 114, 125
  pasta carbonara, 64
  salmon pasta with
    parsley sauce, 50
  spicy Bolognese, 58
  tuna and mixed vegetable
    pasta, 46
pastry, defrosting,
  28, 125
pâté, defrosting, 125
  mushroom pâté, 39
peaches, cooking, 116
  peeling, 27

pears, cooking, 116
  spiced pears in cider, 83
peas, 109, 112
  peas, split, 113
pilaff, seafood, 50
pineapple, cooking, 116
pizzas, defrosting, 125
plaice, 99, 118–19
  Mediterranean plaice, 43
plums, cooking, 117
  plum and walnut
    crumble, 81
popcorn, 31
poppadoms, 29
pork, 105, 123

porridge, 26
portable microwave
  cookers, 11
potatoes, cooking, 109
  jacket potatoes, 25
  lamb pie with a potato
    crust, 55
  potato, leek and tomato
    bake, 76
  potato-topped fish pie, 44
poultry, 8, 54–61, 101–2
  defrosting, 120–21
  see also chicken; duck etc
power, microwave, 31
prawns, 99, 119
  chilli prawns, 36
  prawn curry, 49
pulses, 9, 113–14
pumpkin, 109

Q
quiches, defrosting, 125

R
raspberries, 117

ratatouille: eggs en
  cocotte, 38
ravioli with four cheese
  sauce, 68
red mullet, 99, 119
red snapper, defrosting, 119
redcurrants, 117
reheating food, 23
rhubarb, cooking, 117
rice, 9, 114, 125
  seafood pilaff, 50
  spiced lentils and rice, 70
  stuffed vine leaves, 40
  vegetable rice, 26
  see also risotto

rigatoni with spicy sausage
  and tomato, 66
risotto: mushroom, leek and
  cashew nut, 69
rotating food, 16
rye, cooking, 114

S
sage soda bread, 89
salads: chicken and fruit, 60
  chicken liver, 61
  salade Niçoise, 79
salmon, 99, 119
  salmon pasta with parsley
    sauce, 50
  whole cooked salmon, 52
  see also smoked salmon
salmon trout, 119
sauces: caper, 24
  cheese, 24
  hollandaise, 25
  one-stage, 24
  parsley, 24
  white, defrosting, 126
  white pouring, 24

sausages, 8, 105, 123
  rigatoni with spicy sausage
    and tomato, 66
scallops, 99, 119
  scallops with ginger, 36
scampi, defrosting, 119
scones, defrosting, 126
  cheese and marjoram, 90
scoring foods, 16
shellfish, 7, 42–53, 98–100
  defrosting, 118–9
  seafood pilaff, 50
  see also prawns;
    scallops etc
shielding food, 18

shrimps, 99, 119
smoked cod: creamy cod
  chowder, 35
smoked haddock, 100, 119
smoked salmon,
  defrosting, 119
soda bread: sage, 89
sole, 100, 119
soups, 33–35, 126
  chunky bean and
    vegetable, 33
  creamy cod chowder, 35
  Italian fish, 34
spinach, 109, 112
spring vegetable medley, 74
squash, cooking, 109
standing times, 20
stirring, 16
stocks, defrosting, 126
  giblet, 24
strawberries, cooking, 117
summer vegetable
  braise, 77
swedes, 109, 112
sweetcorn, 112

corn-on-the-cob, 25, 110
Swiss chard, 110

T
tangerine trifle, 86
tea breads: blueberry
  crumble, 92
  maple and banana, 93
techniques, 16–20
terrines: broccoli and
  chestnut, 78
thermometers, 14
tomatoes, 110
  peeling, 27
  potato, leek and tomato
    bake, 76
  stuffed tomatoes, 57
trifle, tangerine, 86
trout, 100, 119
tuna: salade Niçoise, 79
  tuna and mixed vegetable
    pasta, 46
turkey, 102, 121
turnips, cooking, 110

U
upside-down pudding,
  gingerbread, 82
utensils, 13–15

V
veal, 105, 123
vegetables, 9, 106–112
  chunky bean and vegetable
    soup, 33
  golden vegetable
    paella, 67
  Middle-Eastern vegetable
    stew, 75
  spring vegetable
    medley, 74
  summer vegetable
    braise, 77
  sweet vegetable
    couscous, 71
  tuna and mixed vegetable
    pasta, 46
  vegetable rice, 26
vine leaves, stuffed, 40

W
walnuts: plum and walnut
  crumble, 81
wheat, cooking, 114
white pouring
  sauce, 24
white sauce,
  defrosting, 126
whiting, 100, 119
wine: mulled wine, 30

Y
yeast dough, proving, 28
yogurt, defrosting, 126
  honey fruit yogurt
    ice, 84